DOGMATIC THEOLOGY

IV

CHRISTOLOGY

A DOGMATIC TREATISE ON THE INCARNATION

BY

THE RT. REV. MSGR. JOSEPH POHLE, Ph. D., D.D.

ADAPTED AND EDITED

BY

ARTHUR PREUSS

B. HERDER BOOK CO.
15 & 17 SOUTH BROADWAY, ST. LOUIS, MO.
AND
33 QUEEN SQUARE, LONDON, W. C.
1952

TABLE OF CONTENTS

TABLE OF CONTENTS

PREFACE

In treating of God as the Author of Nature and the Supernatural,[1] we showed how the harmony of angelic as well as human nature was seriously disturbed by sin.

For some reason not revealed to us the fallen angels were beyond redemption. St. Thomas thinks that, as they were pure spirits, once they had determined upon evil, their free will became unalterably fixed therein. Other divines hold that the fallen angels were unable to undo their choice because the decision they had made terminated the *status viae.*

The human race immediately after the Fall was reinstated in grace by virtue of the Protevangelium, *i. e.,* God's solemn promise that the Second Person of the Trinity should redeem the sinful race and reconstitute it in the state of adoptive sonship. "Where sin abounded, grace did more abound." [2]

Intimately bound up with the mystery of the Incarnation is that of the Redemption. Jesus Christ, the Redeemer, Son of God, and Himself

---

[1] Pohle-Preuss, *God the Author of Nature and the Supernatural.*

[2] " *Ubi autem abundavit delictum, superabundavit gratia.*" Rom. **V,** 20.

true God,[3] offered Himself up as a sacrifice (in His human nature), and gave adequate satisfaction for our sins by His agonizing death on the Cross. "For God indeed was in Christ, reconciling the world to himself by Christ, not imputing to them their sins." [4]

In this dogmatic treatise on the Incarnation, we assume the existence of Jesus Christ as a historical fact, leaving it to Apologetics to refute such infidel objections as that the Gospel story is merely a legendary reflex of the Gilgamesh epic,[5] etc.

In regard to the mysteries of the Incarnation and Redemption, Divine Revelation proposes to our belief two distinct series of truths. Those which concern the Person of the Redeemer form the ground-work of the dogmatic treatise called *Christology;* those which refer specifically to the Redemption are dealt with in *Soteriology,* to which we shall devote a separate volume. The Blessed Virgin Mary, as Deipara, is causally related both to the Incarnation and the Redemption, and must therefore be treated in connection with both. This gives us another separate treatise, called *Mariology,* which will form the sixth volume of the present series.

3 Cfr. Pohle-Preuss, *The Divine Trinity,* St. Louis, Mo., 1912, pp. 49 sqq.

4 2 Cor. V, 19.

5 See P. Jensen, *Das Gilgamesch-Epos,* Vol. I: *Die Ursprünge der* alttestamentlichen Patriarchen-, Propheten- und Befreiersage und der neutestamentlichen Jesus-Sage, p. 1030, Strassburg 1906. Cfr. *The Catholic Fortnightly Review,* Vol. XVII (1910), Nos. 4 and 5.

INTRODUCTION

1. In treating of the dogma of the Divine Trinity we based our exposition upon the "Athanasian Creed." [1] According to this same ecclesiastical symbol we will also divide the treatise on Christology, treating (1) of "Duality in Unity," [2] or the constitutive elements of Christ, and (2) of "Unity in Duality," or the Hypostatic Union. [3]

The significant parallel between the two dogmatic treatises seems to point to an analogical relation between their respective subjects. Such a relation does indeed exist. Both treatises are concerned with transcendental mysteries which revolve about the concepts of "Nature" and "Hypostasis," and their mutual relations.

It would not, however, be correct to conclude from this analogy that Christ, in respect of the relation of Nature to Person, is a perfect image of the Trinity. There is a very essential distinction. In the Blessed Trinity one Divine Nature subsists in three divine Hypostases (or Persons), who possess a real and identical nature in common; whereas in Christ two distinct and complete natures, one divine, the other human, subsist in one Hypostasis, i. e., the Divine Person of the Logos. Or, to put it somewhat differently, the Blessed

1 Cfr. Pohle-Preuss, *The Divine Trinity*, pp. 5 sqq.
2 *Dualitas in unitate.*
3 *Unitas in dualitate, unio hypostatica.*

3

Trinity forms a real Trinity of Persons in an absolute Unity of Nature, whereas in Christ there is a duality of Natures in an absolute Unity of Person.

This twofold element in the constitution of the God-man is clearly stated in the "Athanasian Creed": *"Est ergo fides recta, ut credamus et confiteamur, quia Dominus noster Iesus Christus Dei Filius, Deus et homo est.*[4] *Deus est ex substantia Patris ante saecula genitus, et homo est ex substantia matris in saeculo natus: perfectus Deus, perfectus homo, ex anima rationali et humana carne subsistens, aequalis Patri secundum divinitatem, minor Patre secundum humanitatem. Qui licet Deus sit et homo, non duo tamen, sed unus est Christus;*[5] *unus autem non conversione divinitatis in carnem, sed assumptione humanitatis in Deum, unus omnino non confusione substantiae, sed unitate personae."* Anglice: "For the right faith is that we believe and confess that our Lord Jesus Christ, the Son of God, is God and Man; God, of the Substance of the Father, begotten before the worlds; and Man, of the substance of His mother, born in the world; perfect God, and perfect Man: of a reasonable soul and human flesh subsisting; equal to the Father, as touching His Godhead: and inferior to the Father, as touching His Manhood. Who although He be God and Man: yet He is not two, but one Christ; one; not by conversion of the Godhead into flesh: but by taking of the Manhood into God; one altogether; not by confusion of substance: but by unity of Person." [6]

4 *Dualitas in unitate.*

5 *Unitas in dualitate.*

6 *Enchiridion Symbolorum, Definitionum et Declarationum de Rebus Fidei et Morum Auctore Henrico Denzinger. Editio undecima, Emendata et Aucta, quam paravit Clemens Bannwart, S. J.,* Friburgi Brisgoviae 1911, n. 40. For brevity's sake we shall hereafter cite this work as Denzinger-Bannwart, *Enchiridion.* Our translation of the Athanasian Creed is that of the English *Book of Common Prayer.* We quote *verbatim, literatim et punctatim* from the Oxford edition of

2. Defining the essential constitution of man in our treatise on Dogmatic Anthropology[7] we answered two questions, *viz.:* (1) How many constitutive elements are there in man? and (2) How are these elements united? We ascertained by the light of Divine Revelation that there is in man a real "duality in unity," in as much as he is composed of a material body essentially informed by a spiritual soul.

Similarly, though not in precisely the same sense, we may ask: (1) What is the number of constitutive elements in Christ? and (2) How are these elements united?

Revelation answers these two questions thus: (1) There are two constitutive elements in Christ, a divine nature and a human nature; and (2) these two natures are united hypostatically. The "Athanasian Creed" points out this analogy when it says: "For as the reasonable soul and flesh is one man: so God and Man is one Christ."[8]

According to Cardinal Franzelin the dogma of the Incarnation may be most effectively expounded from the following points of view:[9] (1) *Who* assumed human nature? (2) *What* did the Son of God assume? (3)

1834. Cfr. Pohle-Preuss, *God: His Knowability, Essence, and Attributes,* p. 318, note 6.

7 See Pohle-Preuss, *God the Author of Nature and the Supernatural,* pp. 124 sqq.

8 " *Nam sicut anima rationalis et caro unus est homo, ita Deus et homo unus est Christus.*"

9 Cfr. Franzelin, *De Verbo Incarnato,* thes. 1, 4th ed., Rome 1910.

How are Divinity and humanity united in Christ? (4)
Why did the Son of God hypostatically assume a human
nature? The answer to the first question (*quis?*) is:
The Divine Logos. The answer to the second question
(*quid?*) is: A real and genuine human nature. The answer to the third question (*quomodo?*) is: Godhead and
manhood are hypostatically united in Christ. The answer
to the fourth question (*ad quid?*) is: The Son of God
assumed flesh in order to redeem the human race.

Of these questions the first three alone belong to Christology proper; the fourth finds its place in Soteriology.

The division we have chosen coincides materially,
though not formally, with that suggested by Cardinal
Franzelin. The only difference is that we base our exposition on the " Athanasian Creed." Our reasons for so
doing are purely didactic. The concept " duality in
unity " contains the reply to the questions *quis?* and *quid?*,
while the answer to *quomodo?* is supplied by the concept
of " unity in duality."

It may be objected that the so-called Athanasian
Creed is not the work of St. Athanasius and lacks the
authority of a primitive symbol. We reply that, though
" of Western origin and . . . composed (probably)
during the fifth century in Southern Gaul," [10] this
symbol is " an admirable résumé of the doctrine of
Athanasius. . . . In the West it was recited at Prime
since the ninth century, was used by the clergy in giving
popular instruction as a summary of Christian doctrine,
and was held in particular esteem as a basis and criterion
of ecclesiastical faith." [11] Dr. Künstle holds [12] that the

10 Its authorship is variously attributed to Honoratus of Arles,
Eusebius of Vercelli, and Vincent
of Lerins.

11 Bardenhewer-Shahan, *Patrol-*

ogy, p. 255, Freiburg and St. Louis
1908.

12 *Antipriscilliana,* pp. 204 sqq.,
Freiburg 1905.

INTRODUCTION 7

Athanasian Creed was written in Spain against Priscil-
lianism, while H. Brewer [13] attributes it to St. Ambrose.

We now enter upon the treatment of Christology according to the division already indicated, *viz.:* (1)
Duality in Unity, or the Constitutive Elements of Christ,
and (2) Unity in Duality, or the Hypostatic Union of
the two Natures in Christ.

GENERAL READINGS: — Among the Fathers: Athanasius, *De Incarnatione Verbi* (Migne, *P.G.,* XXV, 95 sqq., 938 sqq.).—* Cyril
of Alexandria (Migne, *P.G.,* LXXV, LXXVI).— Leontius, *Adv.
Nest. et Eutych.* (Migne, *P.G.,* LXXXVI, 1267 sqq.).— Maximus
Confessor (Migne, *P.G.,* XC, XCI).— The teaching of these
writers is summarized by St. John Damascene, *De Fide Orthodoxa, l. III* (Migne, *P.G.,* XCIV).— On the teaching of Theodoret see A. Bertram, *Theodoreti Episcopi Cyrensis Doctrina
Christologica,* Hildesheim 1883.— On the doctrine of St. Cyril,
cfr. A. Rehrmann, *Die Christologie des hl. Cyrillus von Alexandrien,* Hildesheim 1902.

The student may also consult with profit St. Augustine's *Enchiridion* (Migne, *P.L.,* XC; English translation by J. F. Shaw,
in Vol. IX of *The Works of Aurelius Augustine, Bishop of Hippo,*
3rd ed., Edinburgh 1892); St. Ambrose, *De Incarnat. Dominicae
Sacram.* (Migne, *P.L.,* XVI, 817 sqq.), and Fulgentius, *De Incarnatione Filii Dei* (Migne, *P.L.,* LXV).

Among the Schoolmen: * St. Thomas, *S. Theol.,* 3a, qu. 1–
26 (summarized in Freddi-Sullivan, *Jesus Christ the Word In-
carnate,* St. Louis 1904); A. Vonier, O. S. B., *The Personality of
Christ,* London 1915.—*IDEM, *Contr. Gent.,* IV, 27 sqq. (Rickaby, *Of God and His Creatures,* pp. 359 sqq., London 1905).—
Billuart, *De Incarnatione,* t. V, ed. Lequette.— Salmanticenses,
De Incarn., Vols. 13–16, ed. Paris 1870 sq.— Suarez, *De Incarn.,*
Lugd. 1592.—*Bellarmine, *De Christo,* t. I, ed. Vivès, Paris 1870.—
* De Lugo, *De Mysterio Incarnationis,* t. II, III, ed. Vivès, Paris
1890–92.—Gregory of Valentia, *De Incarn. Divini Verbi,* Venice
1600.—*Ysambert, *De Mysterio Incarnationis,* Paris 1639.— Wirce-
burgenses (Holtzclau, S. J.), *De Incarn. Verbi,* Vol. VI, ed. Paris
1879.— Legrand, *Tract. de Incarn. Verbi Divini* (Migne, *Cursus
Compl.,* t. IX, Paris 1860).— Fr. I. Bertieri, *De Verbo Dei Incarnato,* Vindob. 1773.

13 *Das sogenannte Athanasianische Glaubensbekenntnis ein Werk des hl.
Ambrosius,* Paderborn 1909.

Among later writers: Bautz, Einig. B. Jungmann, Heinrich, Hurter, Hunter, van Noort, in their respective textbooks.— Also *Franzelin, *De Verbo Incarnato,* ed. 6, Romae 1910.—*F. A. Stentrup, *De Verbo Incarnato, I: Christologia,* 2 vols., Oeniponte 1882.—*L. Billot, *De Verbo Incarnato,* ed. 5, Romae 1912.— Chr. Pesch, *Praelect. Dogmat.,* t. IV, ed. 3, Friburgi 1909.— G. B. Tepe, *Instit. Theol.,* Vol. III, Paris 1896.—*L. Janssens, *De Deo-Homine, I: Christologia,* Friburgi 1901.—*P. Galtier, S. J., *De Incarnatione et Redemptione,* Paris 1926.— C. v. Schäzler, *Das Dogma von der Menschwerdung Gottes,* Freiburg 1870.— Oswald, *Die Erlösung in Christo Jesu,* 2 vols., 2nd ed., Paderborn 1887.— Scheeben, *Dogmatik,* Vols. II and III, Freiburg 1878 sq.— IDEM, *Die Mysterien des Christentums,* 3d ed., Freiburg 1912.— H. P. Liddon, *The Divinity of Our Lord and Saviour Jesus Christ,* Cambridge 1867.— E. C. Minjard, *L'Homme-Dieu,* 2 vols., Paris 1898–99.— I. Souben, *Le Verbe Incarné,* Paris 1902.— E. Krebs, *Der Logos als Heiland im ersten Jahrhundert,* Freiburg 1910.— E. Hugon, *The Mystery of the Incarnation,* London 1925.— C. Lattey, S. J., *The Incarnation* (Cambridge Summer School Lectures for 1925), Cambridge 1926.— J. P. Arendzen, *Whom Do You Say? A Study in the Doctrine of the Incarnation,* London 1927.— Cfr. also W. Drum, art. "Incarnation" in Vol. VII of the *Catholic Encyclopedia.*

On the history of the dogma, consult *Schwane, *Dogmengeschichte,* Vols. I and II, 2nd ed., Freiburg 1892–95.—*J. Bach, *Dogmengeschichte des Mittelalters vom christologischen Standpunkte,* 2 vols., Vienna 1873–75.— H. Kihn, *Patrologie,* 2 vols., Paderborn 1904–08.— J. Tixeront, *History of Dogmas,* Vol. I. English ed., St. Louis 1911; Vol. II, 1914; Vol. III, 1916.— B. J. Otten, S. J., *A Manual of the History of Dogmas,* St. Louis 1917.— Ed. Weigl, *Christologie vom Tode des Athanasius bis zum Ausbruch des nestorianischen Streites,* Munich 1925.

Against Modernism: M. Lepin, S. S., *Christ and the Gospel, or Jesus the Messiah and Son of God,* Engl. tr., Philadelphia 1910. — M. E. Mangenot, *Christologie, Commentaire des Propositions XXVII–XXXVIII du Décret du Saint-Office "Lamentabili,"* Paris 1910.

On the Christological teaching of St. Paul, cfr. F. Prat, S. J., *La Théologie de Saint Paul,* Vol. II, pp. 165–243, Paris 1912.

PART I

DUALITY IN UNITY, OR THE CON-
STITUTIVE ELEMENTS
OF CHRIST

Jesus Christ is true God; more specifically, He is the Son of God, or Logos, and consequently the Second Person of the Divine Trinity. As Son of the Virgin-Mother Mary He is also true man.

We therefore divide the first part of this volume into two Chapters: (1) The Divinity of Christ, and (2) His Humanity.

CHAPTER I

THE DIVINITY OF CHRIST

1. STATE OF THE QUESTION.—Having given a full dogmatic demonstration of the Divinity of Jesus Christ in our treatise on the Trinity,[1] we here confine ourselves to showing how that demonstration is to be regarded for the purposes of Christology.

In our treatise on the Blessed Trinity we had merely to establish the fact that there are Three Divine Persons in one Divine Nature, viz.: Father, Son, and Holy Ghost. That the Son of God became man did not concern us there. In expounding the dogma of the Trinity, therefore, it would not have been necessary to deal with the historic fact of the Incarnation were it not for the circumstance that nearly all the Scriptural and Patristic texts which can be adduced to prove the existence of the Divine Logos (λόγος ἄσαρκος) are based on the existence of Jesus Christ as the Godman or Word Incarnate (Λόγος ἔνσαρκος).

St. John the Evangelist, in describing the Logos as He existed before all time in His eternal Godhead,[2] did not fail to add the significant statement: "And the

1 Pohle-Preuss, *The Divine Trinity*, pp. 63-96, St. Louis 1912.
2 John I, 1 sqq. Cfr. J. H. Newman, *Tracts Theological and Ecclesiastical*, pp. 228 sq., new ed., London 1895.

Word was made flesh." [3] Following his example the Fathers invariably identified the Divine Logos, or Son of God, with Jesus of Nazareth. Accordingly, nearly all the texts which can be gathered from Patristic literature in favor of the dogma of the Divine Trinity, have a Christological as well as a Trinitarian bearing. In other words, the Scriptural and Patristic teaching on the Divinity of Christ proves the existence of a Second Person in the Blessed Trinity (and therefore the dogma of the Trinity) quite as clearly and stringently as the Scriptural and Patristic teaching on the Incarnation of the Logos demonstrates the dogma of Christ's Divinity. [4] It is due to this close interrelation of the two dogmas that the fundamental Christological thesis with which we are here concerned has really, for the most part, been already established in the treatise on the Divine Trinity.

Generally speaking, the Divinity of Christ may be demonstrated either dogmatically or apologetically.

The dogmatic argument rests on the inspiration of Holy Scripture and the dogmatic validity of the evidence furnished by Tradition.

The apologetic argument has a much broader basis. It is both historical and philosophical. It takes the Bible as a genuine and credible document and from it, in connection with pagan and Jewish sources, proves that Jesus Christ is true God.

[3] Καὶ ὁ Λόγος σὰρξ ἐγένετο. John I, 14.

[4] On the Incarnation in the Gospel of St. John see C. C. Martindale, S. J., in *The Incarnation*, edited by

C. Lattey, S. J., Cambridge 1926, pp. 68–83.

For the apologetic argument in proof of Christ's Divinity we may refer the reader to any approved text-book of Christian Apologetics.[5] The dogmatic argument, as we have already noted, is set forth with considerable fulness in our own treatise on the Divine Trinity. We will merely recapitulate it here.

2. THE DOGMATIC ARGUMENT.—Holy Scripture teaches that Jesus Christ is the Son of God, that He is true God and the Divine Logos. With this teaching Ecclesiastical Tradition is in perfect accord. The contrary doctrine was rejected as heretical very early in the Church's history, and we may therefore truly say that modern Rationalism stands condemned at the bar of Primitive Christianity.

a) The Scriptural doctrine concerning the Second Person of the Blessed Trinity culminates in these three propositions: (1) Christ is truly and properly the Son of God, consubstantial with the Father; therefore (2) He is not an ordinary man, but true God as well as man; (3) "Logos" is merely another name for the Second Person of the Divine Trinity, who became incarnate in Jesus Christ.

5 For instance, Devivier-Sasia, Christian Apologetics, or A Rational Exposition of the Foundations of Faith, Vol. I, pp. 33 sqq., San José, Cal., 1903. Cfr. also Bougaud-Currie, The Divinity of Christ, New York 1906; Hettinger-Bowden, Revealed Religion, pp. 130 sqq., 2nd ed., London s. a.; P. Schanz, A Christian Apology, 4th ed., New York s. a.; O. R. Vassall-Phillips, The Mustard Tree. An Argument on Behalf of the Divinity of Christ, London 1912.

a) The Biblical argument for the Divinity of Christ rests upon the fact that Scripture describes and declares Him to be really and truly the Son of God. How absolutely conclusive this argument is, appears from the desperate efforts made by contemporary Rationalists and Modernists to weaken its force by attributing to Christ a divine sonship wholly foreign to that meant by the inspired writers.

Thus Harnack writes: "The Gospel, as Jesus proclaimed it, has to do with the Father only and not with the Son."[6] According to this Rationalist theologian "the whole of the Gospel is contained" in the formula: "God and the soul, the soul and its God."[7] But did not Christ Himself put His Divine Sonship prominently in the foreground — so much so that our belief in the existence of the Father as the First Person of the Blessed Trinity, in its last analysis really rests upon this emphatic self-assertion of the Son?[8] Harnack cannot deny that "this Jesus who preached humility and knowledge of self, nevertheless named himself, and himself alone, as the Son of God."[9] But he prefers to call this astonishing fact a psychological riddle and pleads ignorance of its meaning. "How he [Jesus] came to this consciousness of the unique character of his relation to God as a Son . . . is his secret, and no psychology will ever fathom it."[10] To solve this enigma, if

6 A. Harnack, *Das Wesen des Christentums*, p. 91, Leipzig 1902 (English translation, *What is Christianity?* by T. B. Saunders, 2nd ed., p. 154, London 1908).

7 *Ibid.*, p. 90 (English translation, p. 153).

8 Cfr. Pohle-Preuss, *The Divine Trinity*, pp. 44.

9 *Das Wesen des Christentums*, p. 81 (English translation, p. 139).

10 *Ibid.*, p. 81 (English translation, p. 138).

Harnack's theory were true, would be the business of psychiatry rather than of psychology, for in that case Jesus Christ was either a fool or a knave. Unwilling to take either horn of the dilemma, Harnack can find no other way out of the difficulty than the assumption that " The sentence ' I am the Son of God ' was not inserted in the Gospel by Jesus himself, and to put that sentence there side by side with the others is to make an addition to the Gospel." [11]   It is difficult to imagine a more frivolous asseveration.   Even the superficial reader can easily see that to obliterate this sentence would be to take away an essential part of the Gospel. Cfr. John IX, 35 sqq.: " Dost thou believe in the Son of God? He answered, and said: Who is he, Lord, that I may believe in him? And Jesus said to him: Thou hast both seen him, and it is he that talketh with thee." [12]

To realize the hollowness of Harnack's contention we need but reflect that Jesus suffered torture and death deliberately and with a solemn oath in confirmation of His claim that He was the Son of God.[13]

The appellation " Son of man," [14] which Jesus applied to Himself with predilection, and which in no wise detracts from His other name, " Son of God," was no doubt designed to safeguard the doctrine of His humanity against future errors, such as that of the Docetae.[15] We should remember, however, that in calling Him-

---

11 *Ibid.,* p. 92 (English translation, p. 156).

12 On the teaching of St. John and St. Paul concerning the Logos, see Pohle-Preuss, *The Divine Trinity,* pp. 88 sqq., St. Louis 1912; on that of St. Paul in particular, F. Prat, *La Théologie de Saint Paul,* Vol. II, pp. 67 sqq., 165 sqq., Paris 1912; D. Somerville (Prot.), *St. Paul's Conception of Christ,* Edin-burgh 1897. Cfr. also H. P. Liddon, *The Divinity of Our Lord and Saviour Jesus Christ,* pp. 311 sqq., 454 sqq., and J. Lebreton, *Les Origines du Dogme de la Trinité,* pp. 291 sqq., 364 sqq., 495 sqq., 515 sqq., Paris 1910.

13 Pohle-Preuss, *op. cit.,* pp. 54 sqq.

14 ὁ υἱὸς τοῦ ἀνθρώπου.

15 See *infra,* pp. 41 sqq.

self "Son of Man," Jesus evidently had in mind the famous prophecy of Daniel, which heralded the Messias by this very name. *"Aspiciebam ergo in visione noctis, et ecce cum nubibus coeli quasi Filius hominis* (כְּבַר אֱנָשׁ) *veniebat et usque ad antiquum dierum pervenit: et in conspectu eius obtulerunt eum. Et dedit ei potestatem et honorem et regnum, et omnes populi, tribus et linguae ipsi servient; potestas eius potestas aeterna, quae non auferetur, et regnum eius, quod non corrumpetur* — I beheld therefore in the vision of the night, and lo, one like the son of man came with the clouds of heaven, and he came even to the Ancient of days: and they presented him before him. And he gave him power, and glory, and a kingdom: and all peoples, tribes, and tongues shall serve him: his power is an everlasting power that shall not be taken away: and his kingdom that shall not be destroyed." [16] With unmistakable reference to this prophecy Christ tells His Apostles that " the Son of man shall be betrayed " and delivered to the Gentiles, " to be mocked, and scourged, and crucified, and the third day he shall rise again." [17] With this same text in mind He assures Caiphas that he " shall see the Son of man sitting on the right hand of the power of God, and coming in the clouds of heaven." [18]

β) If Christ is truly the Son of God, it logically follows that He is true God.[19] For He

---

16 Dan. VII, 13 sqq.
17 Matth. XX, 18 sq.
18 Matth. XXVI, 64. Cfr. B. Bartmann, *Das Himmelreich und sein König nach den Synoptikern,* pp. 85 sqq., Paderborn 1904; H. Schell, *Jahwe und Christus,* pp. 332 sqq., Paderborn 1905; Fr. Tillmann, *Der Menschensohn.* Frei-

burg 1907; A. Seitz, *Das Evangelium vom Gottessohn, eine Apologie der wesenhaften Gottessohnschaft Christi,* pp. 310 sqq., Freiburg 1908.
19 Cfr. Pohle-Preuss, *God: His Knowability, Essence, and Attributes,* pp. 63 sqq.

who originates in the substance of God must be consubstantial with God, because He participates in the Divine Nature by eternal generation. In the mouth of Christ, therefore, "Son of God" signifies nothing less, but rather something more than "God," because it is through our Lord's Sonship rather than through His Divinity that we arrive at a knowledge of the truth that there are three Persons in one Godhead.[20]

The Divinity of Christ can also be proved from the various divine attributes ascribed to Him in Sacred Scripture, the divine worship (*latria*) which He exacted and received,[21] and the application to Him of the predicate "God."[22] The arguments based on the divine attributes ascribed to Jesus and the latreutic adoration offered to Him, sufficiently disprove the Rationalist contention that He is called "God" in a metaphorical sense only, as, *e. g.*, Moses was called the "god of Pharaoh." [23] Moreover, Christ is called "God" in precisely the same sense in which the Old Testament applies the term to Yahweh Himself.[24]

Our main proof rests upon the ascription to Christ by Holy Scripture of such distinctively divine attributes as self-existence, eternity, immutability, creative power, om-

20 Cfr. J. Kleutgen, *Theologie der Vorzeit,* Vol. III, pp. 38 sq., 2nd ed., Münster 1870.

21 *V. infra,* pp. 282 sq.

22 See Pohle-Preuss, *The Divine Trinity,* pp. 63 sqq.

23 Ex. VII, 1.

24 Pohle-Preuss, *l. c.,* pp. 79 sqq.

niscience, universal dominion, etc., rather than upon the fact that it applies to Him the abstract predicate of " God."

In our treatise on the Blessed Trinity we cited five New Testament texts in which Christ is expressly called " God." [25]   There is a sixth, which would be even more conclusive, were it not for the fact that textual criticism throws a doubt upon its authenticity. A few Greek codices, and several of the Fathers,[26] interpret this obscure passage as referring to the " apparition of God in the flesh." It reads as follows: *" Et manifeste magnum est pietatis sacramentum, quod manifestatum est in carne."* Our English Bible renders it thus: " And evidently great is the mystery of godliness, which was manifested in the flesh." [27] The *textus receptus* has: Καὶ ὁμολογουμένως μέγα ἐστὶ τὸ τῆς εὐσεβείας μυστήριον· ὅς [Θεὸς] ἐφανερώθη ἐν σαρκί. It is easy to see how in a large-letter Greek manuscript ΘΣ (= θεός) could be misread for ΟΣ (= ὅς).

The Scriptural argument for the Divinity of Christ, as set forth in our treatise on the Trinity, may be supplemented from other New Testament writers.

That St. Peter really addressed Jesus as his " God" and " Saviour," as the Evangelists relate,[28] is confirmed by the opening words of his Second Epistle: *" Simon Petrus . . . iis qui coaequalem nobiscum sortiti sunt fidem in iustitia Dei nostri et Salvatoris Iesu Christi —* Simon Peter . . . to them that have obtained equal faith with us in the justice of our God and Saviour

25 John XX, 28; Tit. II, 13; 1 John V, 20; Rom. IX, 5; and John I, 1.

26 E. g., Gregory of Nyssa; on his Christological teaching see J. Lenz, *Jesus Christus nach der Lehre* *des hl. Gregor von Nyssa,* Treves 1925.

27 1 Tim. III, 16.

28 Matth. XIV, 28; XVI, 16; John VI, 69; XXI, 17; cfr. Acts III, 6, 15; IV, 10.

Jesus Christ," [29] and in 2 Pet. I, 11: "*Sic enim abundanter ministrabitur vobis introitus in aeternum regnum Domini nostri et Salvatoris Iesu Christi* — For so an entrance shall be ministered to you abundantly into the everlasting kingdom of our Lord and Saviour Jesus Christ." The apposition "our Lord and Saviour" manifestly refers to Christ, and the parallelism running through the whole passage demands that the attributes "our God" and "Saviour" in the first verse of the Epistle be applied to the one person of "Jesus Christ." This interpretation is confirmed by the circumstance that the definite article is used but once (τοῦ Θεοῦ ἡμῶν καὶ [no τοῦ here] σωτῆρος)." [30]

St. Jude attests that it was Jesus who "saved the people out of the land of Egypt." [31] Jesus must therefore be identical with Yahweh, who said: "I am the Lord thy God, who brought thee out of Egypt." [32] According to St. Jude,[33] "Jesus . . . hath reserved the angels [who kept not their principality, but forsook their own habitation] under darkness in everlasting chains, unto the judgment of the great day." And St. Peter assures us that "God [34] spared not the angels that sinned, but delivered them, drawn down by infernal ropes to the lower hell, unto torments, to be reserved unto judgment." By comparing these two passages we arrive at the equation: Jesus = God, and the context moreover shows that the term "God" must be taken in its strict sense.[35]

---

[29] τοῦ Θεοῦ ἡμῶν καὶ σωτῆρος Ἰησοῦ Χριστοῦ. 2 Pet. I, 1.

[30] On the Christological teaching of St. Peter cfr. Liddon, *The Divinity of Our Lord and Saviour Jesus Christ*, pp. 435 sqq.

[31] ὅτι Ἰησοῦς λαὸν ἐκ γῆς Αἰγύπτου σώσας. Epistle of St. Jude, verse 5.

[32] Ex. XX, 2.

[33] Epistle of St. Jude, verse 6.

[34] ὁ Θεός.

[35] Cfr. Cardinal Bellarmine, *De Christo*, I, 4.

In conclusion we will quote a passage from the Epistle of St. James: " You have heard the patience of Job, and you have seen the end of the Lord,[36] that the Lord is merciful and compassionate." [37] " *Misericors Dominus et miserator*" is a standing phrase which the Bible applies exclusively to God,[38] and in this same sense, writing to the witnesses of the Ascension, St. James predicates it of Christ the " Lord."

γ) The use of the term "Logos" (*Verbum Dei*) to designate the "Son of God" who became incarnate in Jesus Christ, is peculiar to St. John.[39]   He ascribes to the Logos eternal pre-existence,[40] aseity, creative power, and the authorship of supernatural grace, truth, and divine sonship. Hence the fundamental teaching of the Johannean Gospel, that "the Logos [Word] was God," [41] can have but one meaning, *viz.:* that the Logos is God in the strict sense of the term, not merely figuratively or metaphorically.   Now St. John Himself tells us that Jesus Christ is the Word made flesh,[42] and consequently Jesus Christ, being the Logos, must be true God.

In the light of these Scriptural texts it is passing strange to hear Harnack declare: " The most impor-

---

36 τὸ τέλος Κυρίου εἴδετε.

37 Ep. of St: James V, 11.

38 Cfr. Pohle-Preuss, *God: His Knowability, Essence, and Attributes,* pp. 464 sqq.

39 John I, 1 sqq.; 1 John I, 1; V, 7; Apoc. XIX, 13. Cfr. Pohle-Preuss, *The Divine Trinity,* pp. 88 sqq.

40 This eternal pre-existence is real, not merely logical in the Divine Intellect or Knowledge, because the Logos is " *unigenitus in sinu Patris* — only-begotten in the bosom of the Father " (John I, 18).

41 John I, 1.

42 John I, 14, 17.

tant step that was ever taken in the domain of Christian
doctrine was when the Christian apologists at the beginning of the second century drew the equation: the
Logos = Jesus Christ." [43]   In matter of fact St. John
" drew this equation " long before the apologists. He
employed the term " Logos " in a higher sense than that
of " a mere predicate," [44] by ascribing to Him a variety of
indisputably divine attributes.[45]

b) Because of the importance of this dogma
we proceed to develop the argument from Tradition.[46]

a) The belief of the Primitive Church is
clearly recorded in the writings of the Apostolic
Fathers.

St. Clement of Rome,[47] who was a disciple and fellow-
laborer of St. Paul,[48] and the third successor of St.
Peter in the See of Rome,[49] invariably refers to Christ
as " the Lord," [50] — a title proper to God alone.[51]   He
furthermore expressly teaches that " The scepter of the

[43] *Das Wesen des Christentums,*
p. 127 (English translation, p. 218).
[44] Harnack, *l. c.*
[45] Cfr. Pohle-Preuss, *The Divine
Trinity,* pp. 91 sqq. For a detailed
refutation of Harnack's denial of
the genuinity of the Fourth Gospel,
see Al. Schäfer, *Einleitung in das
Neue Testament,* pp. 255 sqq., Paderborn 1898. We need hardly add
that the above argument abundantly
refutes the contention of the Modernists, that " the Divinity of
Christ cannot be demonstrated from
the Gospels." (Cfr. Syllabus of
Pius X, *apud* Denzinger-Bannwart,

Enchiridion, n. 2027). On the
teaching of the Modernists see F.
Heiner, *Der neue Syllabus Pius X.,*
pp. 114–159, Mainz 1907.
[46] On certain difficulties connected with the Patristic argument
cfr. Pohle-Preuss, *The Divine Trinity,* pp. 142 sqq.
[47] Died about the year 96.
[48] Phil. IV, 3.
[49] Cfr. St. Irenæus, *Adv. Haer.,*
III, 3, 3.
[50] *Dominus, ὁ Κύριος.*
[51] Cfr. Pohle-Preuss, *God: His
Knowability, Essence and Attributes,* pp. 140 sqq.

majesty of God,[52] the Lord Jesus Christ, did not come with arrogance of pride and overbearing, which He might have done, but with humility." While this text does not embody an explicit profession of faith in the Divinity of Christ, it involves such a profession, inasmuch as no mere creature, whether man or angel, could without blasphemy be called " the scepter of the majesty of God." Had St. Clement not believed in the Divinity of Christ, he could not reasonably have asserted that our Lord, had He so desired, instead of coming " with humility," might have come " *cum iactantia superbiae,*" that is, with a just claim to divine honors.

The so-called Second Letter of St. Clement, though now generally admitted to be the work of a writer living in the middle of the second century,[53] may yet, because of its antiquity and the high esteem in which it has always been held in the Church,[54] claim considerable dogmatic authority. It begins with the significant exhortation: " Brethren, thus we must think of Jesus Christ as God, as the Judge of the quick and the dead." [55]

The so-called Epistle of St. Barnabas, though reckoned among the non-canonical writings by Eusebius,[56] is as old as, if not older than St. Clement's undoubtedly genuine First Letter to the Corinthians.[57] As a witness

[52] τὸ σκῆπτρον τῆς μεγαλοσύνης τοῦ Θεοῦ. 1 Cor. XVI, 2 (ed. Funk, I, 41, Tübingen 1887).

[53] This opinion is based on both internal and external evidence. The complete Greek text of this " Second Letter," as first published in 1875, makes it evident that it is not a letter but a sermon, probably preached at Corinth. Cfr. Bardenhewer-Shahan, *Patrology,* p. 29.

[54] The " Letter " is first men-tioned by Eusebius (*Hist. Eccl.,* III, 38, 1) as purporting to be the Second Letter of St. Clement.

[55] *Patres Apostolici,* Ed. Funk, I, 81.

[56] *Hist. Eccl.,* VI, 13, 6.

[57] According to the most approved conjectures (Funk, Hilgenfeld) this Letter was composed in the reign of the Emperor Nerva (A. D. 96–98). Cfr. Bardenhewer-Shahan, *Patrology,* pp. 22 sqq.

to primitive Tradition its authority is unexceptionable. It teaches: " Jesus is not [only] the Son of man, but the Son of God, though as to form revealed in the flesh. But because they would say that He was the son of David, David himself, apprehending and foreseeing the error of impious men, prophesied: ' The Lord spoke to my Lord ' . . . Behold how David calls Him ' Lord ' and not son." [58]

The author of the work known as the *Shepherd of Hermas* was not, as he represents himself, a contemporary of St. Clement of Rome, but probably a brother of Pope Pius I (about 140–155).[59] Funk justly charges him with teaching a false Christology.[60] Nevertheless he may be cited as a witness to primitive Tradition. He says: " The Son is older than any creature, so much so that He ministered as counsellor to the Father at the creation of the creature." [61] And again: " The name of the Son of God is grand and immeasurable and supports the whole world." [62] Pre-existence, the power of creation and preservation are divine attributes, and He to whom they are ascribed (the " Son of God," or Christ), must be Divine. However, as the phraseology of the *Shepherd* occasionally savors of Adoptionism, it will be well not to attach too much importance to his testimony.[63]

58 *Ep. Barnabae*, XII, 10, ed. Funk, I, 41. On the testimony of Polycarp and St. Ignatius of Antioch, cfr. Pohle-Preuss, *The Divine Trinity*, p. 137, and Nirschl, *Die Theologie des hl. Ignatius*, Mainz 1880.

59 This theory, upon which competent critics are now almost unanimously agreed, is based on a passage of the Muratorian Fragment, which the reader will find quoted in Bardenhewer-Shahan, *Patrology*, p. 40.

60 Hermas identifies the " Son of God " with the Holy Ghost, and the Holy Ghost, as it would seem, with the Archangel Michael. Cfr. Pohle-Preuss, *The Divine Trinity*, p. 151.

61 *Pastor Hermae*, l. III, sim. 9, c. 12, 2.

62 *Ibid.*, c. 14, 5.

63 Cfr. Tixeront, *History of Dogmas* (Engl. ed.), Vol. I, pp. 115 sqq., St. Louis 1911.

THE DIVINITY OF CHRIST 23

β) The Christian apologists of the second century are a unit in their Logos-teaching, though it should be borne in mind that their theory of the Λόγος σπερματικός, as well as the distinction they make between λόγος ἐνδιάθετος and λόγος προφορικός are not derived from Revelation but from the philosophical systems of the Platonists and Stoics.[64]

A most important witness to primitive Christian belief in the Divinity of Jesus is Aristides of Athens. His *Apology,* already mentioned by Eusebius,[65] was regarded as lost until the year 1878, when the Mechitarists of San Lazzaro published a fragment of an Armenian translation. In 1891, Rendel Harris made known a complete Syriac translation, and a Greek recension of the text was simultaneously edited by Armitage Robinson.[66] The original of this Apology was probably offered to the Emperor Antoninus Pius (138–161). "The Christians," says Aristides,[67] "date the beginning of their religion from Jesus Christ. He, Himself, is

[64] "The view of the Logos as ἐνδιάθετος and as προφορικὸς, as the Word conceived and the Word uttered, the Word mental and the Word active and effectual — to distinguish the two senses of Logos, thought and speech — came from the Stoics, and is found in Philo, and was, under certain limitations, allowed in Catholic theology. (Damasc., *F. O.,* II, 21). To use, indeed, either of the two absolutely and to the exclusion of the other, would have involved some form of Sabellianism, or Arianism, as the case might be; but each term might correct the defective sense of the other. That the use was not over-safe would appear from its history in the Church, into which the above theologians [Tatian, Tertullian, Novatian, etc.], by their mode of teaching the γέννησις of the Word, introduce us." (Newman, *Select Treatises of St. Athanasius,* Vol. II, p. 340, 9th impression, London 1903.) On the history of these terms see the same eminent author's *Tracts Theological and Ecclesiastical,* pp. 209 sqq., new ed., London 1895.
[65] *Chron. ad a. Abrah. 2140;* cfr. *Hist. Eccl.,* IV, 3, 3.
[66] Cfr. Bardenhewer-Shahan, *Patrology,* p. 46.
[67] *Apol.,* II, 6.

called the Son of God the Most High, and they teach
of Him that God descended from heaven and assumed
flesh from a Hebrew virgin.   Therefore the Son of God
hath dwelled in a daughter of man."

To the same Emperor Antoninus Pius, and to his
adopted sons, Marcus Aurelius and Lucius Verus, is addressed the "First" Apology of St. Justin Martyr, composed about A. D. 150.[68]   Justin attempts to demonstrate
from the Old Testament [69] that "Jesus Christ is the
Son of God," and thereupon continues: "Who, being
the first-born word of God, is also God." [70]   On the
authority of Sacred Scripture he rejects the contention
of the Ebionites that Christ is a "mere man," [71] and
declares that He is "alone" called "Son of God" in
"the proper sense." [72]   St. Justin concludes his argument against the Jew Trypho with the remark: "That
Christ the Lord, therefore, is both God and the Son of
God,[73] . . . has been repeatedly proved."   He accordingly does not hesitate to assign to Jesus Christ, as
Second Person of the Divine Trinity, a place in the
baptismal form, saying that all Christians are baptized
"in the name of the Parent of all things, the Lord God,
and of our Saviour Jesus Christ, and of the Holy
Ghost." [74]

68 On St. Justin's teaching concerning the Logos cfr. Pohle-Preuss,
The Divine Trinity, p. 144.

69 *Apol.*, I, n. 63 (Migne, *P. G.*,
VI, 423 sq.).

70 *Ibid.* (Migne, *P. G.*, VI, 426):
ὃς καὶ Λόγος πρωτότοκος ὢν τοῦ
Θεοῦ, καὶ Θεὸς ὑπάρχει.

71 *Dial. c. Tryph.*, 48 (Migne, *l.
c.*, 579).

72 *Apol.*, II, n. 6 (Migne, *l. c.*,
453): ὁ μόνος λεγόμενος κυρίως
υἱός, ὁ Λόγος πρὸ τῶν ποιημάτων·

73 *Dial. c. Tryph.*, 128 (Migne,
l. c., 774): καὶ Θεὸς Θεοῦ υἱὸς
ὑπάρχων.

74 *Apol.*, I, n. 61 (Migne, *l. c.*,
419): "*In nomine Parentis uni-
versorum ac Domini Dei, ac Salvatoris nostri Iesu Christi, et Spiritus
Sancti.*" On the Christological
teaching of St. Justin consult A. L.
Feder, S.J., *Justins des Märtyrers
Lehre von Jesus Christus*, Freiburg
1906.

One of the most beautiful professions of faith in the Divinity of Christ that has come down to us from the early days is contained in the Letter to Diognetus, which on internal evidence is commonly ascribed to the era of the persecutions.[75] The author of this Letter [76] devotes an entire chapter (the seventh) to Christ as " the Logos sent upon this earth by the invisible Creator," and who is " no angel," but the " Creator of the Universe " Himself.[77]

γ) An important doctrinal rôle in the tradition of our dogma must be assigned to St. Irenæus of Lyons (born about 140). He was a disciple of St. Polycarp of Smyrna (d. 155), who had received the faith from St. John, the Apostle.

St. Irenæus emphasizes the fact that Christ is truly the Son of God, and consequently true God. " No one else, therefore," he writes, . . . " is called God or Lord, except He who is the God and Lord of all [*i. e.*, the Father] . . . and His Son Jesus Christ, our Lord." [78]

75 Cfr. Bardenhewer-Shahan, *Patrology*, p. 68.

76 The authorship of the Letter to Diognetus has been variously attributed: by Bunsen to Marcion, by Dräseke to Apelles, by Doulcet, Kihn, and Krüger to Aristides of Athens. Bardenhewer says that " the latter hypothesis alone merits attention." (Bardenhewer-Shahan, *l. c.*)

77 *Ep. ad Diognet.*, VII, 2, 4 (ed. Funk, I, 321): "*Ipse vere omnium regenerator et omnium conditor et invisibilis Deus* (= *Pater*) *ipse e coelis veritatem et Verbum sanctum et incomprehensibile* (τὸν Λόγον τὸν ἅγιον καὶ ἀπερινόητον) *inter homines locavit et cordibus*

eorum infixit; non quemadmodum aliquis coniicere possit, hominibus ministrum aliquem mittens aut angelum aut principem, . . . sed ipsum opificem et creatorem omnium (τὸν τεχνίτην καὶ δημιουργὸν τῶν ὅλων), *per quem coelos condidit. . . . In clementia et lenitate ut rex mittens Filium regem misit eum, ut Deum misit, ut hominem ad homines misit.*"

78 "*Nemo igitur alius. . . . Deus nominatur aut Dominus appellatur nisi qui est omnium Deus et Dominus* [*i. e., Pater*] *. . . et huius Filius Iesus Christus Dominus noster.*" *Contr. Haer.*, III, 6, 2 (Migne, *P. G.*, VII, 861).

"He [*i. e.*, Christ] alone of all men who lived up to that time is properly called God, and Lord, and Eternal King, and Only-Begotten, and Word Incarnate, by all the prophets and Apostles, and by the [Holy] Spirit Himself, as any one can see who has attained to even a modicum of truth. The Scriptures would not give such testimony of Him if He were a mere man like the rest of us." [79] In virtue of this belief St. Irenæus unhesitatingly identifies Christ with the Second Person of the Divine Trinity: "The Church received from the Apostles and their disciples that faith which is in one God, the Father Almighty . . . and in one Jesus Christ, the Son of God, who was made Flesh for our salvation, and in the Holy Ghost." [80]

As for Origen (185–255), he is quite orthodox in his Christological teaching when he speaks as a simple witness to ecclesiastical Tradition. It is only when he engages in philosophical speculation that he seems to deviate from the truth. In his first-mentioned capacity he says in the preface to his famous work Περὶ Ἀρχῶν: "Jesus Christ, who has come, was begotten from the Father before all creatures. And having ministered to the Father at the creation of all things — for through Him all

---

[79] *Contr. Haer.*, III, 19, 2 (Migne, *P. G.*, VII, 910): "*Quoniam autem ipse* [*i. e., Christus*] *proprie praeter omnes, qui fuerunt tunc homines, Deus et Dominus et Rex aeternus et Unigenitus et Verbum incarnatum praedicatur et a Prophetis omnibus et Apostolis et ab ipso Spiritu, adest videre omnibus, qui vel modicum de veritate attigerint; haec autem non testificarentur Scripturae de eo, si similiter ut omnes homo tantum fuisset.*"

[80] *Ibid.*, I, 10, 1–2 (Migne, *l. c.*, 549, 550): "*Ecclesia et ab Apostolis et a discipulis eorum accepit eam fidem, quae est in unum Deum Patrem omnipotentem . . . et in unum Iesum Christum Filium Dei incarnatum pro nostra salute* (καὶ εἰς ἕνα Χριστὸν Ἰησοῦν, τὸν υἱὸν τοῦ Θεοῦ, τὸν σαρκωθέντα ὑπὲρ τῆς ἡμετέρας σωτηρίας) *et in Spiritum Sanctum.*" A cognate text from the writings of Clement of Alexandria is cited in Pohle-Preuss, *The Divine Trinity*, p. 141. On traces of Subordinationism in Irenæus cfr. Tixeront, *History of Dogmas*, p. 234.

things were made — He emptied Himself in recent days, became man and assumed flesh, notwithstanding He was God, and having become man, He nevertheless remained what He was, namely God." [81] Of the author of the Johannine Gospel Origen observes: " None of the Evangelists has proclaimed the Divinity of Christ so clearly as John." [82]

δ) Among the ecclesiastical writers of the West, Tertullian taught and defended the Divinity of Christ and the dogma of the Trinity. In his *Apologeticum* (or *Apologeticus*)[83] he says: *"Verum neque de Christo erubescimus, quum sub nomine eius deputari et damnari iuvat, neque de Deo aliter praesumimus.   Necesse est igitur pauca dicamus de Christo ut Deo. . . . Hunc ex Deo prolatum didicimus et prolatione generatum et idcirco Filium Dei et Deum dictum ex unitate substantiae; nam et Deus spiritus. . . . Quod de Deo profectum est, Deus est et Dei Filius et unus ambo."* [84]

---

81 *Orig., De Princ.*, Praef., 5.

82 *Tract. in Ioa.*, 6 (Migne, *P. G.*, XIV, 29). On the controversy between Dionysius the Great of Alexandria (d. 265) and Pope Dionysius, cfr. Pohle-Preuss, *The Divine Trinity*, pp. 121 sqq., 142. On Origen's Christological teaching cfr. Liddon, *The Divinity of Christ*, pp. 573 sqq.; Tixeront, *History of Dogmas*, I, 264 sqq.

83 The most ancient text-witnesses do not agree with regard to the precise title of this famous book.

84 *Apologet.*, 21. Bardenhewer ob-serves that Tertullian " in his defense of the personal distinction between the Father and the Son . . . does not, apparently, avoid a certain Subordinationism, although in many very clear expressions and turns of thought he almost approaches the decision of the Nicene Council." (Otto Bardenhewer, *Patrologie*, 2nd ed., p. 162, Freiburg 1901. Shahan's translation, p. 185. We have slightly altered Dr. Shahan's wording, in order to bring out our point more effectively). The difficulty is one of terminology

The writings of St. Cyprian, Bishop of Carthage (about
A D. 200–258), who was a countryman of Tertullian,
abound in passages affirming the Divinity of Christ and
the dogma of the Trinity. " If he has obtained forgiveness of his sins . . .," Cyprian says in one place,
" he has been made a temple of God. I ask: Of which
God? Not of the Creator, because he does not believe
in Him. Not of Christ, because he denies that Christ
is God. Not of the Holy Ghost, because, if the Three
are One, how can the Holy Ghost be pacified in regard
to him who is an enemy of either the Father or the
Son? " [85]

The Patristic texts which we have quoted show how
utterly groundless is the Modernist assertion, solemnly
condemned in the " Syllabus of Pius X," that " the
Christ of history [*i. e.,* Jesus as depicted in the four Gos-
pels] is far inferior to the Christ who is the object of
faith." [86]

3. THE APOLOGETIC ARGUMENT.—Apologetically, the Divinity of Christ can be demonstrated
in a twofold manner: (1) against the Jews, by
showing that the Messianic prophecies were fulfilled in Christ; (2) against unbelievers, from
internal and external criteria furnished by His
life and teaching and by the testimony of His

rather than real. Cfr. Pohle-Preuss,
The Divine Trinity, pp. 141 sqq.;
also, Tixeront, *History of Dogmas,*
Vol. I, p. 312

[85] *Ep. ad Iubaian.,* 23, 12.

[86] " *Concedere licet Christum,
quem exhibet historia, multo inferi-
orem esse Christo, qui est obiectum
fidei.*" Cfr. Heiner, *Der neue Syl-*

labus, pp. 121 sqq., Mainz 1907.
On the Nicene decision see Pohle-
Preuss, *The Divine Trinity,* pp. 125
sqq. On the testimony of the martyrs to the Divinity of Christ, *ibid.,*
pp. 137 sqq. On the teaching of the
Nicene and post-Nicene Fathers,
ibid., pp. 153 sqq.

Apostles. It belongs to Fundamental Theology to develop this argument fully; in the present, purely dogmatic treatise we shall merely sketch its outlines.

a) Against the Jews we must prove that Jesus Christ is the " Messias" [87] promised in the Old Testament.   If He *is* the Messias, He is true God, for as such the prophets predicted that He would appear.[88]   If He were not the Messias, the Jewish religion would be based on fraud, because the idea of the Messias forms its very foundation-stone.[89]

All the Messianic prophecies were fulfilled in that historic personage known as Jesus of Nazareth, who proved Himself by word and deed to be the true Messias.[90]

The well-known prediction of Jacob (Gen. XLIX, 10 sqq.) : " The sceptre shall not be taken away [91] from Juda, nor a ruler from his thigh, till he come that is to be sent, etc.," either has not yet been fulfilled, and must forever remain unfulfilled, or it is fulfilled in Jesus Christ.[92]   The same holds good of the famous prophecy

87 'Ο Χριστός, *i. e., unctus.*

88 Cfr. Pohle-Preuss, *The Divine Trinity,* pp. 15 sq.

89 Cfr.   Hettinger-Bowden,   *Revealed Religion,* pp. 149 sqq., 2nd ed.; A. J. Maas, S. J., *Christ in Type and Prophecy,* 2 vols., New York 1893; J. P. Arendzen, "The Preparation of Jewry," in *The Incarnation,* edited by C. Lattey, S. J., Cambridge 1926, pp. 19–38.

90 On the Messianic expectations of the Jews and Gentiles at the time of Christ cfr. Hettinger, *Fundamentaltheologie,* pp. 339 sqq.; C. Gutberlet, *Lehrbuch der Apologetik,* Vol. II, pp. 192 sqq., Münster 1895; H. P. Liddon, *The Divinity of Our Lord and Saviour Jesus Christ,* pp. 109 sqq., London, Oxford, and Cambridge 1867; Maas, *Christ in Type and Prophecy,* Vol. I, pp. 56 sqq., New York 1893; H. J. Coleridge, S. J., *The Preparation of the Incarnation,* pp. 59 sqq., 2nd ed., London 1894.

91 On this rendering of the Hebrew text, as well as on the whole passage, see Maas, *Christ in Type and Prophecy,* Vol. I, pp. 288 sqq.

92 On certain strange Jewish at-

30   DUALITY IN UNITY

of Daniel (Dan. IX, 24–27: "Seventy weeks are shortened upon thy people, etc."). No matter how we may interpret it in detail, as a whole it was either realized in Christ or must remain forever unfulfilled.[93] Now there can be no reasonable doubt that the Danielic prediction has found its consummation in Christ, for since His time the Jewish sacrifices have ceased and the city of Jerusalem with its Temple has been destroyed. Similar arguments can be constructed from the prophecies of the "virgin birth" (Is. VII, 14), the passion (Ps. XXI; Is. LIII, 1 sqq.), the "clean oblation" (Mal. I, 11 sqq.), and so forth.[94]

Furthermore, all Old Testament types, both personal and real, have been fulfilled in Christ and His Church.[95] Hence, for an orthodox Jew to deny the Messiahship and consequently the Divinity of Christ, means to reject the Jewish religion as an empty superstition.

b) Against unbelievers the Divinity of Jesus Christ can be demonstrated: (1) from internal criteria such as the divine character of His teaching and the superhuman majesty of His Person; and (2) from external evidence, especially His

tempts at evading this dilemma cfr. Billuart, *De Incarn.*, diss. 2, art. 2, §1.

[93] Cfr. Fraidl, *Die Exegese der 70 Wochen Daniels in der älteren und mittleren Zeit*, Graz 1883; Düsterwald, *Die Weltreiche und das Gottesreich nach den Weissagungen des Propheten Daniel*, Freiburg 1890; Maas, *Christ in Type and Prophecy*, Vol. I, pp. 299 sqq.

[94] Cfr. G. B. Tepe, S. J., *Instit. Theol.*, Vol. I, pp. 132 sqq.; H. E. Hall, *The Miraculous Birth of Our Lord*, London 1919; Durand-Bruneau, *The Childhood of Jesus*

Christ, Philadelphia 1910, and G. Oussani, "The Virgin Birth of Christ and Modern Criticism" in the *New York Review*, Vol. III (1907), No. 2–3 (1908), No. 4–5; Coubé, *Revue des Objections*, Paris, Mai 1924; M. J. Scott, S. J., *The Virgin Birth*, N. Y. 1925.

[95] Cfr. J. Selbst, *Die Kirche Jesu Christi nach den Weissagungen der Propheten*, Mainz 1883; A. Schöpfer, *Geschichte des Alten Testamentes*, 4th ed., pp. 370 sqq., Brixen 1906; A J. Maas, S. J., *Christ in Type and Prophecy*, New York 1893.

prophecies and the miracles wrought by Him in confirmation of His mission and teaching.

This argument derives additional force from the admission of modern Rationalists, that " the historical criticism of two generations has resulted in restoring the credibility of the first three Gospels " (which had been impugned by David Friedrich Strauss),[96] and that St. Paul " understood the Master and continued His work." [97]

a) The Rationalists are forced to admit that Christ's religious and moral teaching was as sublime as it was simple, and that not the slightest moral taint attaches to His Person.

" That Jesus' message is so great and so powerful," says, *e. g.*, Harnack,[98] " lies in the fact that it is so simple and on the other hand so rich; so simple as to be exhausted in each of the leading thoughts which he uttered; so rich that every one of these thoughts seems to be inexhaustible and the full meaning of the sayings and parables beyond our reach. But more than that — he himself stands behind everything that he has said. His words speak to us across the centuries with the freshness of the present. It is here that that profound saying is truly verified: ' Speak, that I may see thee.' " Sublime indeed, born of superhuman wisdom and celestial holiness is the teaching of Jesus Christ,[99] and consequently, He Himself must be more than a mere man.[100]

96 A. Harnack, *Das Wesen des Christentums*, p. 14. (English edition, p. 22).

97 *Ibid.*, p. 110. (English ed., p. 189.)

98 *Ibid.*, p. 33. (English translation, pp. 55 sq.)

99 Consider, for instance, the Lord's Prayer and the Sermon on the Mount.

100 The student will find this thought forcefully developed by P. Hake in his *Handbuch der allge-*

By the compelling majesty of His Person Jesus looms as the ideal " Superman." His very features, His words and actions, are so human and yet at the same time so exalted, that we instinctively feel He is a superior being. We are justified in asking Professor Harnack whether his own description of Christ would fit a mere man: " The sphere in which he lived, above the earth and its concerns, did not destroy his interest in it; no, he brought everything in it into relation with the God whom he knew, and he saw it as protected in him: ' Your Father in heaven feeds them.' The parable is his most familiar form of speech. Insensibly, however, parable and sympathy pass into each other. Yet he who had not where to lay his head does not speak like one who has broken with everything, or like an heroic penitent, or like an ecstatic prophet, but like a man who has rest and peace for his soul and who is able to give life and strength to others. He strikes the mightiest notes; he offers men an inexorable alternative; he leaves them no escape; and yet the strongest emotion seems to come naturally to him, and he expresses it as something natural; he clothes it in the language in which a mother speaks to her child." [101]

There is another characteristic which, even more than those we have already mentioned, stamps the Person of Jesus Christ with the seal of Divinity,— His absolute exemption from error and sin. No mere man is immune from sin and error. If any man really enjoyed these prerogatives, he could not proclaim the fact to his fellow men without making himself the butt of ridicule. Jesus, the Godman, speaking ' as one hav-

meinen Religionswissenschaft, Vol. II, pp. 131 sqq., Freiburg 1887.
[101] *Das Wesen des Christentums,*
pp. 23 sq. (English translation, pp. 39–40.)

ing power," [102] fears not error, nor doubt, nor contradiction. He bases His instructions on a categorical: " I tell you," and meets the objections of His opponents in the majestic posture of a true sovereign. Still more marvellous is His freedom from sin. Neither His friends [103] nor His enemies, [104] including Judas the traitor, were able " to find a cause " in Him. Nay, more — He Himself was in a position to say without the slightest conceit: " I am meek and humble of heart," [105] and to ask: " Which of you shall convince me of sin? " [106]— the same Jesus who taught His Apostles to pray: " Father . . . forgive us our debts, as we also forgive our debtors." [107]

Christ thus stands before us both in the intellectual and the moral order as a wondrous apparition, a superhuman, heavenly Being of divine origin. Closely bound up with His character and teaching is His own assertion of His Divine Sonship and Divinity. It puts all men face to face with the terrible dilemma: " Either Jesus Christ is true God, or the Christian religion is a blasphemous deception, and its Founder a knave or a fool. This alternative ought to convince all who are able and willing to use their reason, that Christ is true God and that the Christian religion is a divine institution." [108]   In vain does Harnack declare it unevangelical to " put a Christological creed in the forefront of the Gospel " and to " teach that before a man can approach [the Gospel] he must learn to think rightly about Christ." [109]   Christ

102 Matth. VII, 29.

103 Cfr. Acts III, 14; XIII, 35; Heb. IV, 15; 1 Pet. I, 19; 1 John III, 7; II, 1.

104 Cfr. Luke XXIII, 4.

105 Matth. XI, 29.

106 John VIII, 46.

107 Matth. VI, 12.

108 J. Kleutgen, *Theologie der Vorzeit*, Vol. III, p. 17, 2nd ed., Münster 1870.   Cfr. M. Lepin, *Christ and the Gospel*, English tr., pp. 128 sqq., Philadelphia 1910.

109 *Das Wesen des Christentums*, p. 93. (English translation, p. 158.)

Himself imposed " a Christological profession of faith on
His Apostles," [110] and confronted the Jews with the categorical question: "What think you of Christ? whose
son is he?" [111] In proof of His own conviction and
of His assertion that He is the Messiah and the true
Son of God, He suffered ignominious death.[112] Upon a
right conception of the Person of Christ, therefore, depends the truth or falsity of the Christian religion. It is
a question of eternal life or death.[113]

β) External proofs for the Divinity of Christ's Person and mission are the *prophecies* He uttered and the *miracles* He performed.

His prophecies concern partly His own future,[114]
partly the fate of His Church,[115] partly the destruction
of Jerusalem and its Temple,[116] and the dispersion of
the Jews.[117] The fact that these predictions were fulfilled to the letter, furnishes a sufficient guaranty that
those which still remain unfulfilled (*e. g.*, the resurrection of the dead and the last judgment), will also come

110 Matth. XVI, 16 sqq.
111 Matth. XXII, 42.
112 Matth. XXVI, 23 sqq.; Luke XXII, 66 sqq.; John XIX, 7.
113 Cfr. K. Hennemann, *Die Heiligkeit Jesu als Beweis seiner Gottheit*, Würzburg 1898; A. Seitz, *Das Evangelium vom Gottessohn*, Freiburg 1908, pp. 171 sqq., 343 sqq.; H. P. Liddon, *The Divinity of Christ*, pp. 243 sqq.; F. Sawicki, *Die Wahrheit des Christentums*, pp. 355 sqq., Paderborn 1911.
114 As, *e. g.*, His betrayal at the hands of Judas, the denial of Peter, the Passion and the Resurrection.
115 For instance, the sending of the Holy Ghost, the heathen per-
secutions, the conversion of the Gentiles, the indestructibility of His Church.
116 Cfr. Matth. XXIV, 5; Luke XIX, 43 sqq.
117 Cfr. Luke XXI, 24. On the literal fulfillment of these proph-
ecies cfr. P. Hake, *Handbuch der allgemeinen Religionswissenschaft*, Vol. II, pp. 193 sqq.; G. B. Tepe, *Instit. Theol.*, Vol. I, pp. 193 sqq. On the destruction of Jerusalem in particular, see Josephus, *Bell. Iud.*, II, 13; VI, 3 sqq.; VII, 1; Tacitus, *Hist.*, I, 2; Ammian. Marcellin., *Rer. Gest.*, XXIII, 1 sqq. (Kirch, *Enchiridion Fontium Historiae Ecclesiasticae*, n. 606, Friburgi 1910).

true. Meanwhile the Catholic Church resides among us
as a living tangible proof of Christ's prophetic power.
Her existence, teaching, character, and indefectibility
supply the earnest inquirer with a sufficiently strong argument for the Godhead of her Founder.[118]

The historicity of the Gospel miracles cannot be
brushed aside on Harnack's frivolous pretext that " what
happens in space and time is subject to the general laws
of motion, and that in this sense, as an interruption of
the order of Nature, there can be no such thing as
'miracles.' " If the Gospels are authentic and genuine documents,— and Harnack admits that at least
three of them are,— the wonderful events which they
record must be accepted as historic facts, because they
are inseparably bound up with the narrative as a whole.
The moral character of Jesus stands or falls with His
miracles, to which He so frequently appeals in proof
of His doctrine and mission.[119]   In matter of fact these
miracles were wrought before the eyes of the whole
Jewish nation, their genuineness is attested alike by
friend and foe, and at least one of them was established
by a searching legal investigation.[120]   Harnack arbi-
trarily disrupts the texture of the Gospel miracles when
he says: " That the earth in its course stood still, that
a she-ass spoke, that a storm was quieted by a word,
we do not believe and we shall never again believe; but
that the lame walked, the blind saw, and the deaf
heard, will not be so summarily dismissed as an illu-

118 This argument is well developed by O. R. Vassall-Phillips, C.
SS. R., *The Mustard Tree: An Argument on Behalf of the Divinity of
Christ,* London 1912.

119 Harnack, *Das Wesen des
Christentums,* p. 17 (English translation, pp. 28 sq.) Cfr. Matth. XI,
4, 5; XII, 25 sqq.; Luke V, 23
sqq.; John V, 21, 36; VI, 30; X, 37
sq.; XI, 42; XIV, 10 sq., etc., etc.
On the historic character of the
Gospels see P. Batiffol, *The Credibility of the Gospel,* tr. by G. C. H.
Pollen, S. J., London 1912.

120 Cfr. John IX, 1 sqq.

sion." [121]   The miracles of the Gospel cannot be divided off
into credible cures and incredible interruptions of the
order of Nature without destroying the harmonious
unity of the sacred narrative. Furthermore, such
unwarranted discrimination would cast a slur on the
moral character of Jesus, who in His sermons constantly appeals to both classes of miracles. If some of
them were unreal, Christ would be a contemptible im-
postor.[122]

And now to the final question: What attitude does
modern Rationalism take with regard to the Resurrection,
that pivotal miracle which constitutes the climax of
our Lord's earthly career and the foundation stone of
Christian belief? [123]   Will Harnack here too make the
reservation: " We are not yet by any means acquainted
with all the forces working in it [i. e., the order of
Nature] and acting reciprocally with other forces "? [124]
It is here that the unbeliever meets with his final Water-
loo. The hypothesis that the death of Christ was
merely apparent, and that His disciples were impostors,
has now been universally abandoned. The so-called
vision theory is flatly contradicted by the facts.[125]   Therefore our Lord's triumphant Resurrection forms the
pillar and groundwork of the Christian dispensation and
the test and touchstone of true belief.[126]

---

121 *Das Wesen des Christentums,*
p. 18 (English translation, pp. 30
sq.).

122 Cfr. Luke VII, 13 sqq.;
Matth. VII, 18 sqq.; John XI, 43.

123 " If Christ be not risen again,
then is our preaching vain, and
your faith is also vain." (1 Cor.
XV, 14.)

124 *Das Wesen des Christentums,*
p. 18 (English translation, p. 30).

125 The doubting Thomas was

surely neither a visionary nor a
day-dreamer.

126 The student will find this sub-
ject more fully developed in Tepe,
Instit. Theol., Vol. I, pp. 97 sqq.
He may also consult with profit:
P. Hake, *Handbuch der allgemeinen
Religionswissenschaft,* Vol. II, pp.
171 sqq.; F. Hettinger, *Fundamen-
taltheologie,* 2nd ed., pp. 368 sqq.,
Freiburg 1888; Fl. Chable, *Die
Wunder Jesu in ihrem inneren*

READINGS : —* St. Thomas Aquinas, *Contr. Gent.*, IV, 2 sqq. (Rickaby, *Of God and His Creatures,* pp. 340 sqq., London 1905). — Suarez, *De Incarnatione,* disp. 2.—* Prudentius Maranus, *De Divinitate Domini Nostri Iesu Christi,* ed. Wirceb., 1859.— P. Hake, *Handbuch der allgemeinen Religionswissenschaft,* Vol. II, §§ 30 sqq., Freiburg 1887.—* C. Gutberlet, *Apologetik,* 2nd ed., Vol. II, 2, §§ 5–10, Münster 1895.—* Fr. Hettinger, *Apologie des Christentums,* I, 1, Vortr. 14–18, 9th ed., Freiburg 1906. (English tr. by H. S. Bowden, *Revealed Religion,* pp. 130 sqq., 2nd ed., London *s. a.*) — J. Bade, *Christotheologie oder Jesus Christus, der Sohn Gottes und wahre Gott,* 2nd ed., Paderborn 1870.— L. Reinke, *Die messianischen Psalmen,* 2 vols., Giessen 1857–58.— IDEM, *Die messianischen Weissagungen bei den Propheten,* 4 vols., Giessen 1859–62.— M. Lendovšek, *Divina Maiestas Verbi Incarnati Elucidata ex Libris Novi Testamenti,* Graz 1896.— Endler, *Apologetische Vorträge über die Gottheit Iesu,* Prague 1900.— W. Capitaine, *Jesus von Nazareth, eine Prüfung seiner Gottheit,* Ratisbon 1904.— H. Schell, *Jahwe und Christus,* Paderborn 1905.— G. W. B. Marsh, *Messianic Philosophy, an Historical and Critical Examination of the Evidence for the Existence, Death, Resurrection, Ascension, and Divinity of Jesus Christ,* London 1908.— IDEM, *Miracles,* London 1906.— IDEM, *The Resurrection of Christ, Is it a Fact?* London 1905.— Devivier-Sasia, *Christian Apologetics,* Vol. I, pp. 33 sqq., San José, Cal., 1903.— Bougaud-Currie, *The Divinity of Christ,* New York 1906.— J. H. Newman, *An Essay in Aid of a Grammar of Assent,* New York ed., 1870, pp. 420 sqq.— Freddi-Sullivan, S. J., *Jesus Christ the Word Incarnate,* pp. 12 sqq., St. Louis 1904.— V. Rose, O. P., *Studies on the Gospels,* English tr. by R. Fraser, London 1903.— * H. Felder, O. M. Cap., tr. by J. L. Stoddard, *Christ and the Critics, A Defence of the Divinity of Jesus Against the Attacks of Modern Sceptical Criticism,* 2 vols., London 1924.—H. Lepin, *Christ and the Gospel,* Philadelphia 1910.—O. R. Vassall-Phillips, C. SS. R., *The Mustard Tree: An Argument on Behalf of the Di-*

Zusammenhang, Freiburg 1897; H. Schell, *Jahwe und Christus,* pp. 278 sqq., Paderborn 1905; L. Fonck, S. J., *Die Wunder des Herrn im Evangelium,* 2nd ed., Innsbruck 1907; H. P. Liddon, *The Divinity of Our Lord and Saviour Jesus Christ,* pp. 232 sqq., London, Oxford, and Cambridge 1867; J. B. Disteldorf, *Die Auferstehung Christi,* Trier 1906; G. W. B. Marsh, *The Resurrection of Christ,* London 1905; E. Mangenot, *La Resurrection de Jésus,* Paris 1910.

vinity of Christ, London 1912.— F. X. Kiefl, *Der geschichtliche Christus und die moderne Philosophie*, Mainz 1911.— P. Batiffol, *The Credibility of the Gospels* (tr. by G. C. H. Pollen, S. J.), London 1912.— H. Schumacher, *Die Selbstoffenbarung Jesu bei Mat. 11, 27 (Luc. 10, 22)*, Freiburg 1912.— *Jesus Christus, Vorträge von Braig, Hoberg, Krieg, Weber, Esser,* 2nd ed., Freiburg 1911.— A. L. Williams (Prot.), *The Hebrew-Christian Messiah*, London 1917.— F. Clarke, "Sources of St. John's Logos Doctrine," *Irish Eccles. Record*, 1922–23, Nos. 659 sqq.—L. de Grandmaison, *Jésus dans l'Histoire et dans le Mystère*, Paris 1925.

Additional literature in Pohle-Preuss, *The Divine Trinity*, pp. 95 sqq., St. Louis 1912.

CHAPTER II

THE HUMANITY OF CHRIST

In this Chapter we shall first demonstrate (Sect. 1) the reality of the human nature of Christ as defined by the Church against the Docetae (Art. 1), and its integrity as defined against Arianism and Apollinarianism (Art. 2). Then we shall proceed to show the Adamic origin of Christ, *qua* man, from the Virgin Mary, as defined against Valentinus and Apelles (Sect. 2), and, finally, the passibility of His human nature, *i. e.,* its capacity for suffering, with special reference to the atonement. (Sect. 3).

GENERAL READINGS : —* J. Grimm, *Das Leben Jesu,* 2nd ed., 7 vols., Ratisbon 1890 sqq.— P. Didon, *Jesus Christ,* 2 vols., London 1908.— J. Duggan, *The Life of Christ,* London 1897.— M. Meschler, S. J., *The Life of Our Lord Jesus Christ the Son of God,* 2 vols., Freiburg and St. Louis 1909.—* J. Kleutgen, S. J., *Theologie der Vorzeit,* Vol. III, pp. 7 sqq., Münster 1870. — Alb. a Bulsano, *Instit. Theol. Dogmat.* (ed. a Graun), t. I, pp. 570 sqq., Oeniponte 1893.—* St. Thomas Aquinas, *S. Theol.,* 3a, qu. 5-6 (summarized in English in Freddi-Sullivan, *Jesus Christ the Word Incarnate,* St. Louis 1904).—* Suarez, *De Incarnatione,* disp. 2, sect. 1; disp. 15, sect. 1 sqq.— Thomassin, *De Incarn.,* IV, 1-11.— L. Janssens, O. S. B., *De Deo-homine,* Vol. I, pp. 240 sqq., Friburgi 1901.— Durand-Bruneau, *The Childhood of Jesus Christ According to the Canonical Gospels,* Philadelphia 1910.— H. J. Coleridge, S. J., *The Preparation of the Incarnation,*

2nd ed., London 1894.— IDEM, *The Nine Months,* London 1895.
— IDEM, *The Thirty Years,* new ed., London 1893.— Rivière-Cappadelta, *The Doctrine of the Atonement,* 2 vols., London 1909.
— Fr. Schmid, *Quaestiones Selectae ex Theologia Dogmatica,* qu. 6, Paderborn 1891.

SECTION 1

REALITY AND INTEGRITY OF CHRIST'S SACRED HUMANITY

ARTICLE 1

THE REALITY OF CHRIST'S SACRED HUMANITY, AS DEFINED AGAINST THE DOCETAE

1. DOCETISM AND THE CHURCH.—In the course of the first four centuries of the Christian era sundry heretics asserted that our Blessed Redeemer was not a real man, but merely bore the semblance of a man, and that His body was a mere phantasm (δόκημα, φάντασμα). Against this heresy the Church vigorously upheld the true and genuine character of Christ's humanity.

a) The Docetæ[1] were recruited partly from the Gnostics of the second century,[2] and partly from the

[1] Δοκηταί, from δόκησις, "appearance" or "semblance," because they taught that Christ only "appeared" or "seemed" to be a man, to be born, to live, and to suffer. The word *Docetae* is best rendered in English by "Illusionists." (Cfr. J. P. Arendzen, art. "Docetae," in the *Catholic Encyclopedia*, Vol. V). Arendzen does not fail to point out the noteworthy fact that this early heresy is being renewed in modern Theosophic and Spiritistic circles in a form "scarcely less phantastic than the wildest vagaries of old." The name Docetae did not designate a sect properly so called. It applied to all the sects which taught the non-reality of the material body of Christ. Of this number were the Valentinians, the Basilidians, the Ophites, the Marcionites, and other Gnostics. Cfr. Milman's notes on Gibbon's *Decline and Fall of the Roman Empire,* Vol. I, Ch. XXI.

[2] Saturnilus, Basilides, Marcion, *et al.*

Manichæans and Priscillianists of the third and fourth.
These heretics were at one in contending that matter
(*hyle*) is the seat of evil and that God would have subjected Himself to contamination by assuming a material
body.[3]

b) In the early days of Christianity the Church simply
bound her children to her official form of Baptism (now
called the Apostles' Creed), which in its articles on the
conception, birth, and crucifixion of Christ plainly de-
bars the illusionist theory.

We have no authentic record of any formal definition
of the faith against the Priscillianists. The anti-Pris-
cillianist profession of faith erroneously attributed to a
Council of Toledo (A. D. 447) is in reality the work
of an anonymous Spanish bishop.[4] "*Credimus,*" we
read therein, ". . . *nec imaginarium corpus aut phan-
tasmatis alicuius in eo* [*scil. Christo*] *fuisse, sed solidum
et verum; hunc et esuriisse et sitiisse et doluisse et
flevisse et omnes corporis iniurias pertulisse* — We believe
that the body of Christ was not imaginary, nor a mere
phantasm, but real and substantial, and that He experienced hunger, and thirst, and pain, and grief, and all the
sufferings of the body."[5]

The Docetic heresy was repeatedly condemned. At
the Second Council of Lyons (A. D. 1274) a profession
of faith was submitted by a number of bishops who rep-
resented the Greek Emperor Michael Palæologus.[6] This
document contains the following passage: "*Credimus
ipsum Filium Dei . . . Deum verum et hominem verum,*

---

3 Funk-Cappadelta, *A Manual of
Church History,* Vol. I, pp. 83 sqq.,
90 sqq., London 1910.

4 See K. Künstle, *Antipriscilliana,*
pp. 30 sqq., Freiburg 1905.

5 Cfr. Denzinger-Bannwart, *Enchiridion,* n. 19.

6 Cfr. Alzog-Pabisch-Byrne, *Manual of Universal Church History,*
Vol. II, pp. 814 sqq.

*proprium in utraque natura atque perfectum, non adopti-
vum, nec phantasticum, sed unum et unicum filium Dei*
— We believe that the Son of God [is] true God and
true man, proper and perfect in both natures, not an
adoptive or fantastic, but the one and only-begotten Son
of God." [7]

A very important dogmatic definition is the famous
Decretum pro Iacobitis, promulgated by Pope Eugene
IV at the Council of Florence, A. D. 1439. This decree
condemns seriatim all Christological heresies, beginning
with those of Ebion, Cerinthus, and Marcion, down to
the Monothelite vagaries of Macarius of Antioch.
Against Docetism it says: " *Anathematizat [Ecclesia]
etiam Manichæum cum sectatoribus suis, qui Dei Filium
non verum corpus, sed phantasticum sumpsisse somnian-
tes humanitatis in Christo veritatem penitus sustulerunt,
necnon Valentinum asserentem Dei Filium nihil de Virgine Maria cepisse, sed corpus coeleste sumpsisse atque
transiisse per uterum Virginis, sicut per aquaeductum
defluens aqua transcurrit* —[The Church] anathematizes
also Mâni, together with his followers, who, imagining
that the Son of God assumed not a true but an apparitional body, utterly deny Christ's manhood. [She
likewise condemns] Valentinus, who asserts that the Son
of God took naught from the Virgin Mary, but assumed
a celestial body and passed through the Virgin's womb
as water flows through an aqueduct." [8]

2. THE TEACHING OF DIVINE REVELATION.—
The ecclesiastical definitions just quoted are
firmly grounded in Sacred Scripture and Tradition.

[7] Cfr. Denzinger-Bannwart, *Enchiridion,* n. 462.

[8] Cfr. Denzinger-Bannwart, *Enchiridion,* n. 710.

4

a) Christ's manhood is so manifestly in evidence throughout the Synoptic Gospels that we can content ourselves with citing but a few of the many available texts. Again and again He speaks of Himself as the "Son of Man." [9]   While it may be readily allowed that in the mouth of the Redeemer this title means far more than a mere assertion of His humanity,[10] it can surely not be reconciled with the assumption of a merely fictitious or apparitional body; for else He could not have told the Jews: [11] "Now you seek to kill [12] me, a man who have spoken the truth to you." In manifesting Himself to the two disciples at Emmaus, after the Resurrection, He showed them His glorified body, which bore the marks of the Crucifixion, saying: [13] "See my hands and feet, that it is I myself; handle, and see: for a spirit [14] hath not flesh and bones, as you see me to have." A visible and tangible body of flesh and bone cannot be a phantasm; it must be real and material. In perfect consonance with this realism is the Scriptural use of the term "flesh," which leaves no doubt whatever as to the materiality of the man Jesus. St. John does not say: "The Word was made man"; he employs the far more graphic phrase: "The Word was made *flesh*." [15]

9 *Filius hominis.*
10 *V. supra*, pp. 16 sq.
11 John VIII, 40.
12 ἀποκτεῖναι.

13 Luke XXIV, 39.
14 *Spiritus*, πνεῦμα, *i. e.*, a pure spirit, wraith.
15 John I, 14.

In vain did the Docetæ bolster their contention by
an appeal to Rom. VIII, 3: "God sending his own
Son, in the likeness of sinful flesh and of sin."[16]
"Likeness" here is not synonymous with "semblance,"
but denotes identity of nature. St. Paul wishes to say
that the flesh of Christ was consubstantial with ours except as touching sin. Cfr. Heb. IV, 15: "For we have
not a high priest, who cannot have compassion on our
infirmities: but one tempted in all things like as we are,
without sin." Another favorite passage with the Docetæ
was Phil. II, 7, where St. Paul attributes to the Son
of God "the form of a servant."[17] But the expression
"form of a servant" can no more mean "semblance
of man" than "form of God"[18] in the preceding verse
means "semblance of God."[19]

b) The Fathers rigorously maintained the
reality of Christ's manhood, as is evidenced by
the sharply anti-Docetic tenor of the seven genuine Epistles[20] of St. Ignatius of Antioch.

a) To quote but one passage:[21] "And He
[Christ] suffered truly, even as He truly raised
Himself up, not as some unbelievers say, that He
suffered in appearance, existing themselves in ap-

---

[16] "Deus Filium suum mittens in
similitudinem carnis peccati (ἐν
ὁμοιώματι σαρκὸς ἁμαρτίας)."

[17] "Who being in the form of
God, thought it not robbery to be
equal with God; but emptied himself, taking the form of a servant
(forma servi, μορφὴ δούλου)."

[18] Forma Dei, μορφὴ Θεοῦ.

[19] Cfr. Pohle-Preuss, The Divine
Trinity, p. 62.

[20] On these Epistles cfr. Bardenhewer-Shahan, Patrology, pp. 30
sqq.

[21] Καὶ ἀληθῶς ἔπαθεν, ὡς καὶ
ἀληθῶς ἀνέστησεν ἑαυτόν, οὐχ
ὥσπερ ἄπιστοί τινες λέγουσι, τὸ
δοκεῖν αὐτὸν πεπονθέναι, αὐτοὶ τὸ
δοκεῖν ὄντες." (Ep. ad Smyrn., c.
2.) Cfr. Funk's Latin translation
of the passage and his note on it in
the Patres Apostolici, i. h. l.

pearance;"—that is to say, if Christ suffered only
in appearance, they who assert this, themselves
have a merely apparitional existence, and thus we
should land in utter scepticism.

In the West Tertullian vigorously refuted the Docetic
errors of Marcion and his adherents by pointing out
their absurd consequences: "*Quomodo in illo* [*scil.
Christo*] *vera erunt, si ipse non fuit verus, si non vere
habuit in se, quod* [*cruci*] *figeretur, quod moreretur,
quod sepeliretur et resuscitaretur? Carnem scilicet sanguine suffusam, ossibus structam, nervis intextam, venis
implexam, quae nasci et mori novit?*" [22]

β) But the early Fathers were not satisfied
with a bare statement of the dogma; they sought
to explain our Lord's humanity theologically and
philosophically. Their favorite mode of argu-
mentation was that familiarly known as *deductio
ad absurdum*.

Docetism is subversive of the very foundations of
Christianity, they said, for if Christ had not a genuine
human body, the entire work of Redemption would
be nugatory. "*Sequitur*," says Tertullian,[23] "*ut omnia
quae per carnem Christi gesta sunt, mendacio gesta sint.
. . . Eversum est igitur totum Dei opus, totum Chri-
stiani nominis et pondus et fructus; mors Christi negatur,
. . . . negatâ vero morte nec de resurrectione constat.*"
The Docetic heresy is also opposed to the dogma of
Christ's Divinity. "*Non erat*," says the same writer,[24]

---

22 *De Carne Christi*, c. 5.   24 Tertullian, *l. c.*, III, 8.
23 *Adv. Marcion.*, III, 8.

" quod videbatur, et quod erat, mentiebatur: caro nec caro, homo nec homo, proinde Christus Deus nec Deus. Cur enim non etiam Dei phantasma portaverit?" And St. Augustine writes: " If the body of Christ was a mere phantasm, Christ was a deceiver; and if He was a deceiver, He is not the truth. But Christ *is* the truth; consequently His body was not a phantasm." [25] Needless to remark, the Docetic theory was not apt to kindle enthusiasm for the faith or eagerness to lay down one's life in its defense. " If all this was a mere semblance [*i. e.,* if Christ suffered only in appearance]," [26] exclaims St. Ignatius,[27] " my handcuffs, too, are an illusion. Why, then, did I give myself up to death, to fire, to the sword, to wild beasts?" [28] The Docetic hypothesis is furthermore destructive of natural certitude. For to assert that Christ and His Apostles were either idiots or impostors, is to fly in the face of historic evidence and common sense. Such a proceeding must lead to absolute scepticism. St. Irenæus effectively urges this argument: " How can these [Docetic heretics] imagine that they are engaged in a real controversy, if their master [Christ] had merely an imaginary existence? . . . Whatever they say and do is purely imaginary, and we may well ask: Since they are not men, but brute beasts, are not they themselves parading in the guise of human beings?" [29]

25 " *Si phantasma fuit corpus Christi, fefellit Christus, et si fefellit, veritas non est. Est autem veritas Christus: non igitur fuit phantasma corpus eius."* (*LXXXIII, Quaest.,* qu. 14.)

26 τὸ δοκεῖν.

27 *Ep. ad Smyrn.,* c. 4.

28 On the Christology of Ignatius, see J. C. Granbery, *Outline of New Testament Christology,* pp. 110 sqq., Chicago 1909; Tixeront, *History of Dogmas,* I, pp. 124 sq.

29 " *Quomodo enim ipsi vere se putant disputare, quando magister eorum putativus fuit? . . . Putativum est igitur et non veritas omne apud eos. Et nunc iam quaeritur, ne forte, quum et ipsi homines non sint sed muta animalia, hominum umbras apud plurimos perferant."* (*Adv. Haer.,* IV, 33, 5.)

READINGS : — Mead, *Fragments of a Faith Forgotten,* London 1906.— J. H. Blunt, *Dictionary of Sects, Heresies,* etc., London 1874.— J. P. Arendzen, art. " Docetae " in the *Catholic Encyclopedia,* Vol. V.

ARTICLE 2

THE INTEGRITY OF CHRIST'S SACRED HUMANITY AS DEFINED AGAINST ARIANISM AND APOLLINARIANISM

1. THE HERESY AND ITS CONDEMNATION BY THE CHURCH.—The dogmatic definition of the humanity of Jesus Christ against the Docetae clearly involved the inference that the manhood of our Blessed Redeemer was essentially composed of a material body and a spiritual soul. Nevertheless Arius declared Christ to be a synthesis of the Logos with inanimate flesh, while Apollinaris argued that, though our Lord had a soul, He lacked reason.

a) The Arians were consistent with themselves in affirming that Christ, whom they believed to be a synthesis of the Logos with soulless flesh, had no human soul.

The Arian idea was that the Logos simply supplied and exercised the functions of a human soul. The impiousness of this heresy lay in its denial of the Divinity of the Logos,— which explains the remark made by St. Athanasius: " The Arians vainly have recourse to subtleties, saying that the Saviour assumed mere flesh, and impiously ascribing the passion to the impassible God-head." [1]

Thus Arianism was a Christological heresy only indirectly and by implication, whereas Apollinarianism expressly attacked the integrity of our Lord's manhood.

Apollinaris was Bishop of Laodicea in Syria and died in the year 390. After having valiantly supported St. Athanasius in his defense of the Homoöusion, he fell away from the orthodox faith and asserted that the body of Christ was animated by an inferior life-principle (ψυχὴ ζωτικὴ ἄλογος), but had no human or rational soul (ψυχὴ λογική, νοερά) ; the place of the missing νοῦς being supplied by the Divine Logos.[2]   In other words, the Son of God actually assumed living flesh (σάρξ, i. e., an animated body), but the place of the human νοῦς or πνεῦμα was supplied by the Godhead.   This new heresy [3] was based on two separate and distinct errors: (1) A wrong notion of the human synthesis, which Apollinaris imagined to consist of three separate and distinct elements, viz.: flesh, soul, and reason; [4] (2) a misconception of the true nature of the Hypostatic Union, by virtue of which Divinity and humanity subsist side by side in the personal unity of the Logos.   If Christ were a perfect man, argued Apollinaris, He would have two na-tures, which means two persons, and hence there would be two Sons of God, one begotten and the other adopted, be-

---

1 *Contr. Apollin.*, I.

2 Cfr. Funk-Cappadelta, *A Manual of Church History*, Vol. I, pp. 153 sq., London 1910; Pohle-Preuss, *God the Author of Nature and the Supernatural*, p. 145.

3 Bardenhewer-Shahan, *Patrology*, pp. 242 sq.

4 σάρξ, σῶμα, ψυχή ἄλογος; νοῦς, πνεῦμα, ψυχὴ λογική. This di-vision is Platonic.

cause two beings each of which is perfect in itself, can
never be united into one (δύο τέλεια ἓν γενέσθαι οὐ δύναται).[5]

b) In condemning Apollinarianism the Church simultaneously struck at the Christological heresy of the Arians.

a) Regardless of his early friendship for Apollinaris,
St. Athanasius persuaded the Council of Alexandria
(A. D. 362) to anathematize the errors of that heretic.   A
more important definition is contained in the seventh
anathema of Pope Damasus at the Council of Rome, 380:
"*Anathematizamus eos, qui pro hominis anima rationabili
et intelligibili dicunt Dei Verbum in humana carne ver-
satum* — We pronounce anathema against those who say
that the Word of God is in the human flesh in lieu
and place of the human, rational, and intellective soul."
The phrase ἐκ ψυχῆς λογικῆς καὶ σώματος recurs in the decrees of many subsequent councils, especially that of Chalcedon (A. D. 451),[6] and soon takes rank as a technical
term.   Among Western creeds the "Athanasian" is mod-
elled upon the symbol of Chalcedon in the passage which
reads: "*Perfectus Deus, perfectus homo, ex anima rationali et humana carne subsistens* — Perfect God and
perfect man, of a reasonable soul and human flesh subsisting."[7]   Arianism and Apollinarianism were again
condemned in the fifteenth century by Eugene IV in his
Decretum pro Iacobitis, published at the Council of
Florence: "*Anathematizat [Ecclesia] Arium etiam, qui*

5 Cfr.   St.   Athanasius, *Contra
Apoll.,* I, 2; J.Dräseke, *Apollinaris
von Laodicea,* Leipzig 1892; G.
Voisin, *L'Apollinarisme,* Louvain
1901; J. F. Sollier, art. "Apollinarianism" in the *Cath. Ency.,* Vol. I;

C. E. Raven, *Apollinarianism: An
Essay on the Christology of the
Early Church,* Cambridge, 1923.

6 Also in that of Constantinople,
A. D. 381.

7 Cfr.   Denzinger-Bannwart, *Enchiridion,* n. 40, 65.

*asserens corpus ex virgine assumptum animâ caruisse
voluit loco animae fuisse deitatem; Apollinarem quoque,
qui intelligens, si anima corpus informans negetur in
Christo, humanitatem veram ibidem non fuisse, solam
posuit animam sensitivam, sed deitatem Verbi vicem rationalis animae tenuisse* —[The Church] pronounces
anathema also against Arius, who, asserting that the
body [which Jesus] assumed from the Virgin lacked a
soul, held that the Godhead took the place of the soul;
and likewise against Apollinaris, who, aware that if we
deny the existence in Christ of a soul informing the
body, He cannot have possessed a true human nature,
taught that Jesus had only a sensitive soul and that
the Godhead of the Logos supplied the place of the rational soul." [8]

β) Of exceptional importance among the ecclesiastical definitions of our dogma is a decree
of the Council of Vienne,[9] which not only asserts
the co-existence in Jesus Christ of a body and a
rational soul, but defines their mutual relation.
*"Confitemur, unigenitum Dei Filium in iis omni-
bus, in quibus Deus Pater existit, una cum Patre
aeternaliter subsistentem, partes nostrae naturae
simul unitas, ex quibus ipse in se verus Deus
existens fieret verus homo, humanum videlicet
corpus passibile et animam intellectivam seu ra-
tionalem ipsum corpus vere per se et essentialiter
informantem assumpsisse ex tempore in virginali
thalamo ad unitatem suae hypostasis et personae."*

8 Cfr. Denzinger-Bannwart, *Enchiridion*, n. 710.
9 A. D. 1311.

Anglice: "We profess that the only-begotten
Son of God, who eternally subsists with the
Father in all those respects in which the Father
exists, assumed in time, in the virgin's bridal
chamber, the parts of our nature united together,
by which He, being in Himself true God, became
true man; *viz.*: a passible human body and an intellective or rational soul informing that body
truly *per se* and essentially; and that He assumed
them into the unity of His Hypostasis and
Person." [10]

2. THE TEACHING OF REVELATION.—The dogmatic teaching of the Church in regard to the
integrity of Christ's human nature is merely the
technical formulation of a truth plainly contained
in Holy Scripture and Tradition.

a) The New Testament writings, especially
the Gospels, portray Jesus Christ in His daily
intercourse with men, in His joys and sorrows.
They tell how He suffered hunger and thirst,
weariness and exhaustion. It is impossible to
assume that He who conversed as a man with
men and shared their sentiments, had no human
(*i. e.* rational) soul.

That He Himself expressly claimed such a soul is
evidenced by a number of unmistakable texts; *e. g.* John
X, 17: *"Ego pono animam meam* (τὴν ψυχήν μου), *ut*

10 On the bearing of this definition see Pohle-Preuss, *God the Author of
Nature and the Supernatural*, pp. 142 sqq.

iterum sumam eam." Our English Bible renders this passage as follows: "I lay down my life, that I may take it again." But even if *anima* were here synonymous with "life" (*vita, ζωή*), we should evidently have to assume the existence of a soul, because without a soul there can be neither life nor death. Our Divine Redeemer exclaims on the Cross: "Father, into thy hands I commend my spirit." [11] "Spirit" in this context manifestly does not mean the "Divinity" of the Logos, but His human soul, about to leave His body. For St. Luke adds: "And saying this, he gave up the ghost." [12] What is here called "spirit" (*spiritus, πνεῦμα*) is elsewhere referred to as "soul" (*anima, ψυχή*), so that we have solid Scriptural warrant for saying: Spirit = soul, *i. e.,* spiritual soul (*anima rationalis*).

Probably the text most fatal to Arianism and Apollinarianism is Matth. XXVI, 38: "My soul is sorrowful even unto death." Here Christ unequivocally asserts that He has a soul susceptible to the spiritual affection of sorrow. Such a soul cannot be other than a spiritual soul.[13]

The mutual relationship of body and soul in the sacred humanity of our Lord, as defined by the Council of Vienne, has a solid Scriptural foundation in the fact that the Bible again and again refers to Jesus Christ as "true man," "the Son of man," and "Son of Adam." One of the most effective texts is 1 Tim. II, 5: "There is one God, and one mediator of God and men, the man Christ Jesus." Obviously Christ would not be true man, nor could He act as mediator between God and men if,

---

11 τὸ πνεῦμά μου. Luke XXIII, 46.

12 ἐξέπνευσεν, *expiravit.* See Luke XXIII, 46.

13 Cfr. St. Ambrose, *In Luc.,* l. X: *"Tristis est non ipse Deus, sed anima; suscepit enim animam meam, suscepit corpus meum; non me fefellit, ut alius esset et alius videretur."*

instead of being united in an essential unity of nature, body and soul had existed separately in His Person.

But does not the Johannine dictum: [14] *"Et verbum caro* [15] *factum est"* preclude the existence of a spiritual soul in Christ? It does not, because the synecdochical use of " flesh " for " man " is quite common throughout the Bible.[16]

b) In formulating the Patristic argument for our thesis it will be advisable to regard the Fathers (1) as simple witnesses of Tradition and (2) as theologians or philosophers concerned with the speculative demonstration of the dogma.

a) Let us first consider their testimony as that of simple witnesses to Tradition.

Those of the Fathers who lived *after* the termination of the Arian and Apollinarist controversy, express themselves with unmistakable clearness.[17] The case is different with certain earlier Fathers, who are charged by Protestant writers [18] with having held Arian or Apollinarist views on the subject of Christology. It is easy to show that this charge is unfounded. Some of the earliest among the Fathers believed that Christ was constituted of "flesh" (*caro,* σάρξ) and "spirit" (*spiritus,* πνεῦμα); but they were far from regarding Him as a compound of Divinity and in-

---

14 John I, 14.

15 σάρξ.

16 For the necessary references consult Card. Franzelin, *De Verbo Incarnato,* thes. 11.

17 Cfr. Thomassin, *De Incarnatione,* IV, 8 sq.

18 E. g., Münscher, De Wette, Neander.

animate flesh. By "spirit" they simply understood His Divinity, and for this reason they
could not and did not attach to "flesh" any other
meaning than does the Bible when it employs the
term by synecdochy for "man."

Take, *e. g.*, St. Ignatius of Antioch, who stands in the
front row of the Fathers thus accused. Though he repeatedly describes the Saviour as σαρκοφόρος (flesh-
bearer), he is careful to explain that our Lord was a
" perfect man " (τέλειος ἄνθρωπος).[19]

St. Irenæus employs " flesh " and " man " as synonymous terms when he teaches that " The Word of God
was made flesh, . . . because the Word of God was also
true man." [20] The correctness of this interpretation is
confirmed by the fact that in another passage of the
same work Irenæus expressly mentions the *soul* of Christ.
Adopting a similar expression from St. Clement of
Rome,[21] (who has also been accused of heresy), Irenæus
says : " The mighty Word was also true man . . . since
He redeemed us with His blood and gave up His soul
for our souls [22] and His flesh for our flesh." [23]

Not even Tertullian, who notoriously held false views
on the metaphysical essence of spiritual substances (*e. g.*,
God, the soul),[24] can be convicted of heresy in his
Christological teaching. It is sufficient for our present
purpose to note that, in common with the rest of the
Fathers, Tertullian attributes to the Godman a soul sub-

19 *Epist. ad Smyrn.*
20 *Contr. Haer.*, V, 18, 3: " *Verbum Dei caro factum est, . . . quoniam Verbum Dei et homo verus.*"
21 1 *Ep. ad Cor.*, n. 49.
22 δόντος τὴν ψυχὴν ὑπὲρ τῶν
ἡμετέρων ψυχῶν.

23 *Contr. Haer.*, V, 1, 1.
24 Cfr. Pohle-Preuss, *God: His
Knowability, Essence and Attributes*, pp. 293 sqq.; and also Pohle-
Preuss, *God the Author of Nature
and the Supernatural*, pp. 166 sq.

stantially like ours. Distinguishing clearly between body and soul,[25] he asserts the existence in Christ of two constitutive elements, *viz.*: a material body and a human soul, and indignantly combats Marcion's assertion that Christ, in His outward appearance, was merely a soul clothed in the semblance of flesh (*anima carnalis*).[26] Towards the end of his anti-Docetic treatise *De Carne Christi,* Tertullian gives the following perfectly orthodox account of the constitution of our Blessed Redeemer: " *Homo, qua caro et anima, et filius hominis; qua autem Spiritus Dei et Virtus Altissimi, Deus et Dei Filius* — As flesh and soul, He was a man, and the Son of man; but as the Spirit of God and the Power of the Most High, he is God and the Son of God." [27]

β) In order to obtain a more accurate notion of the teaching of the Fathers on this subject, we must study the explanations they give with a view to bringing Christ's humanity as nearly as possible within the grasp of reason. All we can do within the limits of this treatise is to call attention to two important points of view.

Not a few of the Fathers [28] demonstrate the necessity of a rational soul in Christ by

25 The soul he identifies with the Ego. Cfr. *De Carne Christi,* c. 12: " *In hoc vana distinctio est, quasi nos seorsum ab anima simus, quum totum quod sumus anima sit; deinde sine anima nihil sumus, ne hominis quidem, sed cadaveris nomen."*

26 *De Carne Christi,* c. 11: " *Redde igitur Christo fidem suam, ut qui homo voluerit incedere ani-mam quoque humanae conditionis ostenderit, non faciens eam carnem, sed induens eam carne."*

27 *De Carne Christi,* c. 14. On the Christological teaching of Tertullian cfr. J. Tixeront, *History of Dogmas,* Vol. I (English ed.), pp. 315 sqq., St. Louis 1911.

28 Cfr. Petavius, *De Incarnatione,* V, 11.

the famous soteriological axiom: *"Quod assumptum non est, non est sanatum,"* or, as St. Gregory of Nazianzus expresses it: Τὸ γὰρ ἀπρόσληπτον ἀθεράπευτον.[29] The meaning of this axiom is: Our own souls would remain unredeemed, had not the Son of God assumed a spiritual soul. Gregory develops this thought as follows: "If any one put his hope in a man destitute of reason, he is indeed unreasonable and unworthy of being wholly redeemed. For that which has not been assumed, is not cured; but that which is united with God [*i. e.* the Logos] partakes of salvation. If only half of Adam fell, let but half of him be assumed and saved. But if the whole [Adam] sinned, He [*i. e.* the Logos] is also united with the whole, and the whole [man] attains to salvation."[30] Similar passages can be cited from Tertullian and St. Ambrose.[31]

Another Christological principle, which some of the Fathers effectively urged against Apollinaris, and which was subsequently incorporated into the Scholastic system, is this: *"Verbum assumpsit carnem mediante animâ (rationali),"* *i. e.,* The Word assumed flesh through the mediation of the rational soul.

---

29 *Ep. 101 ad Cledon.*, 7.
30 *Ibid.*
31 Ambros., *Ep. 48 ad Sabin.*, 5: " Si enim aliquid ei [*i. e.* Christo] defuit, non totum redemit . . . totum utique suscepit, quod erat humanae perfectionis." Cfr. St. Augustine, *De Civitate Dei*, X, 27; St. Fulgentius, *Ad. Trasamundum*, I, 6.

This does not mean that the Son of God first assumed a spiritual soul and then, flesh. Nor does it signify that the spiritual soul of Christ constituted, as it were, a permanent bond of union between His body and His Divinity. The Fathers wished to say that the only kind of flesh capable of being assumed by the Godhead was flesh animated by a truly human, *i. e.* rational soul, as its *forma essentialis,* because it would have been altogether unbecoming for God to enter into Hypostatic Union with a body animated by a mere brute soul. But did not the Logos remain united with the body of Christ during the three days from His death to His Resurrection? Yes, but our axiom loses none of its truth for that. For, as St. Bonaventure explains, *"Anima non recedebat a corpore simpliciter, sed solum ad tempus; et corpus illud ex prima coniunctione sui ad animam dispositionem ad incorruptionem habebat: et ideo propter separationem ipsius animae congruitatem ad unionem [hypostaticam] non amittebat; et ideo quamvis anima separaretur a carne, non tamen oportebat divinitatem a carne separari."* [32] It is only by taking *anima rationalis* as the *forma essentialis* of the body that we shall be enabled to understand why the Fathers, after the time of Apollinaris, so strongly emphasized the " rationality of Christ's flesh "— which is really a somewhat paradoxical expression. Thus St. Athanasius says: " The Saviour having become man, it is impossible that His body should lack reason." [33] And St. Cyril of Alexandria teaches: " We must believe that He who is by nature God, was made flesh, *i. e.,* a man animated by a rational soul." [34] The same

---

[32] *Comment. in Quatuor Libros Sent.,* III, dist. 2, art. 3, qu. 1. Cfr. Petavius, *De Incarnatione,* IV, 13, and St. Thomas, *Summa Theol.,* 3a, qu. 6, art. 1 sq.

[33] ἀνόητον εἶναι τὸ σῶμα αὐτοῦ. *Ep. ad Antiochen.* (Migne, *P. G.,* XXVI, 795 sqq.).

[34] ὅτι κατὰ φύσιν Θεὸς ὢν γέγονε σάρξ, ἤγουν ἄνθρωπος ἐμψυχομέ-

Saint habitually employs the phrase σῶμα ψυχωθὲν νοερῶς. Sophronius even speaks of a σὰρξ ἔμψυχος λογική.[35] All of which proves that the dogmatic definition of the Council of Vienne was firmly rooted in Tradition.

3. THE THEOLOGICAL FORMULA OF THE "THREE SUBSTANCES."—Apollinarianism raised a new problem, *viz.:* Must Christ be conceived dichotomically, as consisting of Divinity and humanity, or trichotomously, of "three substances," *i. e.,* Logos, soul, and body?

A tacit compromise finally led to the adoption of the famous Scholastic formula: "*Duae naturae et tres substantiae.*" By expressly emphasizing the two natures in Christ, this formula was calculated to prevent the misconception that body and soul are, like the Logos, each a complete nature or substance, while in fact they are merely component parts of Christ's sacred humanity. The sole excuse for speaking of "three substances" was the necessity of safeguarding the integrity of our Lord's human nature against Arianism, and especially against Apollinarianism. In this sense alone was the phrase employed by the Fathers. Justin Martyr enumerates σῶμα καὶ λόγος καὶ ψυχή as the three constitutive elements of Christ.[36] The teaching of St. Augustine is more definite still: "Man consists of a soul and flesh," he says, "and consequently Christ consists of the Logos, a soul, and flesh." [37]

In spite of this legitimate use, the phrase did not always meet with favor on the part of the Church. The

vos ψυχῇ λογικῇ. *Ep. ad Nestor.,* 3, n. 19.

35 Cfr. Pohle-Preuss, *God the Au-* thor *of Nature and the Supernatural,* p. 146.

36 *Apol.,* II, n. 10.

37 *Serm. Contr. Arian.,* IX, n. 7.

Eleventh Council of Toledo (A. D. 675) taught that "Christ exists in two natures, but in three substances." [38] But when the Fourteenth Council of Toledo, held only nine years later, repeated this phrase, Pope Sergius the First demanded an "explanation." The demand was complied with by St. Julian of Toledo, and His explanation satisfied the Pope.[39] A century later (A. D. 794) the formula was expressly disapproved by a provincial council held at Frankfort against the Adoptionists. The decrees of this council, which are vested with special authority on account of their formal approbation by Pope Hadrian I, contain the following passage: "*In professione Nicaeni symboli non invenimus dictum, in Christo 'duas naturas et tres substantias' et 'homo deificatus' et 'Deus humanatus.' Quid est natura hominis nisi anima et corpus? Vel quid est inter naturam et substantiam, ut 'tres substantias' necesse sit nobis dicere? . . . Consuetudo ecclesiastica solet in Christo duas substantias nominare, Dei videlicet et hominis.*" [40] In spite of this reprimand, however, the formula of the "three substances" continued in use and ultimately became part of the approved Scholastic terminology. St. Bonaventure unhesitatingly speaks of a "threefold substance" in Christ, and St. Thomas Aquinas teaches: "The name 'man,' applied to Christ, also signifies His Divine Person, and thus implies three substances." [41] The orthodoxy of the formula, therefore, when used in the sense which we have explained, cannot be questioned.[42]

---

[38] "*Christus in his duabus naturis, tribus exstat substantiis.*" (Cfr. Denzinger-Bannwart, *Enchiridion,* n. 284).

[39] Cfr. Vasquez, *Comment in S. Th.,* III, disp. 37, c. 2-3.

[40] Cfr. Denzinger-Bannwart, *Enchiridion,* n. 312.

[41] "*Hoc nomen 'homo' dictum de Christo, dicit etiam divinam personam, et sic dicit tres substantias.*" (*Comment. in Quatuor Libros Sent.,* III, dist. 6, qu. 1, art. 3.)

[42] Cfr. L. Janssens, *De Deo-Homine,* I, 156 sqq., Friburgi 1901; De Lugo, *De Myst. Incarn.,* disp. 13, sect. 1 (ed. Paris. 1890, t. II, pp. 636 sqq.).

SECTION 2

THE ADAMIC ORIGIN OF THE HUMAN NATURE OF CHRIST

The dogma that Christ is true man, implies not only the reality and integrity of His human nature, but likewise the origin of that nature from Mary. It is this latter fact which beyond aught else guarantees the reality and integrity of our Lord's sacred manhood. In other words, Christ is truly and integrally a man because, by maternal generation from the Virgin-mother Mary, He is a " Son of Adam " according to the flesh, and consequently our " Brother." To establish unity of species between Himself and us it would have been sufficient for the Logos to have brought His humanity with Him from Heaven. But his humanity is specifically identical with ours. It is founded upon kinship of race and blood relation. By His " real incorporation with our kind " in Adam, Jesus Christ is " bone of our bone and flesh of our flesh."

1. HERETICAL DOCTRINES ON THIS SUBJECT VS. THE TEACHING OF THE CHURCH.—a) Certain Gnostics of the second century, notably Valentinus [1] and Apelles, a disciple of Marcion,[2] who held an attenuated Docetism, admitted

---

1 Valentinus flourished about A. D. 150. His false teaching (see Burt, *Dictionary of Sects*, pp. 612 sqq.) was refuted by St. Irenæus.

2 Cfr. Bardenhewer-Shahan, *Patrology*, p. 80; Tixeront, *History of Dogmas*, Vol. I, pp. 183 sqq.

the reality and integrity of Christ's human nature only after a fashion. Their theory was that He possessed a "celestial body." This teaching involved a denial (1) of the earthly origin of Christ's manhood, and (2) of His conception and birth by the Virgin Mary. In describing the latter Valentinus employed the simile of "water flowing through a channel." [3] Similar errors were harbored by the Paulicians of Syria,[4] and, in modern times, by the Anabaptists, the Quakers, and certain pseudo-mystics of the sixteenth century.[5]

b) The Church never for a moment left her faithful children in doubt as to the true origin and descent of Jesus. The Ecumenical Council of Chalcedon (A.D. 451) defined: *"Docemus, eundemque [Christum] perfectum in deitate et eundem perfectum in humanitate, Deum verum et hominem verum, eundem ex anima rationali et corpore, consubstantialem Patri secundum deitatem, consubstantialem nobis eundem secundum humanitatem* (ὁμοούσιον τῷ πατρὶ κατὰ τὴν θεότητα, καὶ ὁμοούσιον ἡμῖν τὸν αὐτὸν κατὰ τὴν ἀνθρωπότητα), *per omnia nobis similem absque peccato; ante saecula qui-*

---

[3] ὡς διὰ σωλῆνος ὕδωρ. Cfr. Epiphanius, *Haer.*, XXXI, 7.

[4] The Paulicians were "but the Priscillianists of the East." For an account of their curious beliefs see Alzog-Pabisch-Byrne, *Manual of Universal Church History*, Vol. I,

pp. 761 sqq.; cfr. also Funk-Cappadelta, *A Manual of Church History*, Vol. I, pp. 265 sq., London 1910; Conybeare, *The Key of Truth*, London 1898.

[5] Weigel, Petersen, Dippel, and others.

dem de Patre genitum (γεννηθέντα) *secundum deitatem, in novissimis autem diebus eundem propter nos et propter nostram salutem, ex Maria Virgine Dei genitrice* (ἐκ Μαρίας τῆς παρθένου τῆς θεοτόκου)
secundum humanitatem — We teach that He
[Christ] is perfect in Godhead and perfect in
manhood, being truly God and truly man; that
He is of a rational soul and body, consubstantial with the Father as touching the Godhead,
and consubstantial with us as touching His manhood, being like us in all things, sin excepted;
that, as touching His Godhead, He was begotten
of the Father before the worlds; and, as touching
His manhood, He was for us and for our salvation born of Mary, the Virgin, Mother of God." [6]

This is a most important dogmatic definition, and in
order to grasp its full import the student should ponder
the following points:

(1) Christ's *homoousia* with the Father and His consubstantiality with the human race are not co-ordinate
relations. The divine *homoousia* is based on " numerical
identity " or " *tautousia*," [7] whereas Christ's consubstantiality with man rests on a purely " specific identity,"
which, however, in consequence of our common descent
from Adam, is a true blood-relationship.

(2) This blood-relationship arises formally and immediately from the fact of Christ's being engendered in
the Virgin Mary. Had He merely passed through her
virginal womb, as Valentinus and his fellow sectaries

6 Denzinger-Bannwart, *Enchiridion*, n. 148.

7 Cfr. Pohle-Preuss, *The Divine
Trinity*, pp. 255 sqq.

held, no blood-relationship would have been established between Him and us. Hence the need of accentuating the phrase: γεννηθέντα ἐκ Μαρίας.

(3) In order to show that Christ's temporal generation from His mother is equally true and real with His divine generation from the Eternal Father, the Council applies to both the one word γεννηθέντα, without, of course, thereby denying the fundamental distinction between divine and creatural generation.

(4) The dogma would not be complete without a distinct reference to the purpose of the Redemption, inasmuch as the Adamic origin of Christ is intimately bound up with His mediatorial office and the redemption of the human race. The creeds, including that of Chalcedon, bring out this soteriological relation by the typical additament: *"Propter nos et propter nostram salutem* (δι' ἡμᾶς καὶ διὰ τὴν ἡμετέραν σωτηρίαν)."

2. THE TEACHING OF REVELATION.—Holy Scripture teaches that Christ became consubstantial with man by descent from Adam, for the purpose of redeeming the human race, of which He is a member and a scion.

a) In the Old Testament the Redeemer was promised, first as "the seed of the woman," [8] later as "the seed of Abraham," and in fine as "the seed of David." The New Testament frequently refers to Him as "the Son of David." [9]

---

[8] Gen. III, 15 (the "Protevangelium"). Cfr. H. P. Liddon, *The Divinity of Our Lord and Saviour Jesus Christ,* pp. 109 sqq.

[9] *"Filius David."* Matth. I, 1; IX, 27; XII, 23; Luke I, 32; Rom. I, 3; Apoc. V, 5. Cfr. H. J. Coleridge, S. J., *The Preparation of the Incarnation,* pp. 209 sqq., London 1894.

Whenever the inspired writers of the New Testament wish to point to the fulfilment of the Old Testament prophecies in the life of Jesus Christ, they strongly emphasize His conception and birth from the Virgin Mary.[10] Cfr. Luke I, 31 sq.: *"Ecce concipies in utero et paries filium. . . . Filius Altissimi vocabitur, et dabit illi Dominus Deus sedem David patris eius*— Behold thou shalt conceive in thy womb, and shalt bring forth a son. . . . He . . . shall be called the Son of the Most High; and the Lord shall give unto Him the throne of David his father." Luke I, 35: *"Quod nascetur ex te sanctum, vocabitur Filius Dei*— The Holy which shall be born of thee shall be called the Son of God." Matth. I, 16: *"Iacob autem genuit Ioseph, virum Mariae, de qua natus est Iesus, qui vocatur Christus* (ἐξ ἧς ἐγεννήθη Ἰησοῦς ὁ λεγόμενος Χριστός) — And Jacob begot Joseph, the husband of Mary, of whom was born Jesus, who is called Christ." Rom. I, 3: *"Factus ex semine David secundum carnem* — Who was made of the seed of David, according to the flesh." Gal. IV, 4: *"Misit Deus Filium suum factum ex muliere*— God sent his Son, made of a woman." These and many similar texts prove, (1) that Christ is a genuine descendant of Adam, and (2) that He traces his lineage by maternal generation through Mary, who was a daughter of Adam.

The soteriological aspect is sharply accentuated by St. Paul when he says that the human race was redeemed by One who was not only God made man, but also of the blood of Adam. Heb. II, 11 and 14: *"Qui enim sanctificat et qui sanctificantur, ex uno [scil. Adamo] omnes; propter quam causam non confunditur* (ἐπαισχύνεται)*fratres eos vocare . . . ut per mortem destrue-*

<hr>

10 Cfr. M. J. Scott, S.J., *The Virgin Birth*, N. Y. 1925, pp. 4 sqq.

ret eum, qui habebat mortis imperium, id est, diabolum
— For both he that sanctifieth, and they who are sanctified, are all of one. For which cause he is not ashamed to call them brethren . . . that, through death, he might destroy him who had the empire of death, that is to say, the devil." [11]

b) In considering the Patristic tradition we note the remarkable fact that the early Fathers and ecclesiastical writers, down to the time of Fulgentius, attribute very great importance to the preposition *ex* in the Scriptural formula *"factus ex muliere."* [12]

Thus Tertullian observes in his work *De Carne Christi:* *" Per virginem dicitis natum, non ex virgine, et in vulva, non ex vulva. Quia et angelus in somnis ad Ioseph: ' nam quod in ea natum est,' inquit, ' de Spiritu S. est,' non dixit ex ea. Nempe tamen, etsi ex ea dixisset, in ea dixerat; in ea enim erat, quod ex ea erat. . . . Sed bene, quod idem dicit Matthaeus originem Domini decurrens ab Abraham usque ad Mariam: ' Iacob,' inquit, ' generavit Ioseph, virum Mariae, ex qua nascitur Christus.' Sed et Paulus grammaticis istis silentium imponit: ' misit,' inquit, ' Deus Filium suum factum ex muliere.' Numquid per mulierem, aut in muliere?"* [13]
And St. Basil in his treatise on the Holy Ghost says: " To show that the God-bearing flesh was formed of human material,[14] the Apostle chose a striking phrase;

---

[11] On Satan's " reign of death " cfr. Pohle-Preuss, *God the Author of Nature and the Supernatural,* pp. 291, 344 sqq.

[12] γενόμενον ἐκ γυναικός. Gal. IV, 4.

[13] Tertullian, *De Carne Christi,* c. 20.

[14] ἐκ τοῦ ἀνθρωπείου φυράματος.

for the expression 'through the woman' might suggest the notion of a mere transit; but this other [phrase]: 'out of the woman,' sufficiently explains the communication of nature existing between Him who was born and His mother." [15]

We note in passing that Christ's descent from Adam, and His blood-relationship with us, is not impaired by the circumstance that His conception was effected without male coöperation. For, as St. Ignatius observes, "Our God Jesus Christ was conceived [16] by Mary as the fruit of her womb, according to the decree of God,— from the seed of David, 'tis true, but of the Holy Ghost." [17] Whoever is born of a daughter of Adam, though without male coöperation, is a genuine descendant of Adam in all respects except original sin.[18]

Why did Christ choose to enter into blood-relationship with the children of Adam? Following St. Paul the Fathers hold that the reason is to be found in the ulterior purpose of the Redemption. According to the classic dictum of St. Irenæus, Christ, as man, was not, like Adam, formed of "the slime of the earth," but born of a daughter of Adam, "*ut non alia plasmatio fieret neque alia esset plasmatio, quae salvaretur, sed eadem ipsa recapitularetur,*" [19] or, in the words of St. Athanasius, "in order that the nations be of the same body and have a share with Christ." [20] Some of the Fathers

15 St. Basil, *De Spiritu Sancto*, c. 5, n. 12. Other Patristic comments on Gal. IV, 4 in Petavius, *De Incarn. Verbi*, V, 16. Cfr. Durand-Bruneau, *The Childhood of Jesus Christ*, pp. 149 sqq., Philadelphia 1910.

16 ἐκυοφορήθη.

17 *S. Ign. M., Ep. ad Ephes.*, n. 18.

18 Cfr. Pohle-Preuss, *God the Au-*thor of Nature and the Supernatural, pp. 279 sqq. The perpetual virginity of Mary will be treated in Mariology. Cfr. Durand-Bruneau, *The Childhood of Jesus Christ*, pp. 153 sqq.

19 *Contr. Haeres.*, III, 21, 10.

20 ὥστε εἶναι τὰ ἔθνη σύσσωμα καὶ συμμέτοχα τοῦ Χριστοῦ. *Contr. Apollin.*, II, 5.

say that Christ assumed the flesh of the entire human race for the purpose of redemption. Thus, *e. g.,* St. Hilary: "The Word was made flesh and dwelt among us, *i. e.,* by assuming the nature of the entire human race." [21] And, still more graphically St. Leo the Great: "He dwelled among us, whom the Godhead of the Word had fitted to itself, whose flesh, taken from the womb of the Virgin, we are. . . . He made His own the substance of our body, not of any material whatever, but of our proper substance." [22] Of course, these are hyperboles.

3. INCIDENTAL THEOLOGICAL QUESTIONS.— a) Although Sacred Scripture frequently refers to the Blessed Virgin Mary as "the mother of Jesus," [23] it cannot but surprise the careful student that Christ Himself never calls her by the tender name of "mother."

In Matth. XII, 46 sqq. He even expressly rejects this name and with a semblance of harshness points to the higher duty incumbent on Him of performing the will of His Heavenly Father. At the marriage of Cana Mary is worried because "they have no wine; and Jesus saith to her: Woman,[24] what is that to me and to thee? My hour is not yet come." [25] From the cross He charged her: "Woman, behold thy son," and committed her to the care of his favorite Apostle with the

---

[21] "*Verbum caro factum est et habitavit in nobis, naturam scilicet universi humani generis assumens.*" *In Ps.,* 51, 7.

[22] *Serm. de Nativ.,* X, c. 3: "*Habitavit in nobis, quos sibi Verbi divinitas coaptavit, cuius caro de utero Virginis sumpta nos sumus. . . . Substantiam nostri corporis suam fecit, non de quacunque materia, sed de substantia proprie nostra.*" Cfr. Franzelin, *De Verbo Incarnato,* thes. 14; Stentrup, *Christologia,* thes. 9.

[23] Cfr. Matth. I, 18; II, 21; Luke I, 43; John II, 1, *et passim.*

[24] *Mulier,* γύναι.

[25] John II, 4.

words: "Behold thy mother." [26]   Though this manner of speaking, under the circumstances, is pathetic rather than surprising, the two passages Matth. XII, 46 sqq. and John II, 4 cannot be satisfactorily explained by the observation that the word "woman" among the Jews and Greeks denoted respect and esteem for the one thus addressed. We must seek for a deeper theological explanation. This may be found (1) in the fact that it was eminently proper for our Divine Redeemer to put His relations to His Heavenly Father above the ties of flesh and blood, and (2) in the consideration that, beginning with the Protevangelium, all through Isaias and the Gospels down to the Apocalypse, there runs the name of a "woman," which organically connects the "first Gospel" with the "second," and both in turn with the "last," i. e., St. John's Revelation.[27]   Professor (now Bishop) Schäfer deserves credit for having brought out this important point of view, which enables us to solve certain knotty exegetical problems in a perfectly satisfactory way. "Thus," he says, "the last book of Divine Revelation points back to the first. The 'woman' of the first promise of salvation in Paradise, the mother of Him who was to crush the head of the Serpent, and through Him the mother of all those who possess spiritual life, and conjointly with her, in this sense, the Church itself, is the 'sign' heralded by Isaias and visioned by St. John on the isle of Patmos." [28]

26 John XIX, 26 sq.

27 Cfr. Apoc. XII, 1: "Mulier amicta sole."

28 Alois Schäfer, Die Gottesmutter in der Hl. Schrift, 2nd ed., p. 251, Münster 1900. For another equally satisfactory explanation see the recently published work of B. Bartmann, Christus ein Gegner des Marienkultus? Jesus und seine Mutter in den heiligen Evangelien, Freiburg 1909.

b) Regarding the outward aspect of Christ's human nature we have no reliable information.[29]

Tertullian asserts that our Lord closely resembled Adam, and he attributes this resemblance to the alleged fact that, in fashioning the body of our proto-parent, the Creator had before Him as in a vision the portrait of " the Second Adam." [30]   But this is an entirely gratuitous assumption.   The conjecture of several Fathers [31] that the bodily presence of our Divine Lord was contemptible, arose from a misinterpretation of Is. LIII, 2 sqq., where the Messias is pictured in His cruel suffering.   It has been asserted that the impression of our Lord's face (Volto Santo) on the so-called Veil of St. Veronica, which is preserved in St. Peter's Basilica at Rome,[32] bears a certain family resemblance to a portrait found on an ancient monument at Karnak and believed to represent the Jewish King Roboam, a bodily ancestor of our Lord.   But, as has been pointed out, the name appended to this portrait, which was at first deciphered as " *Reha-beam*," is really the name of a city, and the picture itself was most probably intended to be a composite portrait representing the population.[33]

The description of our Divine Lord contained in the report of the alleged ambassadors of King Abgar, is,

29 On this subject cfr. Vavasseur, *De Forma Christi*, Paris 1649; G. A. Müller, *Die leibliche Gestalt Jesu Christi nach der Urtradition*, Graz 1908; S. J. Hunter, *Outlines of Dogmatic Theology*, Vol. II, pp. 463 sqq.; F. Johnson, *Have We the Likeness of Christ?* Chicago 1902; G. E. Meille, *Christ's Likeness in History and Art*, London 1924; J. P. Arendzen, *Men and Manners in the Days of Christ*, London, 1928, pp. 80–93.

30 Cfr. Pohle-Preuss, *God the Au-*

thor of Nature and the Supernatural, pp. 130 sq.

31 *E. g.*, Clement of Alexandria, Cyprian, and also Tertullian.

32 Cfr. P. J. Chandlery, S. J., *Pilgrim-Walks in Rome*, p. 27, 2nd ed., London 1905. On this and other apocryphal portraits of Christ cfr. C. M. Kaufmann, *Christliche Archäologie*, pp. 406 sqq., Paderborn 1905.

33 F. Kaulen in the *Kirchenlexikon*, 2nd ed., Vol. X, 1225, Freiburg 1897.

of course, quite as spurious as the apocryphal correspondence of Christ with the toparch of Edessa, which has come down to us in the so-called Legend of Thaddeus.[34]

It is safe to assume that the Son of God, who was conceived by the Holy Ghost, was beautiful in form and figure, of majestic mien and sympathetic presence. The fact that no trustworthy portrait of Him exists may be due to a purposive design on the part of Divine Providence, lest the beauty of His manhood outshine His spiritual form and dignity.[35]

READINGS: — J. Morris, *Jesus the Son of Mary*, 2 vols., London 1851.— P. Vogt, S. J., *Der Stammbaum Christi bei . . . Matthäus und Lukas*, Freiburg 1907.— J. M. Heer, *Die Stammbäume Jesu nach Matthäus und Lukas*, Freiburg 1910.— L. Prestige (Anglican), *The Virgin Birth of Our Lord*, London 1918.— B. L. Conway, C. S. P., *The Virgin Birth*, N. Y. 1924. (A brief answer, with bibliography, to the chief objections brought forward against the dogma of the Virgin Birth from the days of the Gnostics to the Modernists).—* A. Steinmann, *Die jungfräuliche Geburt des Herrn*, Münster 1916.—* IDEM, *Die Jungfrauengeburt und die vergleichende Religionsgeschichte*, Paderborn 1919.— Coubé *Revue des Objections*, Mai 1924 (whole issue devoted to the question of the Virgin Birth).

34 Cfr. Bardenhewer-Shahan, *Patrology*, pp. 109 sq.; H. Leclercq, art. " Abgar " in the *Catholic Encyclopedia*, Vol. I; J. Tixeront, *Les Origines de l'Église d'Edesse et la Légende d'Abgar*, Paris 1888.

35 Cfr. Suarez, *De Incarn.*, disp. 32, sect. 2; L. Janssens, *De Deo-Homine*, Vol. I, pp. 505 sqq.

SECTION 3

THE PASSIBILITY OF CHRIST'S HUMAN NATURE

1. HERETICAL TEACHINGS AND THE CHURCH.
—The term "passibility" (capacity for suffering), when applied to our Divine Saviour, means
bodily infirmity to a degree involving the possibility of death (*defectus corporis*), and in addition thereto, those psychical affections which are
technically called πάθη, *passiones*,[1] by Aristotle
and St. Thomas. It is necessary to assume such
physical defects and psychical affections in Christ
in order to safeguard His human nature and the
genuineness of the atonement. In other words,
the passibility of Christ is a necessary postulate of
His Passion.

a) To deny our Lord's liability to suffering and death,
or the immeasurable richness of His soul-life while
on earth, would be tantamount to asserting that Christ
merely bore the semblance of a man and that His human
actions were apparitional,— just what the Docetists asserted. On the other side we have Monophysitism, the
doctrine of one composite nature in Christ, which logically

---

[1] "*Propriissime dicuntur passiones animae affectiones appetitus
sensitivi, quae in Christo fuerunt,*   *sicut et cetera, quae ad naturam
hominis pertinent.*" (*S. Theol.*, 3a,
qu. 15, art. 4.)

72

leads to the heretical assumption of " Theopaschitism "—
a worthy pendant to Patripassianism,[2] — and to the
equally heretical theory that Christ was absolutely incapable of suffering. Towards the close of the fifth and the
beginning of the sixth century, a Monophysitic sect
under the leadership of Julian of Halicarnassus[3] and
Gajanus,[4] maintained that the body of Christ was in-
corruptible even before the Resurrection, or, more
precisely, that it was not subject to decay (φθορά).
These sectaries "were named by their opponents
Aphthartodocetæ, i. e., teachers of the incorruptibil-
ity of the body of Christ, or Phantasiastæ, i. e., teachers
of a merely phenomenal body of Christ."[5] Julian was
at least consistent, but his opponent Severus, Monophysite Bishop of Antioch (512), contradicted his own
fundamental assumption when He admitted the orthodox
doctrine that Christ before His Resurrection shared in
all the bodily sufferings and infirmities of human nature.
The Severians were therefore called φθαρτολάτραι or cor-
rupticolæ.[6]

b) Meanwhile, at the Ecumenical Council of
Ephesus (A. D. 431), the Church had laid it
down as an article of faith that "the Word of God
suffered in the flesh, and was crucified in the flesh,
and tasted death in the flesh, and that He is 'the
first-born from the dead' [Col. I, 18], as He is life
and life-giver inasmuch as He is God."

2 Cfr. Pohle-Preuss, *The Divine Trinity*, pp. 117 sq.
3 About A. D. 476 and 536.
4 Bardenhewer-Shahan, *Patrology*, p. 533.
5 New Light is thrown on this controversy by R. Draguet, in *Julien d'Halicarnasse et sa Controverse avec Sévère d'Antioche sur la Incorruptibilité du Corps du Christ*, Louvain 1924.
6 See Appendix II, *infra*, p. 248.

Carefully distinguishing between passibility and passion
the *Decretum pro Iacobitis* of Eugene IV, adopted by the
Council of Florence, A. D. 1439, defined: *"Deus et homo,
Dei Filius et hominis filius, . . . immortalis et aeternus
ex natura divinitatis, passibilis et temporalis ex conditione assumptae humanitatis. Firmiter credit [Ecclesia],
. . . Dei Filium in assumpta humanitate ex Virgine vere
natum, vere passum, vere mortuum et sepultum* — God
and man, Son of God and son of man, . . . immortal and
eternal by virtue of [His] Divinity, capable of suffering
and temporal by virtue of [His] assumed manhood.
The Church firmly believes . . . that the Son of God
in [His] assumed humanity was truly born of the Virgin; that He truly suffered, died, and was buried." [7]
Though these and other ecclesiastical definitions professedly deal only with our Saviour's liability to suffering and
death, they plainly include, at least by implication, the
psychical affections which are the common lot of all men,
and which necessarily accompany suffering and death.
It is impossible to conceive of a genuine human soul
devoid of spiritual and sensitive affections, or even of
actual bodily suffering, without a corresponding affliction
of the soul.

2. THE PASSIBILITY OF CHRIST'S HUMAN NA-
TURE DEMONSTRATED FROM DIVINE REVELA-
TION.—The heretical doctrine that Christ was
incapable of suffering is manifestly repugnant to
Holy Scripture and Tradition.

a) One need but open the Gospels at almost
any page to be convinced that, in His human na-

ture, Christ was subject both to the ordinary infirmities of the body and the human affections of the soul.

The story of His life confirms and completes the prophetic picture of the "man of sorrows" painted by Isaias.[8] He "was hungry"[9] and "thirsted."[10] He was "wearied"[11] and fell "asleep."[12] He shed His blood and died. On many occasions He manifested distinctly human emotions. Standing before the tomb of His friend Lazarus, for example, He "groaned in the spirit and troubled himself . . . and . . . wept."[13] Finding in the temple "them that sold oxen and sheep and doves, and the changers of money," He, who was ordinarily so meek, became inflamed with holy anger and drove them out with a scourge.[14] His eyes rested with tender regard on the pious youth who was able to say that he had observed the commandments of God from his boyhood.[15] He rejoiced[16] and sorrowed,[17] He marvelled[18] and was oppressed with fear and heaviness.[19]

St. Paul explains the reason for all this in Heb. II, 16 sq.: "*Nusquam enim angelos apprehendit, sed semen Abrahae apprehendit; unde debuit per omnia fratribus similari,*[20] *ut misericors fieret et fidelis pontifex ad Deum, ut repropitiaret delicta populi*[21]— For nowhere doth he take hold of the angels: but of the seed of Abraham he taketh hold. Wherefore it behooved him in all things

8 Is. LIII, 3 sqq.
9 Matth. IV, 2.
10 John XIX, 28.
11 John IV, 6.
12 Matth. VIII, 24.
13 John XI, 33 sqq.
14 John II, 15.
15 Mark X, 21: ὁ δὲ Ἰησοῦς ἐμβλέψας αὐτῷ ἠγάπησεν αὐτόν.

16 John XI, 15.
17 Matth. XXVI, 37 sq.
18 Matth. VIII, 10.
19 Mark XIV, 33: "*Et coepit pavere et taedere* (ἐκθαμβεῖσθαι καὶ ἀδημονεῖν)."
20 κατὰ πάντα τοῖς ἀδελφοῖς ὁμοιωθῆναι.
21 εἰς τὸ ἱλάσκεσθαι τὰς ἁμαρτίας τοῦ λαοῦ.

6

to be made like unto his brethren, that he might become a merciful and faithful high priest before God, that he might be a propitiation for the sins of the people."

b) The Patristic teaching on this point agrees with that of Sacred Scripture in every detail, except that the Fathers formally exclude from the human nature of Christ all physical and moral defects, which Holy Scripture does rather by implication.

α) St. Ambrose says that Christ must have felt and acted like a man because He possessed a human nature: *" Unde valde eos errare res indicat, qui carnem hominis a Christo aiunt esse susceptam, affectum [autem] negant, . . . qui hominem ex homine tollunt, quum homo sine affectu hominis esse non possit."* [22]   St. Leo the Great points out that the hypostatic Union of the two natures in Christ postulates the co-existence of contrary properties: *" Impassibilis Deus non dedignatus est esse homo passibilis, et immortalis mortis legibus subiacere."* [23]

β) The only dissenting voice is that of St. Hilary (d. 366), who in his principal work, *De Trinitate,* written for the purpose of defining and scientifically establishing the Christological teaching of the Church against Arianism,[24] seems to have taught that Jesus was absolutely insensible to pain and suffering. St. Hilary was accused of heresy by Claudianus Mamertus (d. about

[22] *In Ps.,* 61, n. 5.

[23] *Serm.,* 22, c. 2. Cfr. St. Augustine, *De Civit. Dei,* XIV, 9, 3.

[24] Cfr. Bardenhewer-Shahan, *Patrology,* pp. 404 sq. " The entire work [Hilary's treatise *De Trinitate*] is a sustained and intensely enthusiastic plea for the faith of the Church. In the domain of early ecclesiastical literature it is certainly the most imposing of all the works written against Arianism."

474),[25] and the charge was repeated by Berengar and
Baronius. Erasmus did not scruple to reckon Hilary
among the Docetæ, and a recent writer, Dom Lawrence
Janssens, O.S.B., who has subjected the text to careful
scrutiny, arrives at practically the same conclusion.[26]
The vast majority of Catholic divines, however, headed
by Peter Lombard,[27] defend St. Hilary against the charge
of heresy and interpret his writings in accordance with
the orthodox teaching of the Church. There is a third
group of theologians, chief among them William of Paris
and Petavius,[28] who hold that St. Hilary's original teaching, in his work *De Trinitate,* was false, but that he tacitly
retracted it in his Commentary on the Psalms.

The objections to St. Hilary's teaching seem to us to
rest on hermeneutical rather than dogmatic grounds.
The supposition that he retracted his previous teaching
in his Commentary on the Psalms is altogether gratuitous. It will be far juster to interpret the ambiguous
phrases in his work *De Trinitate* in the light of certain
perfectly orthodox expressions which occur in the *Trac-
tatus super Psalmos.* Had Hilary believed that the
human nature of Christ was absolutely insensible to
pain and suffering, he would surely not have written:
" *Hunc igitur ita a Deo percussum persecuti sunt, super
dolorem vulnerum dolorem persecutionis huius addentes;
pro nobis enim secundum Prophetam dolet.*" [29]

25 " *Nihil doloris Christum in pas-
sione sensisse,*" was the way in
which he formulated Hilary's teaching. (*De Statu Animae,* II, 9.)

26 " *Mentem S. Hilarii ab Aph-
thartodocetarum excessu non tanto-
pere distare.*" (*Christologia,* p. 552,
Friburgi 1901.)

27 *Liber Sent.,* III, dist. 15 sq.

His example was followed by St.
Bonaventure (*in h. l.*), St. Thomas
Aquinas (*in h. l.*), the Maurist Cou-
stant (*Opp. S. Hilarii,* Praef., sect.
4, § 3, n. 98 sqq.), and lately Stentrup (*Christologia,* I, thes. 56).

28 Cfr. *De Incarn.,* X, 5.

29 *In Ps.,* 68, n. 23. Cfr. *In Ps.,*
53, n. 4-7; 54, n. 6.

How, then, are we to interpret the incriminated passages in the treatise *De Trinitate?* Let us examine the text. It reads as follows (X, n. 13) : *" Homo Iesus Christus, unigenitus Deus, per carnem et Verbum ut hominis filius ita et Dei Filius, hominem verum secundum similitudinem nostri hominis, non deficiens a se Deo sumpsit; in quo quamvis ictus incideret aut vulnus descenderet aut nodi concurrerent aut suspensio elevaret, afferrent quidem haec impetum passionis, non tamen dolorem passionis inferrent. . . . Passus quidem est Dominus Iesus, dum caeditur, . . . dum moritur; sed in corpus Domini irruens passio nec non fuit passio nec tamen naturam passionis exseruit, dum . . . virtus corporis sine sensu poenae vim poenae in se desaevientis excepit. . . . Caro illa, id est panis ille de coelis est; et homo ille de Deo est, habens ad patiendum quidem corpus et passus est, sed naturam non habens ad dolendum. Naturae enim propriae ac suae corpus illud est, quod in coelestem gloriam conformatur in monte, quod attactu suo fugat febres, quod de sputo suo format oculos."*

The orthodoxy of these equivocal and awkward phrases has been defended on a twofold plea. Some have contended that St. Hilary, in speaking of " Christ," meant the " Person of Christ," *i. e.,* the Divine Logos, and that, consequently, in referring to the "nature of Christ " he had in mind the " nature of the Logos," *i. e.,* Christ's Divinity, which in matter of fact can be subject neither to *" dolor passionis"* nor *" sensus poenae."* Others have attempted to solve the difficulty by pointing out that St. Hilary's controversial attitude against the Arians led him to insist on the Divinity of Christ so vigorously as to accentuate unduly the *a-priori* excellence of His humanity and its special prerogatives over or-

dinary human nature.[30]   According to the first theory,
the passage: *"Virtus corporis sine sensu poenae vim
poenae excepit"* would convey the perfectly orthodox
meaning: *"Virtus divina corporis [i. e., Verbum existens in corpore] sine sensu poenae fuit."* The phrase
"naturam non habens ad dolendum" would likewise be
unexceptionable if *natura* were taken in the sense of
natura divina. With regard to the second theory we
may remark: St. Hilary undoubtedly teaches that there
is an important difference between the sacred humanity
of Christ and the ordinary human nature common to
all men by virtue of their descent from Adam. He
holds that the human nature of our Lord was different
from, and superior to, ordinary human nature, and he
attributes this difference to Christ's miraculous generation " from the Holy Ghost and the Virgin." [31]   While
he fully admits the reality and passibility of Christ's
manhood, St. Hilary asserts the existence of a threefold
essential difference between the Godman and all other
human beings, *viz.:* (1) It was impossible for Christ to
be overcome by bodily pain, (2) He was under no obligation to suffer, and (3) His suffering did not partake of
the nature of punishment.[32]

In the light of these considerations it cannot be truth-
fully asserted that St. Hilary sacrificed the dogma of the
passibility to his exalted conception of the majesty of
the Godman. We must, however, admit that he did not
succeed in finding the right *via media* between the doc-

---

30 This peculiarity can be traced
also in his other writings.

31 *De Trinit.,* X, 15, 18.

32 Cfr. St. Thomas, *Commentum
in Quatuor Libros Sent.,* III, dist.
15: *"Solutio Magistri consistit in
hoc, quod simpliciter noluit [S. Hi-*
*larius] removere a Christo dolorem,
sed tria quae sunt circa dolorem:
1. dominium doloris, . . . 2. meri-
tum   doloris, . . . 3. necessitatem
doloris . . . Et secundum hoc sol-
vuntur tria difficilia, quae in verbis
eius videntur esse."*

trine of the Arians on the one hand and that of the
Aphthartodocetæ on the other, and that he failed to give
due emphasis to the Scriptural and ecclesiastical teaching with regard to the nature and extent of our Lord's
capacity for suffering. Thus, while he certainly erred,
he may be said to have erred on a minor point. He
had before him the *ideal* Christ, as He might have appeared among men, in the full consciousness of His
divine dignity and without any obligation to suffer. The
historic Christ of the Gospels, whose Divinity he was
called upon to defend against powerful and sagacious
foes, St. Hilary manifestly overrated. His theory may
be briefly stated thus: The entire life and suffering of
our Lord was a continued miracle. It was as if the
suppressed energy of the Divine Logos were constantly
seeking an outlet. The passibility which duty and necessity imposed on Jesus Christ became actual passion
only by dint of His unceasing consent. His capacity
for suffering was abnormal, unnatural, miraculous. The
normal condition of His sacred humanity manifested
itself when he walked upon the waters, when he
penetrated locked doors, when He was transfigured
on Mount Tabor, and so forth.[33] This sublime conception of Christ led St. Hilary to lose sight of the
soteriological character of His mission. The Incarnation of the Son of God was dictated by practical reasons
and required for its consummation a painful atonement
which involved His death on the cross. The passibility
of Christ must, therefore, be held to be wholly natural
and spontaneous. A supernatural or artificial passibility, based upon an unbroken chain of miracles, could
not have accomplished the purposes of the Redemption.

33 Cfr. St. Hilary, *De Trinit.*, X, 23, 35.

Bardenhewer can scarcely be accused of undue severity when he says that the teaching of St. Hilary "makes a very sharp turn around the headland of Docetism." [34]

3. THE LIMITATIONS OF CHRIST'S PASSIBILITY.—In view of the express teaching of Sacred Scripture and the Church, Catholic theologians circumscribe the dogma of Christ's passibility with certain well-defined limitations, by excluding from His human nature all those defects of body and soul which would have been unbecoming to a Godman. They draw a sharp distinction between *passiones universales sive irreprehensibiles,*[35] *i. e.,* defects which flow from human nature as such, and *passiones particulares sive reprehensibiles,*[36] which are due to particular or accidental causes.

Passiones universales are, for instance, hunger and thirst, fatigue and worry, pain and mortality, joy and sorrow, fear and disgust, hope and love. The *passiones* or *defectus particulares* are partly of the body, such as malformation, deafness, blindness, leprosy, and consumption; and partly of the soul, such as feeble-mindedness, idiocy, revengefulness, and concupiscence.[37]

34 Bardenhewer-Shahan, *Patrology,* p. 410. Cfr. A. Beck, *Die Trinitätslehre des hl. Hilarius von Poitiers,* Mainz 1903; IDEM, *Kirchliche Studien und Quellen,* pp. 82 sqq., Amberg 1903.

35 πάθη ἀδιάβλητα.

36 πάθη διάβλητα.

37 Cfr. St. Thomas, *S. Theol.,* 3a, qu. 14, art. 4: " *Quidam autem defectus sunt, qui . . . causantur in aliquibus hominibus ex quibusdam particularibus causis, sicut lepra et morbus caducus et alia huiusmodi, qui quidem defectus quandoque causantur ex culpa hominis, puta ex inordinato victu, quandoque autem ex defectu virtutis formativae: quorum neutrum convenit Christo, quia et caro eius de Spiritu S. concepta*

As the body of Christ was exempt from all so-called
natural defects, so His soul must have been immune
from those psychic defects which arise from, or have any
connection with, sin. That is to say, our Divine Redeemer was not only absolutely exempt from every sinful
affection, such as concupiscence, excessive anger, etc.;
but He was at all times completely master of His
soul. No unfree *motus primo-primi,* not to speak of
other soul-affections, were able to surprise or overpower
Him. St. Jerome expresses this truth in a phrase which
has become technical: "The soul of Christ knew no
passiones (πάθη in the strict sense of the term) but only
προπάθειαι, *propassiones.*" [38] Since, however, the term
passio in the writings of the Fathers is sometimes applied to the Godman, its use cannot be said to be ob-
jectionable.[39]

The Scriptural and Patristic texts already given [40]
leave no doubt that Christ actually assumed the ordinary
defects and affections of human nature. Regarding the
diseases and weaknesses of the body in particular, St.
Thomas gives three reasons why it was proper that the
Saviour should share them. The first is that He came
into the world to make satisfaction for the sins of men;
the second, that without these defects there would have
been room to doubt the genuinity of His human nature;
and the third, in order to give us an example of pa-

*est . . . et ipse nihil inordinatum
in regimine vitae suae exercuit."*

[38] Cfr. St. Jerome, *In Matth.,* 5,
28: "*Inter* πάθος *et* προπάθειαν,
i. e. inter passionem et propassionem, hoc interest, quod passio
reputatur in vitium." In Matth., 26,
37: "Ne passio in animo illius do-
minaretur, per propassionem coepit
contristari; aliud est enim contristari et aliud incipere contristari."*

(Cfr. St. Thom., *S. Theol.,* 3a, qu.
15, art. 7, ad 1).

[39] Cfr. De Lugo, *De Incarn.,*
disp. 22, sect. 1, *sub fin.* St. John
of Damascus, *e. g.,* says: "*Christum omnes naturales et minime reprehensibiles passiones hominis assumpsisse."* (*De Fide Orth.,* III,
20.)

[40] *Supra,* pp. 74 sqq.

tience.[41] In fallen man these defects are punishments
for sin. Not so in Christ, who was absolutely free from
guilt. This truth is technically expressed in the phrase :
" He assumed *poenalitates* which involved no guilt."

4. A Famous Theological Controversy.—
The foregoing explanation will enable the student to form a correct opinion regarding the
merits of the famous controversy which arose
during the lifetime of St. Bernard of Clairvaux
between the Premonstratensian Abbot Philip
of Harvengt [42] and a certain Canon named John.

John correctly defined the passibility of our Divine
Saviour as spontaneous and natural, though voluntarily
assumed, whereas Philip, on what he believed to be the
authority of St. Hilary,[43] held that impassibility was
the normal condition of the Godman, and His actual
surrender to weakness and suffering must be explained
by a series of miracles. It was in fasting for a period
of forty days, in walking upon the waters, and by
other similar miracles, according to Philip's theory,
that Christ manifested His normal nature; the hunger He is reported to have felt after His fast,[44] and His
ordinary dependence upon the law of gravitation were
wholly abnormal and miraculous phenomena. But this
theory is opposed to the plain words of St. Paul [45] and

41 *S. Theol.*, 3a, qu. 14, art. 1.

42 (+ 1183). He is also called
Philippus Bonae Spei, from his ab-
bey of Bonne Espérance in the
Hennegau. For a short sketch of
his life and a list of his writings
see Hurter, *Nomenclator Literarius
Theologiae Catholicae*, vol. II, ed.

3a, col. 187 sq., Innsbruck 1906.
Cfr. also Berlière, *Philippe de Harvengt*, Bruges 1892.

43 Cfr. *supra*, pp. 76 sqq.

44 Cfr. Matth. IV, 2: " *post 4
esuriit.*"

45 Cfr. Heb. II, 17; IV, 15.

to the express teaching of the Church and the Fathers.[46]
That these natural defects were voluntarily assumed did
not make them unreal or unnatural, because their assumption was coincident with the moment of Christ's
voluntary Incarnation,[47] which implied His passion, and
consequently also passibility for the sublime purpose of
the atonement.[48]

READINGS : — St. Thomas, *S. Theol.*, 3a, qu. 14, 15.— G. Patiss,
S. J., *Das Leiden unseres Herrn Jesu Christi nach der Lehre
des hl. Thomas*, Ratisbon 1883.—* J. Rappenhöner, *Die Körper-
leiden und Gemütsbewegungen Christi*, Düsseldorf 1878.— Fr.
Schmid, *Quaestiones Selectae ex Theologia Dogmatica*, qu. 6,
Paderborn 1891.— G. A. Müller, *Die leibliche Gestalt Jesu Christi*,
Graz 1909.

[46] Cfr. St. Athanasius, *De Incarn.
Verbi* (Migne, *P. G.*, XXV, 132):
" *Pro corporis proprietate esurivit.*"
St. Augustine, *De Pecc. Mer. et
Rem.*, II, 29: " Inasmuch as in Him
there was the likeness of sinful
flesh, He willed to pass through the
changes of the various stages of life,
beginning even with infancy, so that
it would seem as if that flesh of
His might have arrived at death by
the gradual approach of old age, if
He had not been killed when a
young man." Hence the conciliar
phrase: " *Passibilis ex conditione
assumptae humanitatis.*"

[47] Cfr. Heb. X, 5 sqq.

[48] Cfr. Phil. II, 7: " *Semetipsum
exinanivit, . . . et habitu inventus
ut homo* — Christ . . . emptied himself, . . . being made in the likeness of men." On the Aphthartodocetae consult J. P. Junglas, *Leontius von Byzanz*, pp. 100 sqq., Paderborn 1908.

PART II

UNITY IN DUALITY, OR THE HYPO-STATIC UNION

We have shown that there are in Christ two natures, a divine and a human.   How are these natures united?

Ordinarily there are two species of unity, *i. e.*, two modes by which separate substances can be united into one.   The first, called accidental (*unitas acciden-talis*), is that by which two substances loosely coexist, as, *e. g.*, wine and water poured into the same cup. The second, called substantial unity (*unitas substan-tialis*), is that by which two substances combine so as to constitute a third, which is identical with neither of the two components but forms an entirely new substance. Thus man results from the union of body and soul, water from a combination of oxygen and hydrogen. Moral unity (*unitas moralis*) is a subdivision of acci-dental unity and obtains chiefly between rational beings, *e. g.*, between Christ and the faithful who receive Him in the Blessed Eucharist, between God and the elect endowed with the beatific vision, etc.   Opposed to moral is physical, which necessarily involves substantial unity.

Both reason and experience tell us that two finite substances can be combined into a new substance only by losing each its own proper self-existence. It is in this manner that soul and body unite in forming man.

The case is different with our Divine Saviour. In Him Divinity and humanity enter into a peculiar kind of physical and substantial union, in which neither loses its substantial existence. The Divine Logos simply possesses both natures without commingling or blending them together — the divine *per modum identitatis realis,* the human *per modum unitionis.* This peculiar kind of physical and substantial union, concerning which we have no knowledge other than that derived from Divine Revelation, is technically called hypostatic (*unitas hypostatica*), in contradistinction to a purely natural or a merely accidental or moral union.

The exceptional rank which this " unity in duality " holds among the different species of substantial unity leads us to expect that it should be subject to extraordinary determinations and productive of peculiar and unique effects. This is indeed the case, as we shall show in explaining (1) the Hypostatic Union as such, and (2) its effects.

CHAPTER I

THE HYPOSTATIC UNION

We shall base our exposition of the Hypostatic Union on the decrees of the Fourth General Council of Chalcedon (A. D. 451). Its definition of the dogma is more explicit even than that of the Third Ecumenical Council of Ephesus (A. D. 431), which is generally utilized for this purpose.

Here is the canon of Chalcedon: "*Sequentes igitur s. Patres, unum eundemque confiteri Filium et Dominum nostrum Iesum Christum consonanter omnes docemus, ... unum eundemque Christum Filium Dominum unigenitum, in duabus naturis inconfuse, immutabiliter, indivise, inseparabiliter agnoscendum,[1] nusquam sublatâ differentiâ naturarum propter unitionem magisque salvâ proprietate utriusque naturae, et in unam personam atque subsistentiam concurrente,[2] non in duas personas partitum aut divisum, sed unum eundemque Filium et unigenitum Deum Verbum Dominum Iesum Christum[3]* — Following, therefore, the holy Fathers, we confess one and the same Son, our Lord Jesus Christ, and we do with one voice teach one and the same Christ, Son, Lord, Only-Begotten, acknowledged to be in two na-

---

[1] Ἐν δύο φύσεσιν [*aliter:* ἐκ δύο φύσεων; on this incorrect reading cfr. Petavius, *De Incarn.*, III, 6, 11] ἀσυγχύτως, ἀτρέπτως, ἀδιαιρέτως, ἀχωρίστως.

[2] Καὶ εἰς ἓν πρόσωπον καὶ μίαν ὑπόστασιν συντρεχούσης.

[3] Οὐκ εἰς δύο πρόσωπα μεριζόμενον ἢ διαιρούμενον, ἀλλ' ἕνα καὶ τὸν αὐτὸν υἱὸν μονογενῆ Θεὸν Λόγον, Κύριον Ἰησοῦν Χριστόν.

tures, without confusion, change, division, separation; the distinction of natures being by no means destroyed by their union; but rather the distinction of each nature being preserved and concurring in one Person and one Hypostasis; not in something that is parted or divided into two persons, but in one and the same and Only-Begotten Son, God the Word, the Lord Jesus Christ." [4]

A careful analysis of this dogmatic definition shows that the Hypostatic Union may be regarded either (1) as the personal unity of Christ in two natures, or (2) as a union of two natures which remain distinct; this union may again be regarded (3) as absolutely inseparable.

GENERAL READINGS : —* St. Thomas Aquinas, *S. Theol.*, 3a, qu. 2–15, and the Commentators.— C. von Schätzler, *Das Dogma von der Menschwerdung des Sohnes Gottes*, § 3 sqq., Freiburg 1870.—* Scheeben, *Dogmatik*, Vol. II, §§ 215–227, Freiburg 1878 (summarized in Wilhelm-Scannell, *A Manual of Catholic Theology*, Vol. II, pp. 70 sqq., 2nd ed., London 1901).—* Card. Franzelin, *De Verbo Incarnato*, thes. 16–40, Rome 1893.— Oswald, *Christologie*, §§ 5–6, Paderborn 1887.—* Stentrup, *Christologia*, Vol. I, thes. 16–38, Innsbruck 1882.—* Maranus, *De Divinitate Christi*, etc., Würzburg 1859.— Dom. Mingoja, O. P., *De Unione Hypostatica*, Catania, Sicily, 1926.— J. P. Arendzen, *Whom Do You Say—? A Study in the Doctrine of the Incarnation*, London 1927, pp. 147 sqq.

On the teaching of the Fathers see * Petavius, *De Incarnatione*, III–IX, Antwerp 1700.—* Schwane, *Dogmengeschichte*, Vol. II, 2nd ed., §§ 29–51, Freiburg 1895.— J. Tixeront, *History of Dogmas*, English tr., Vol. I, St. Louis 1910; Vol. II, 1914; Vol. III, 1916.

4 Denzinger-Bannwart, *Enchiridion*, n. 148.

SECTION 1

THE HYPOSTATIC UNION OF THE TWO NATURES IN CHRIST

ARTICLE 1

THE POSITIVE DOGMATIC TEACHING OF REVELATION, AS DEFINED AGAINST NESTORIUS

1. NESTORIANISM AND THE CHURCH.—The Nestorian heresy, which denied the personal unity of Christ, grew out of the Christological teaching of Diodorus of Tarsus [1] and Theodore of Mopsuestia, who has been called a "Nestorius before Nestorius." [2]   Nestorianism was anathematized by the Third Ecumenical Council held at Ephesus, A. D. 431.   Among its most prominent champions were Theodoret of Cyrus and Ibas of Edessa, whose writings, together with certain excerpts from the works of Theodore of Mopsuestia, were condemned by the Fifth Ecumenical Council of Constantinople (A. D. 553) under the name of the Three Chapters.[3]

1 Died about 394. On Diodorus see Bardenhewer-Shahan, *Patrology,* pp. 315 sqq.

2 Theodore of Mopsuestia, a disciple of Diodorus, died about the year 428. An account of his life and teachings will be found in Bardenhewer-Shahan, *Patrology,* pp. 318 sqq.

3 Cfr. Lévêque, *Étude sur le Pape Virgile,* Paris 1887; W. H. Hutton, *The Church of the Sixth Century,* London 1897.

a) Nestorius was a Syrian by birth and became Patriarch of Constantinople in 428. In this position he at once began to disseminate with great obstinacy the Christological heresies of his master Theodore. These heretical teachings may be summarized as follows: (1) Jesus of Nazareth, the Son of Mary, is a different person from the Divine Logos or Son of God. As there are in Christ two different and distinct natures, so there are in Him also two different and distinct persons, one divine, the other human. (2) These two persons are, however, most intimately united, the Logos or Son of God indwelling in the man Jesus as in a temple. The man Jesus by this indwelling of the Logos becomes a " God-bearer " (*deifer*, θεοφόρος), or God in a figurative sense, like as Moses was called " the god of Pharao." (3) It follows that the Divine Logos is united with the man Jesus not by way of a physical union (ἕνωσις φυσική — καθ' ὑπόστασιν), but by a merely external, accidental, moral union (συνάφεια — ἕνωσις σχετική), and that, consequently, the Incarnation must be defined, not as an assumption of manhood by God, but simply as an indwelling of the Logos (ἐνοίκησις) in the man Jesus. (4) It follows further that Mary is not the " Mother of God " (θεοτόκος), but merely the mother of a man (ἀνθρωποτόκος), and should therefore properly be called Mother of Christ (χριστοτόκος) ; the term " Mother of God " can be applied to her only in a metaphorical sense, inasmuch as she was θεοδόχος, *i. e.*, mother of the θεοφόρος. Nestorius repeatedly referred to this synthesis of the Person of the Divine Logos with the human person of Christ as ἓν πρόσωπον, but he meant one moral or juridical person composed of two different hypostases, as is apparent from the fact that he consistently rejected the term μία ὑπόστασις.[4]

b) As St. Athanasius had defended the orthodox faith against Arianism, and as St. Augustine had stood forth as the champion of revealed truth against Pelagianism, so St. Cyril of Alexandria waged the Church's battle against the heresy of Nestorius. St. Cyril was a man of strong faith and extensive theological knowledge.[5] "If we except Athanasius," observes Bardenhewer, "none of the other Greek Fathers exercised so far-reaching an influence on ecclesiastical doctrine as Cyril; and if we except Augustine, there is none among all the other Fathers whose works have been adopted so extensively by ecumenical councils as a standard expression of Christian faith." [6] As the champion of the true faith against the Nestorians, St. Cyril was commissioned by Pope Celestine I. to preside over the Third General Council of Ephesus, A. D. 431. His twelve anathematisms against Nestorius [7] were approved by that Council as "canonical," i. e., as articles of faith, and Nestorius himself was deposed and excommunicated. The word θεοτόκος, so vehemently opposed by the Nestorian heretics, became the tessera of orthodoxy, and justly so, for it expresses the true doctrine regarding the Person of our divine Redeemer as pregnantly as the Nicene term ὁμοούσιον expresses the true doctrine concerning His Divinity. The first of St. Cyril's anathema-

---

4 Cfr. Marius Mercator (Migne, *P. L.*, XLVIII). On Nestorius' life cfr. Nau, *Nestorius*, pp. v sqq., Paris 1910. On a new view of his teaching, see Appendix, *infra*, pp. 296 sq.

5 He died June 27, 444.

6 Bardenhewer-Shahan, *Patrology*, p. 362.

7 The reader will find the text (in Greek and Latin) of these anathematisms in Alzog-Pabisch-Byrne, *Manual of Universal Church History*, Vol. I, pp. 596 sq., where there is also a good account of the Council of Ephesus. Cfr. Denzinger-Bannwart, *Enchiridion*, n. 113 sqq.

tisms (or Canon 1) reads: "*Si quis non confitetur Deum esse veraciter Emmanuel et propterea Dei geni-tricem* [8] *sanctam Virginem: — peperit enim secundum carnem carnem factum Dei Verbum,* [9] *anathema sit* — If any one do not confess that Emmanuel is truly God and that, therefore, the Holy Virgin is the Mother of God: — for she gave birth, according to the flesh, to the Word of God made flesh — let him be anathema." The second anathematism (Canon 2), while it does not formally define the mode of union between the Logos and His manhood, describes it practically as hypostatic: "*Si quis non confitetur, carni secundum subsistentiam* [10] *unitum Dei Patris Verbum, unumque esse Christum cum propria carne, eundem scil. Deum simul et hominem,* [11] *anathema sit* — If any one do not confess that the Word of God the Father is hypostatically united to the flesh, and that Christ is one with His own flesh, alike God and man, let him be anathema." The remaining ten anathe-matisms (or canons) condemn the Nestorian errors in detail.

2. THE DOGMA OF THE HYPOSTATIC UNION DEMONSTRATED FROM SACRED SCRIPTURE.— Though the term "Hypostatic Union," as in fact the entire technical phraseology in which the Church couches her teaching on the union of the two natures in Christ, is not found in the Bible, the doctrine itself is undoubtedly Scriptural. This can be shown (a) by a general and (b) by a special argument.

---

[8] θεοτόκον.

[9] σάρκα γεγονότα τὸν ἐκ Θεοῦ Λόγον.

[10] καθ' ὑπόστασιν, i. e., hypo-statically.

[11] τὸν αὐτὸν δηλονότι Θεὸν ὁμοῖ καὶ ἄνθρωπον.

a) The general argument may be formulated thus.   Sacred Scripture attributes to Christ two distinct series of predicates, the one divine, the other human.   It represents Him to us both as true God [12] and true man.[13]   Now the Christ who is true God is identical with the Christ who is true man.   Consequently, both classes of attributes belong equally to one and the same person, *i. e.,* the Godman Jesus Christ.   In other words, there are not two persons sharing the divine and the human attributes between them in such manner that the divine attributes belong to the one, while the human attributes belong to the other; but one individual, namely, the Divine Person of the Logos or Son of God, is alike *God and man,* because He possesses both a divine and a human nature.   Technically this truth is expressed in the proposition: Godhead and manhood are hypostatically united in Christ.

b) Of the many texts which can be adduced from Sacred Scripture in proof of this dogma we shall subject only one or two to an analysis from the Christological point of view.

ᵃ) The most pregnant sentence in the Gospels is undoubtedly John I, 14:   *"Et Verbum caro factum est* — καὶ ὁ Λόγος σὰρξ ἐγένετο — And the Word was made flesh."   Who is the subject of the predicate phrase: "was made flesh"?   It is

12 Cfr. *supra,* Part I, Chapter 1.   13 Cfr. *supra,* Part I, Chapter 2.

the "Logos," whom we have shown to be the Son of God, Himself true God, the Second Person of the Divine Trinity.[14] This Logos was made flesh, *i. e.,* became man. Consequently, the one Incarnate Logos is both God and man, and therefore *Godman* (θεάνθρωπος).

And what is the meaning of the word ἐγένετο? A creature can " become " or " be made " (*fieri aliquid*) in a threefold sense. (1) It can simply begin to exist, as, *e. g.,* " the world became," that is, it began to exist. (2) It may undergo a substantial change; thus water was changed into wine at the wedding of Cana. (3) It may assume a new mode of being, over and above that which it already possesses. This new mode of being may be due either to an intrinsic quality, such as learning or sanctity; or to a purely extrinsic relation, such as the generalship of an army. It is quite evident that the Incarnation of the Logos cannot be taken in either the first or the second of the above mentioned meanings. The notion of the divine, eternal, immutable Logos positively excludes a creatural beginning or any transubstantiation of the Godhead into flesh, *i. e.,* manhood. Hence the third meaning alone is the true one. It does not, however, do full justice to the mystery of the Incarnation, because in a creature a new state or condition can never be a substance but is always necessarily an accident, whereas in the Divine Logos the assumption of manhood means a mode of being based upon substantial union, without exercising the slightest intrinsic effect upon the Logos Himself. To express the same truth in simpler terms: The union of the Logos with

14 Cfr. Pohle-Preuss, *The Divine Trinity,* pp. 49 sqq.

human nature results in one Divine Person possessing two distinct natures. This is what theologians call the Hypostatic Union.

β) The teaching of St. Paul agrees with that of St. John. Witness the following passage from Phil. II, 6 sq.: ". . . *qui quum in forma Dei* [15] *esset, non rapinam arbitratus est esse se aequalem Deo,* [16] *sed semetipsum exinanivit formam servi accipiens,* [17] *in similitudinem hominum factus et habitu inventus ut homo* — Who being in the form of God, thought it not robbery to be equal with God: but emptied himself, taking the form of a servant, being made in the likeness of men, and in habit found as man." The subject of this sentence is Christ. St. Paul asserts of Him: (1) That He was "in the form of God," which means that He was consubstantial with God, and therefore Himself God; [18] and (2) that He "took the form of a servant" and was in consequence thereof "found as man." Here we have a clear assertion of the Incarnation of God, which, according to St. Paul, involves self-abasement (*exinanitio,* κένωσις). In what sense are we to take *exinanitio* or *kenosis?* Does it mean that the Godhead annihilated itself, or that God ceased to be God? That would be intrinsically impossible, and, besides, verse 11 of

---

[15] ἐν μορφῇ Θεοῦ.
[16] τὸ εἶναι ἴσα Θεῷ.
[17] μορφὴν δούλου λαβών.

[18] Cfr. Pohle-Preuss, *The Divine Trinity,* pp. 61 sq.

the same chapter of St. Paul's Epistle to the Philippians reads: "The Lord Jesus Christ is in the glory of God the Father." [19] Consequently the phrase "God . . . emptied himself" can only mean that He who was God "took [20] the form of a servant," *i. e.,* assumed human nature, inasmuch as the Son of God appeared among men not alone "in the form of God," but also in "the form of a servant" (human nature). It follows that, according to St. Paul's teaching, the two natures are in Christ combined in a Personal or Hypostatic Union.[21]

All the arguments which prove the Divinity of Christ likewise demonstrate the Hypostatic Union, because Holy Scripture declares that the man Jesus *is* true God. This could not be if Divinity and humanity were not united in Him as in one individual subject. In that case we should have to say with Nestorius: The man Jesus bears in His person the Godhead.

The assertion of certain Modernists, that "the Christological teaching of SS. Paul and John, and of the councils of Nicaea, Ephesus, and

19 Phil. II, 11.

20 *Accipiens,* λαβών.

21 On the Kenosis see P. J. Toner, "The Modern Kenotic Theory," in the *Irish Theological Quarterly,* Vol. I (1906), Nos. 1 and 2; W. T. C. Sheppard, O. S. B., "The 'Kenosis' According to St. Luke," in the same review, Vol. V (1910), No. 19; F. J. Hall (Anglican), *The Kenotic Theory,* New York 1898; M. Waldhäuser, *Die Kenose und die moderne protestantische Christologie,* Mainz 1912; F. Prat, S. J., *La Théologie de Saint Paul,* Vol. II, pp. 239 sqq., Paris 1912; R. A. Knox, "Kenotic Theories," in *The Incarnation* (Cambridge Summer School Lectures) Cambridge 1926, pp. 211–228.

Chalcedon does not represent Christ's own teaching, but merely the upshot of philosophical speculation," [22] cannot stand in the light of our Lord's self-assertion,[23] which substantially agrees with the doctrine of the Apostles, the Fathers, and the Councils.

3. THE PATRISTIC ARGUMENT.—The Fathers of the first four centuries (there is no need of extending the argument beyond 431) condemned the heresy of Nestorius before it was broached. To bring out their teaching effectively we shall consider it (a) as the simple testimony of Tradition, and (b) in its deeper speculative bearings.

a) The ante-Ephesine Fathers testify to the traditional belief of Primitive Christianity in the dogma of the Hypostatic Union whenever, in their characteristic simple language, they ascribe divine attributes to the man Christ, or human attributes to the Divine Logos, and insist on the inseparable unity of Jesus against any and all attempts to make it appear that there are two persons in Him.

α) "Hypostatic Union" as a technical term is foreshadowed in the writings of the Fathers long before

22 Cfr. H. P. Liddon, *The Divinity of Our Lord and Saviour Jesus Christ*, pp. 229 sqq., London, Oxford, and Cambridge 1867; H. Felder, O. M. Cap., *Jesus Christus, Apologie seiner Messianität und Gottheit gegenüber der neuesten ungläubigen Jesus-Forschung*, Vol. I, pp. 291 sqq., Paderborn 1911. The Christological teaching of St. Paul is exposed with great acumen and very fully by Prat, *La Théologie de Saint Paul*, Vol. II.

23 Cfr. Denzinger-Bannwart, *Enchiridion*, n. 2031.

Nestorius. Pre-eminent among the so-called Apostolic
Fathers in this respect is St. Ignatius of Antioch (d.
107), who says: "One is the physician, both bodily
and spiritual [*i. e.* divine], begotten and unbegotten,
God existing in the flesh,[24] both of Mary and of God,
capable of suffering and yet impassible, Jesus Christ our
Lord." [25] It was plainly on the supposition of the Hypostatic Union that St. Melito of Sardes spoke of "God
suffering at the hands of the Israelites." [26]

Of great importance is the teaching of St. Irenæus of
Lyons (d. 202), from which we extract four leading
propositions. He declares: (1) That one and the same
person is both God and man. "*Si enim alter quidem
passus est, alter autem impassibilis mansit, et alter quidem natus est, alter vero in eum qui natus est descendit
et rursus reliquit eum, non unus, sed duo monstrantur.
. . . Unum autem eum, et qui natus est et qui passus
est, novit apostolus: ipse est Verbum Dei, ipse unigenitus
a Patre, Christus Iesus Dominus noster.*" [27] Whence it
follows (2) that God is man and the man Jesus is true
God: "*Verbum caro erit, Filius Dei filius hominis . . .
et hoc factus quod et nos, Deus fortis est et inenarrabile
habet genus.*" [28] It follows further (3) that the Word
Incarnate possesses human as well as divine attributes:
"*Verbum Dei suo sanguine nos redemit et in Eucharistia
calicem suum sanguinem, panem suum corpus* [29] *confirma-
vit.*" [30] And lastly (4) that the union of Godhead and
manhood in Christ must be conceived as hypostatic. For,
as Irenæus points out, St. John Himself refuted the
"*blasphemae regulae quae dividunt Dominum ex altera*

24 ἐν σαρκὶ γενόμενος Θεός.
25 *Ep. ad Eph.*, VII, 2.
26 Fragm. 8 (Migne, *P. G.*, V,
1221).

27 *Adv. Haer.*, III, 16, 9.
28 *Ibid.*, IV, 33, 11.
29 αἷμα ἴδιον, σῶμα ἴδιον.
30 *Ibid.*, V, 2, 2.

*et altera substantia [i. e. hypostasi] dicentes eum fac-
tum."* [31]

Substantially the doctrine of the Hypostatic Union
was also taught by St. Gregory of Nazianzus. He writes:
" If any one introduces two sons, the one of God the
Father, and the other of the mother, but does not [ac-
knowledge them to be] one and the same, he shall forfeit
the adoptive sonship which has been promised to those
who have the true faith. For though there are two natures, the divine and the human, there are not two
sons." [32]

Among the older Latin writers the dogma of the Hypostatic Union was most concisely formulated by Tertullian. *" Videmus duplicem statum [i. e. naturam] non
confusum, sed coniunctum in una persona, Deum et
hominem Iesum."* [33]

St. Ambrose has a beautiful passage on the Person
of Christ: *" Non enim alter ex Patre, alter ex virgine,"*
he says, *" sed idem aliter ex Patre, aliter ex virgine."* [34]

Similarly St. Augustine: *" Nunc vero ita inter Deum
et homines mediator [Christus] apparuit, ut in unitate
personae copulans utramque naturam et solita sublimaret
insolitis et insolita solitis temperaret."* [35]

As the above-quoted Patristic texts show, Irenæus
and Tertullian employed the later ecclesiastical formula
" in unitate personae" (= Hypostatic Union) even before St. Augustine. Hippolytus [36] at least foreshadowed

31 *Ibid.*, III, 16, 6. Cfr. Franzelin, *De Incarn.*, thes. 18.

32 *Ep. ad Cledon.*, I.

33 *Contr. Prax.*, c. 27. Cfr. J. F.
Bethune-Baker, " Tertullian's Use
of *Substantia, Natura,* and *Persona,"* in the *Journal of Theol.
Studies,* Vol. IV (1902–3), pp. 440
sqq.

34 *De Incarn.*, V, 5.

35 *Ep.,* 137, III, 9 (Migne, *P. L.,*
XXXIII, 519). Cfr. Petavius, *De
Incarn.*, III, 11; J. Schwetz, *Theol.
Dogmat.,* Vol. II, pp. 371 sqq.,
Vindobonae 1880.

36 Died about the year 236.

it when, misconceiving the essence of the Most Holy
Trinity, he said: " For neither was the Logos without
His flesh [37] and in Himself the perfect only-begotten
Son, although He was the perfect Logos, nor could the
flesh subsist [38] apart from the Logos, because it had its
subsistence [39] in the Logos." [40]

A most valuable witness is Epiphanius,[41] who in developing his " theory of the Incarnation " says: " The
Logos has united body and spiritual soul in one unity and
one spiritual Hypostasis." [42]   The meaning of this prolep-
tic expression is made clear by a famous parallel passage,
which not only contains the significant term ὑποστήσαντα,
but distinctly accentuates the absence of a human personality in Christ.   " We do not," writes Epiphanius, " introduce two Christs or two kings and sons of God, but the
same God and the same man.   Not as if the Logos dwelled
in the man, but because He wholly became man . . . the
Word was made flesh.   He does not say, ' The flesh became God,' because he wished to emphasize above all
things that the Logos descended from Heaven and took
on flesh from the womb of the Blessed Virgin,[43] and
in a most perfect manner incorporated into Himself a
complete human nature." [44]

As witnesses to Primitive Tradition we may also regard
those among the Fathers who employ the term ὕπαρξις
as a synonym for ὑπόστασις.   Thus St. Athanasius:
" Unum esse Christum secundum indeficientem existen-

---

[37] ἄσαρκος.

[38] ὑποστᾶναι.

[39] σύστασιν.

[40] Contr. Noët., 15.

[41] Died about 403.

[42] Haeres., 20, n. 4 (Migne, P. G.,
XLI, 277): συνενώσας εἰς μίαν

ἐνώτητα καὶ μίαν πνευματικὴν
ὑπόστασιν.

[43] εἰς ἑαυτὸν δὲ ὑποστήσαντα
τὴν σάρκα.

[44] τελείως εἰς ἑαυτὸν ἀναπλα-
σάμενον. Haer., 77, 29 (Migne,
P. G., XLII, 685).

tiam [*i. e. subsistentiam*],[45] *ut unus sit utrumque, perfectus secundum omnia Deus et homo idem."* [46]

No further proof is needed to show that the Fathers who flourished before the Third General Council, inculcated the doctrine of the Hypostatic Union and prepared the technical terminology subsequently adopted by the Church.

β) The argument from Tradition derives special weight from the matter-of-fact references made by the Fathers to the ecclesiastical symbolum, which, because based upon the "Apostles' Creed," was regarded as the most powerful bulwark against Christological heresies.[47]

The Council of Ephesus (A. D. 431) refused to draw up a special symbolum against Nestorius [48] on the express ground that his heretical teaching was sufficiently refuted by the Nicene Creed.   In matter of fact the profession of faith in " the only-begotten Son of God, conceived by the Holy Ghost, born of the Virgin Mary, crucified, dead, and buried " [49] embodies an overwhelming argument for the personal unity of Christ, inasmuch as all these human predicates are attributed directly to the " Son of God," not to the man Jesus. While the Latin translations do not specially stress the " unity " of Christ, the Oriental creeds all, or nearly all,

---

45 καθ' ὕπαρξιν ἀνελιπῇ.

46 *Contr. Apollin.*, I, 16 (Migne, P. G., XXVI, 1124). On Athanasius' rare use of the term *Hypostasis* see Newman, *Select Treatises of St. Athanasius*, Vol. II, p. 158, 9th impression, London 1903.

47 Cfr.   Rufinus,   *Comment. in Symbol.*, 3 sqq.

48 " *Non esse fidem alteram conscribendam.*" *Synod. Ephes. Act.*, VI.

49 Cfr.   Denzinger-Bannwart, *Enchiridion*, n. 1 sqq.

contain the typical locution: εἰς ἕνα Κύριον Ἰησοῦν Χριστόν,
— a formula plainly directed against the oft-repeated attempts, dating from the time of Cerinthus, to " dissolve "
Jesus Christ into two different and distinct persons, *viz.*:
the Son of God and the man Jesus in whom the Logos indwells.[50]   In opposition to this heretical doctrine,
as taught, *e. g.*, by the Patripassionist Noëtus, the
presbyters of Smyrna solemnly emphasized the teaching
of their symbol: Ἕνα Χριστὸν ἔχομεν — We have one
Christ.   St. Epiphanius, to whom we are indebted for
our knowledge of this incident,[51] also reports the in-
structive fact that the Eastern bishops demanded of their
catechumens an elaborate profession of faith in the uni-
personality of Christ, thereby rejecting in advance the
Nestorian as well as the Monophysite heresy.   This
creed contains such passages as the following: " We
believe . . . in one Lord Jesus Christ, the Son of God,
begotten from God the Father, . . . who incorporated
in a sacred union the flesh, not in some other man, but
in Himself.[52] . . . For the Word was made flesh, not by
undergoing a transformation, or by changing His Divinity
into humanity. . . . For the Lord Jesus Christ is one
and not two, the same God, the same King." [53]

b) A still better view of the primitive ecclesiastical Tradition can be obtained from those passages of Patristic literature which professedly
discuss and explain the dogma that there is but
one person in Christ.

---

50 Cfr. 1 John IV, 3: "*Et omnis
spiritus, qui solvit Iesum, ex Deo
non est* — And every spirit that dis-
solveth Jesus, is not of God."

51 *Haer.*, 57.

52 εἰς ἑαυτὸν σάρκα ἀναπλά-
σαντα εἰς μίαν ἁγίαν ἐνότητα.

53 Epiph., *Ancoratus*, V, n. 12.
Cfr. Denzinger-Bannwart, *Enchiridion*, n. 13. For a fuller discussion

a) In voicing their firm belief in the Son of Mary as Son of God, and therefore true God,[54] not a few of the Fathers point out an absurd inference that flows inevitably from the teaching of Nestorius, to wit: If (as Nestorius alleged) there were two Hypostases in Christ, the Divine Trinity would consist of four Persons. Thus the African Bishops, including St. Augustine, compelled the Gallic monk Leporius, who, besides propagating the Pelagian heresy, was also a precursor of Nestorianism, to abjure the doctrine of a twofold personality in Christ on the ground that it would introduce a fourth person into the Trinity.[55]

β) It was quite natural for the Fathers to seek out points of similarity between Christ the Godman and the Blessed Trinity. In developing these analogies, several Patristic writers describe the relation between nature and person in Christ as the opposite of that existing between the Godhead and the Three Divine Hypostases. In the Trinity, they say, there are " three Hypostases (or Persons) in one absolute unity of nature," whereas in Christ there is " only one Hypostasis or Person as against two complete natures." The Council of Ephesus quoted St. Gregory Nazianzen [56] as follows: " *Aliud quidem et aliud sunt ea, ex quibus Salvator, . . . non tamen alius et alius, absit. Ambo enim haec connexione* [57] *unum sunt, Deo nimirum humanitatem atque homine divinita-*

of this point consult Franzelin, *De Verbo Incarnato*, thes. 17; Stentrup, *Christologia*, Vol. I, thes. 12.

54 *V. supra*, Part I, Chapter 1.

55 " *Quartam se subintroducere in Trinitate personam.*"— In his retractation, composed about the year 418, Leporius declares: " *Si ergo ita hominem cum Deo natum esse dicamus, ut seorsum quae Dei sunt*

soli Deo demus, et seorsum quae sunt hominis soli homini reputemus, quartam manifestissime inducimus in Trinitate personam et de uno Filio Dei non unum, sed facere incipimus duos Christos." (*Libell. Emendat. ad Episc. Gall.*, n. 5.)

56 St. Gregory of Nazianzus died about 390.

57 συγκράσει.

tem suscipiente.[58] . . . *Porro aliud et aliud dico, contra
quam in Trinitate res habet: illic enim alius atque alius,
ne personas confundamus, non autem aliud atque aliud,
quoniam tria quoad divinitatem unum et idem sunt."* [59]

γ) The sarcastic objection of certain Pagan and Jewish writers, that the Christians " adored a crucified man
as divine " and " degraded the immutable God " to the
level of a " mutable man born of a woman," was met by
the Fathers with the declaration that Christ, born of the
Virgin Mary, is not merely a man, but also true God,
and that He is consequently both God and man by virtue
of a miraculous and incomprehensible union. Pliny, in
his well-known letter to the Emperor Trajan, says:
" They [the Christians] confessed that they used to assemble together before dawn to say prayers to Christ as
their God.[60] . . ." The notorious scoffer Lucian railed:
" Their chief lawgiver [Christ] has persuaded them that
they were all brethren, one of another, as soon as they
had gone over, *i. e.,* renounced the Greek gods and adored
that crucified sophist and live according to his laws." [61]
The philosopher Celsus reproaches the Christians as follows: " God is good, beautiful, blessed, most magnificent
and beautiful of form. But if he would descend to men,
he must change Himself and become bad instead of good,

[58] Θεοῦ μὲν ἐνανθρωπήσαντος, ἀνθρώπου δὲ θεωθέντος.

[59] *Ep. ad Cledon.,* I (Migne, *P. G.,* XXXVII, 179). Cfr. Franzelin, *De Verbo Incarnato,* thes. 19.

[60] ". . . *essent soliti stato die ante lucem convenire carmenque Christo quasi deo dicere secum invicem." Ep.,* X, 97. (Text of letter and Trajan's rescript in Kirch, *Enchiridion Fontium Hist. Eccl. Antiqu.,* pp. 18 sqq.) and, with English tr., in C. R. Haines, *Heathen Contact with Christianity during its First Century and a Half,* Cambridge 1923, pp. 40 sqq. *"Carmen"* could signify a liturgical dialogue. Lightfoot identifies the scene described by Pliny with the liturgy of baptism and Batiffol is inclined to adopt this view. (*The Credibility of the Gospel,* Engl. tr. of *"Orpheus" et l'Evangile,* pp. 31 sq.)

[61] *De Morte Peregrini,* 13.

ugly instead of beautiful, unhappy instead of happy, the worst instead of the best." [62]

4. PATRISTIC AND CONCILIAR FORMULAS.—By way of deepening and strengthening the argument from Tradition we will devote a few pages to an explanation of the various formulas employed by the Fathers before the Council of Ephesus, and by some of the later councils, to elucidate the dogma of the Hypostatic Union.

a) One of the most popular of these formulas was the following: "Between (Christ's) divinity and (His) humanity there exists a substantial, physical, natural union." [63]

This formula was not, of course, coined in the interest of Monophysitism, but merely to express the truth that the constituent elements of Christ (*termini ex quibus, i. e.,* His Divinity and humanity) are substances, and that the result of their union (*terminus qui*) is a substantial,

[62] Quoted by Origen, *Contr. Celsum,* IV, 14. On the arguments, based upon the "Hypostatic Union," of Tertullian, Justin Martyr, Arnobius, Origen, Lactantius, Cyril of Alexandria (against Julian the Apostate), cfr. Maranus, *De Divinit. Iesu Christi,* II, 2; III, 2–4. On the caricature of the Crucifixion discovered A. D. 1856 beneath the ruins of the Palatine palace, (the figure on the cross bears an ass's head, before which stands a Christian in the posture of adoration), see Garrucci, *Il Crocifisso Graffito,* Rome 1857. The "Graffito blasfemo," as this caricature of the adoration of our crucified Lord is called, is a rough sketch, traced in all probability by the hand of some pagan slave in one of the earliest years of the third century of our era. Cfr. also H. P. Liddon, *The Divinity of Our Lord and Saviour Jesus Christ,* pp. 593 sqq.; C. M. Kaufmann, *Handbuch der christlichen Archäologie,* pp. 254 sqq., Paderborn 1905; P. J. Chandlery, S. J., *Pilgrim-Walks in Rome,* 2nd ed., p. 216, London 1905; H. Grisar, *History of Rome and the Popes,* Vol. III, p. 71, London 1912.

[63] *Unio substantialis, physica, secundum naturam* — ἕνωσις κατ' οὐσίαν, κατὰ φύσιν ἢ φυσική, οὐσιώδης.

physical unity. Thus Justin Martyr calls Christ Λόγον μορφωθέντα καὶ ἄνθρωπον γενόμενον,[64] meaning that the Logos assumed human nature after the manner of a substantial form. Gregory Nazianzen exclaims: "If any one says that the Godhead was operative in Him [Christ] as in a prophet in mode of grace,[65] but was not united with Him and does not unite with Him [66] substantially,[67] let him be devoid of every higher inspiration. . . . Let him who worships not the Crucified, be anathema." [68] St. John of Damascus, who was no doubt the most authoritative interpreter of the teaching of the Greek Fathers, explains the true bearing of this formula against Monophysitic misconstructions as follows: "We call it a substantial,[69] that is a true and not an apparent union. Substantial, not as if two natures had coalesced into one single, composite nature, but because they are united in the one composite Hypostasis of the Son of God." [70]

b) Another formulation of the same truth, and one which admitted of no misunderstanding, was *"Verbum naturam humanam fecit suam propriam,"* i. e., The Logos made human nature entirely His own.

The meaning of this formula is thus explained by St. Cyril: *"Sicut suum cuique nostrum corpus est proprium, eodem modo etiam Unigeniti corpus proprium illi erat et non alterius."* [71] St. Athanasius (d. 373) elucidates it as follows: *"Errant docentes, alium esse qui*

---

64 *Apol.*, I, n. 5. On the Christology of St. Justin see Tixeront, *History of Dogmas*, Vol. I, pp. 222 sq., St. Louis 1910.

65 κατὰ χάριν.

66 συνῆφθαί τε καὶ συνάπτεσθαι.

67 κατ' οὐσίαν.

68 *Ep. ad Cledon.*, I.

69 οὐσιώδη.

70 *De Fide Orth.*, III, 3. Cfr. Petavius, *De Incarn.*, III, 4.

71 *Contr. Nestor.*, I, 1.

passus est Filius, et alium qui passus non est; non est enim alius praeter ipsum Verbum quod mortem et passionem suscepit. . . . Formam servi ipsum Verbum suam propriam fecit physicâ generatione . . . et caro facta est secundum naturam propria Deo; non quasi caro consubstantialis esset divinitati Verbi velut coaeterna, sed ei secundum naturam propria facta est et indivisa per unionem (ἰδία κατὰ φύσιν γενομένη καὶ ἀδιαίρετος κατὰ ἔνωσιν) *ex semine David et Abraham et Adam, ex quo et nos progeniti sumus. . . . Consubstantiale* (ὁμοούσιον) *enim et impassibile et immortale cum consubstantiali non habet unitatem secundum hypostasin, sed secundum naturam, secundum hypostasin vero exhibet propriam perfectionem* (τελειότητα = *totietatem in se*). . . . *Si Filium et Spiritum S. ita dicitis Patri consubstantialem sicut carnem passibilem, . . . vel inviti quaternitatem pro Trinitate inducitis, docentes carnem esse Trinitati consubstantialem.*" [72]

This is a dogmatic *locus classicus* of prime importance. Its salient points may be paraphrased as follows: (1) The union of divinity and humanity is conceived after the manner of an intussusception of humanity by the Divine Logos,— actively, by virtue of " physical generation from the seed of David and Abraham and Adam," [73] formally, by virtue of a " physical and inseparable union." (2) The " physical union " thus consummated does not, however, result in consubstantiality of the flesh with the Godhead (which would be Monophysitism), but is based on an " *unitas secundum hypostasin,*" which attains its climax in the τελειότης and excludes the preposterous inference that there are in Christ two Sons, one who suffers, and another who does not suffer.[74] (3) Disregard of this im-

[72] *Contr. Apollin.,* I, 12 (Migne, P. G., XXVI, 1113).
8

[73] *V. supra,* p. 58 sq.
[74] *V. supra,* p. 97 sq.

portant consideration would involve the error of Tetra-
dism, which is destructive of the Trinity.[75]

This definition of the Hypostatic Union as an appro-
priation of humanity by the Logos accurately expresses
the true meaning of the mystery of the Incarnation, and
it need not surprise us, therefore, to find it in vogue
even after the classic formula *unio secundum hypostasin*
had been definitively fixed by the Church.[76]

　　c) A third formula, employed almost exclusively by St. Cyril, and found hardly anywhere
before his time, reads: *"Una natura Verbi incarnata (μία φύσις τοῦ Λόγου σεσαρκωμένη)."*

Cardinal Newman explains this formula as follows:
" 1. φύσις is the Divine Essence, substantial and personal, in the fulness of its attributes — the One God.
And, τοῦ Λόγου being added, it is that One God, considered in the Person of the Son. 2. It is called μία (1)
because, even after the Incarnation, it and no other nature is, strictly speaking, ἴδια, *His own,* the flesh being
'*assumpta*'; (2) because it, and no other, has been His
from the first; and (3) because it has ever been one
and the same, in nowise affected as to its perfection by
the Incarnation. 3. It is called σεσαρκωμένη in order to
express the dependence, subordination, and restriction of
His humanity, which (a) has neither ἡγεμονικόν nor personality; (b) has no distinct υἱότης, though it involved a

75 *V. supra,* p. 103.

76 It recurs in the numerous
writings of St. Cyril, in the decrees
of the Council of Ephesus (Can. 11,
apud Denzinger-Bannwart, *Enchiridion,* n. 123), in the famous *Epistula Dogmatica ad Flavianum* of
Pope Leo the Great, which played

such an important rôle at the Council of Chalcedon (A. D. 451), and
especially in the decrees of the
Sixth Ecumenical Council held at
Constantinople, A. D. 680, against
the Monothelites. (Cfr. Denzinger-
Bannwart, *Enchiridion,* n. 291.)

new γέννησις; (c) is not possessed of the fulness of characteristics which attaches to any other specimen of our race. On which account, while it is recognized as a perfect nature, it may be spoken of as existing after the manner of an attribute rather than of a substantive being, which it really is, as in a parallel way Catholics speak of its presence in the Eucharist, though corporeal, being after the manner of a spirit." [77]

Theodoret asserts that this formula was consonant with the mode of conception and expression current in Alexandria, and for this very reason was impugned as Monophysitic by John of Antioch and others of the Antiochene school. Leontius of Byzantium tells another story. "You must know," he says,[78] "that St. Cyril was the first among the orthodox to employ the phrase, 'the one incarnate nature of the Divine Logos.' We say, 'among the orthodox,' because Apollinaris often used the same formula, and for this reason the blessed Cyril was looked upon as an Apollinarist by the Orientals. But he was not an Apollinarist. It is unfair to reject everything that the heretics say. We should repudiate only that which is wrong." Had he foreseen the abuse to which this formula and his own authority were later on subjected by the Monophysites, Cyril would no doubt have couched his teaching in clearer terms. But in the sense in which he used it, and wished others to understand it, the formula μία φύσις σεσαρκωμένη was entirely orthodox, and it was only by a gross misconstruction that the Monophysitic heretics were able to twist it in favor of their false teaching of a μόνη φύσις. St. Cyril used the phrase mainly against the Nestorian

[77] Newman, "On St. Cyril's Formula μία φύσις σεσαρκωμένη" in Tracts Theological and Ecclesiastical, New Edition, London 1895, pp. 380 sq.

[78] De Sectis, Act. 8.

figment of "two independently subsisting natures
which would involve a dualism of persons in Christ.
fusion of both natures into one (μία) φύσις was entire
foreign to his mind, as is evidenced by the addition
the word σεσαρκωμένη, to which he calls particular a
tention in his *Ep. 46 ad Succensum,* and also from t
fact that in St. Cyril's mind *natura Verbi* was mere
another term for *Verbum subsistens in natura divi*
i. e., the Divine Hypostasis of the Logos. Manifest
therefore, by μία φύσις σεσαρκωμένη St. Cyril meant pure
and solely the Incarnate Word. In the second place
must be noted that St. Cyril did not fail to defend t
dogma of the inconfusion of both natures in Chr
against his accusers and critics, who were numero
already during his lifetime. Thus he says in his *E
stola ad Acac. Melit.: "Ea, ex quibus est unus Fili
ac Dominus Iesus Christus, consideratione comple
duas naturas dicimus unitas esse, post unitionem ve
utpote sublatâ iam divisione in duos, unam credimus e
Filii naturam, utpote unius, sed inhumanati et incarnati,
quum vero Deus Verbum inhumanatus et incarnat
dicitur, procul abiiciatur conversionis suspicio; man
enim, quod erat."* It is not surprising, therefore (a
this is the third point in our argument), that the fo
mula μία φύσις σεσαρκωμένη was upheld as orthodox
the various synods subsequently held against the Mor
physites. Thus the Fifth Ecumenical Council of Co
stantinople (A. D. 553) defines: *"Si quis ... 'un
naturam Dei Verbi incarnatam' dicens non sic has vo
accipit, sicut Patres docuerunt, quod ex divina nat
et humana, unitione secundum subsistentiam factâ,*[80] *un*

---

[79] μίαν εἶναι πιστεύομεν τὴν τοῦ
Θεοῦ φύσιν, ὡς ἑνός, πλὴν ἐνανθρωπήσαντος καὶ σεσαρκωμένου.

[80] τῆς ἑνώσεως καθ' ὑπόστα
γενομένης.

Christus factus est, sed ex huiusmodi vocibus unam naturam sive substantiam deitatis et carnis Christi[81] *introducere conatur, talis anathema sit."* [82]

d) A fourth formula expresses the truth that there is but one personality in Christ in these terms: *"Duae naturae ratione tantum* (κατὰ θεωρίαν, νοήσει, διακρίσει) *distinguuntur."*

Like the preceding formulas this one too was directed against the dualistic heresy of Nestorius, and therefore the Fathers who employed it, among them St. Cyril, cannot reasonably be suspected of harboring Monophysitic errors. An authentic interpretation of the phrase *ratione tantum* was furnished by the Fifth Ecumenical Council (A. D. 553) as follows: *" Si quis . . . non tantummodo contemplatione*[83] *differentiam eorum accipit, ex quibus et compositus est — non interemptâ proprietate propter unitatem (unus enim ex utraque et per unum utraque) — sed propterea numero utitur, tamquam divisas et propriâ subsistentiâ consistentes naturas habeat,*[84] *talis anathema sit."* [85]   How foreign the idea of identifying the two natures in Christ was to the Fathers and the councils that made use of this formula, is plain from the subjoined expression of Pope Agatho, which was read at the Sixth General Council of Constantinople,

[81] μίαν φύσιν ἤτοι οὐσίαν.
[82] Cfr. Denzinger-Bannwart, *Enchiridion*, n. 220. Cfr. also the Lateran Council of 649, held under Martin I (Denzinger-Bannwart, *l. c.*, n. 258). For a more detailed discussion of St. Cyril's formula and its fortunes consult J. H. Newman, *Tracts Theological and Ecclesiastical*, pp. 331 sqq., new ed., London 1895; Petavius, *De Incarnatione*, IV, 6 sqq.; Franzelin, *De Verbo Incarnato*, thes. 35; Stentrup, *Christologia*, Vol. I, thes. 47; Janssens, *De Christo-Homine*, I, pp. 214 sqq.

[83] μὴ τῇ θεωρίᾳ μόνῃ.

[84] ὡς κεχωρισμένας καὶ ἰδιοϋποστάτους ἔχει τὰς φύσεις.

[85] Can. 7, *apud* Denzinger-Bannwart, *Enchiridion*, n. 219.

A. D. 680: *"Utramque naturam unius eiusdemque Dei Verbi incarnati, i. e. humanati, inconfuse, inseparabiliter, incommutabiliter esse cognovimus, solâ intelligentiâ* [86] *quae unita sunt discernentes . . .: aequaliter enim et divisionis* [*Nestorii*] *et commixtionis* [*Eutychetis*] *detestamur errorem."* [87]

e) A fifth formula, which was employed chiefly against Apollinaris, ran as follows: *"Verbum assumpsit carnem mediante animâ."* [88]

This formula expresses the dogma of the Hypostatic Union in so far as it describes the Logos as "assuming" flesh animated by a rational soul (*i. e.,* a true and complete human nature), into the Divine Person. The Athanasian Creed enunciates the same truth in almost identical terms: "Who, although He is God and man, yet He is not two, but one Christ. One, not by conversion of the Godhead into flesh, but by taking of the manhood into God; One altogether, not by confusion of substance, but by unity of Person."

f) The sixth formula is the classical one: *"Unio naturarum hypostatica seu secundum hypostasin* (καθ᾽ ὑπόστασιν),*"* which has been generally received as a test and touchstone of Catholic belief since the Council of Chalcedon. It was framed against the errors of both Nestorianism

---

86 μόνη νοήσει.

87 Hardouin, *Coll. Conc.,* t. III, p. 1079. Cfr. Petavius, *De Incarnatione,* IV, 10; VI, 9.

88 For an explanation of its meaning see *supra,* p. 57 sq.

and Monophysitism. Against Nestorianism it upholds the physical and substantial, in contradistinction to a purely moral and accidental union of the two natures in Christ. Against Monophysitism it denies any fusion or mixture of the two natures. Hence the union between Godhead and manhood in Christ must be conceived as strictly personal or "hypostatic," *i. e.,* not as a moral but as a physical union of person.

The definitive fixation of the synodal term ὑπόστασις to denote the *Person* of Christ in contradistinction to His twofold οὐσία or φύσις, was the upshot of a lengthy process of development, in the course of which the word gradually changed its meaning.[89] Originally ὑπόστασις denoted " substructure, foundation, mire, broth." [90] In course of time the term came to be applied metaphorically to the " subject-matter " of an address, narrative, or poem; and finally it was used to designate " reality " as opposed to " semblance " or " appearance." [91] Though the transition would seem to be simple and natural enough, we

[89] " Language . . . requires to be refashioned even for sciences which are based on the senses and the reason; but much more will this be the case, when we are concerned with subject-matters, of which, in our present state, we cannot possibly form any complete or consistent conception, such as the Catholic doctrines of the Trinity and Incarnation. Since they are from the nature of the case above our intellectual reach, and were unknown till the preaching of Christianity, they required on their first promulgation new words, or words used in new senses,

for their due enunciation; and since these were not definitely supplied by Scripture or by tradition, nor, for centuries by ecclesiastical authority, variety in the use, and confusion in the apprehension of them, were unavoidable in the interval." (Newman, *The Arians of the Fourth Century,* pp. 433 sq., new ed., London 1901).

[90] Cfr. Diod. Sicul., *Bibliotheca,* XIII, 82; Aristot., *Hist. Animal.,* II, 1.

[91] Cfr. Aristot., *Mund.,* IV, 21: καθ᾽ ὑπόστασιν — κατ᾽ ἔμφασιν.

have no evidence of ὑπόστασις being used in the sense of *substantia prima* (οὐσία πρώτη), *i. e.* an individual.[92] In the Epistles of St. Paul ὑπόστασις never occurs in the sense of " person " or " substance," but only in that of " foundation " or " basis," or at most, " essence." [93] Up to the Nicene Council ὑπόστασις in ecclesiastical usage was synonymous with οὐσία.[94] Even St. Augustine confessed his ignorance of any difference in meaning between the two terms.[95]

But the vagaries of Trinitarian and Christological heretics soon made it imperative to draw a sharp distinction between *substantia prima* (οὐσία πρώτη) and *substantia secunda* (οὐσία δευτέρα). This led to the choice of ὑπόστασις for *substantia prima,* with special emphasis upon the notes of *inseitas* and *integritas,* and particularly upon that of *perseitas.* Thus originated the technical term *Hypostasis,* which, when applied to rational beings, is equivalent to *Person.*[96] Nestorius no doubt attached the same technical meaning to the word ὑπόστασις as we do to-day; else why should he have so stubbornly rejected the phrase μία ὑπόστασις, while he was quite willing to accept ἓν πρόσωπον? His opponent St. Cyril, however, was not so consistent in his use of the term; he repeatedly employs it as synonymous with φύσις.[97]

---

92 " Those who taught the Greek philosophy among the Greeks," observes the church historian Socrates (*Hist. Eccles.,* III, 7), " have defined οὐσία in different ways, but they made no mention of ὑπόστασις."

93 2 Cor. IX, 4; XI, 17; Heb. III, 14; I, 3.

94 Cfr. *Conc. Nicaen.,* I (*apud* Denzinger-Bannwart, *Enchiridion,* n. 54): ἐξ ἑτέρας ὑποστάσεως ἢ οὐσίας.

95 Cfr. *De Trinitate,* V, 8: " I know not what difference they intend to put between οὐσία and ὑπόστασις."

96 For a fuller explanation of the meaning of these terms see Pohle-Preuss, *The Divine Trinity,* pp. 220 sqq.

97 St. Cyril, *Contr. Theodoret., ad anath. 3:* ἡ τοῦ Λόγου ὑπόστασις ἤγουν φύσις.

For this same reason it is probable that ἕνωσις καθ' ὑπόστασιν,[98] found in the decrees of the Council of Ephesus, means "physical," *i. e.*, substantial, rather than "hypostatic" union, though objectively, no doubt, the phrase embodies an expression of belief in the personal unity of our Lord. This ambiguity in the use of the term continued up to the Council of Chalcedon (A. D. 451), which employed ὑπόστασις and πρόσωπον as synonyms, thus rendering the Nestorian distinction between μία ὑπόστασις and ἓν πρόσωπον meaningless.[99] Finally, the Fifth Ecumenical Council of Constantinople (A. D. 553) rejected the phrase δύο ὑποστάσεις ἤτοι δύο πρόσωπα, and expressly defined the union of the two natures in Christ as strictly hypostatic (*unitio secundum subsistentiam*).[100]

READINGS: — Garnerius, *De Haeresi et Libris Nestorii* (Migne, P. L., XLVIII, 1089 sqq.).— J. Kopallik, *Cyrillus von Alexandrien*, Mainz 1881.— Funk-Cappadelta, *A Manual of Church History*, Vol. I, pp. 154 sqq., London 1910.— Bardenhewer-Shahan, *Patrology*, pp. 361 sq., 369, 641.— T. Gilmartin, *A Manual of Church History*, Vol. I, pp. 267 sqq., 3rd ed., Dublin 1909.— L. Fendt, *Die Christologie des Nestorius,* München 1910.— Bethune-Baker, *Nestorius and His Teaching*, London 1908.— F. Nau, *Le Livre de Heraclide de Damas*, Paris 1910.— Loofs, *Nestoriana,* Halle 1905.— Ph. Kuhn, *Die Christologie Leos I. d. Gr.*, Würzburg 1894.— A Sartori, *Il concetto di Ipostasi e l'Enosi Dogmatica ai Concilii di Efeso e di Calcedonia*, Turin 1927.

98 *V. supra*, p. 90.

99 *V. supra*, p. 87 sq.

100 *V. supra*, p. 110 sq. Cfr. Janssens, *De Deo-Homine*, I, pp. 123 sqq.; Petavius, *De Incarn.*, VI, 17; Newman, *Tracts Theological and Ecclesiastical*, pp. 333 sqq. On the terms *ousia* and *hypostasis,* as used in the early Church, see Newman, *The Arians of the Fourth Century,* pp. 186, 432 sqq.; IDEM, *Select Treatises of St. Athanasius*, Vol. II, pp. 426 sqq., 454 sqq. On the fortunes of certain parallel terms applied to the Blessed Trinity consult Pohle-Preuss, *The Divine Trinity*, pp. 224 sqq., 271 sqq.

ARTICLE 2

SPECULATIVE DEVELOPMENT OF THE DOGMA OF THE HYPOSTATIC UNION

1. THE DOGMA IN ITS RELATION TO REASON. —The Hypostatic Union of the two natures in our Lord Jesus Christ is a theological mystery, and as such absolutely indemonstrable. But it is not, as the Rationalists allege, repugnant to reason.

a) A theological mystery is one the very existence of which unaided human reason is unable to discover, and which, to adopt the phraseology of the Vatican Council, by its own nature so far transcends the created intelligence that, even when delivered by Revelation and received by faith, it remains shrouded in a certain degree of darkness, so long as we are wayfarers on this earth.[1]

α) That the Hypostatic Union is a mystery in the above mentioned sense appears from the fact that, unlike the Blessed Trinity, it is not part of the inner divine being and life of the Godhead, but the result of a free decree. Whatever God has freely decreed to effectuate in time, can be perceived by no other medium than the manifestation of the divine Will itself, either as an actual fact (*e. g.*, the Creation) or through supernatural revela-

1 *Conc. Vatican., Sess. III, de Fide et Rat.,* can. 1 (Denzinger-Bannwart, *Enchiridion,* n. 1816).

tion (*e. g.*, the end of the world).   The whole question therefore comes to this, whether human reason can subsequently, that is, after the event, perceive the intrinsic possibility of the Hypostatic Union or demonstrate it by stringent arguments.   Fathers and theologians agree in answering this question in the negative.   St. Cyril of Alexandria speaks of " the mystery of Christ " as something so ineffably profound as to be altogether incomprehensible.[2]   Leo the Great confesses: "*Utramque substantiam in unam convenisse personam, nisi fides credat, sermo non explicat.*"[3]   Suarez is in perfect accord with St. Thomas Aquinas,[4] in fact he voices the belief of all the Schoolmen when he says: "*Non potest humanâ vel angelicâ cognitione naturali evidenter cognosci seu demonstrari, incarnationem esse possibilem; est communis theologorum.*"[5]

Whether the angels could by their natural powers conjecturally attain to a probable knowledge of the intrinsic possibility of the Incarnation, is a question on which theologians differ.   Some say no, while others[6] hold that the angelic intellect is sufficiently acute to perceive the abstract possibility of the Hypostatic Union. Cardinal De Lugo, who favors the last-mentioned view, readily admits, however, that any such knowledge on the part of an angel would needs be so largely mixed with doubt, as practically to amount to ignorance.[7]

[2] *Contr. Nestor.*, I, 3 (Migne, P. G., LXXVI, 112).

[3] *Serm. in Nativ.*, 29, IX, 1.   Cfr. Petavius, *De Incarn.*, III, 1.

[4] *Contr. Gent.*, IV, 27.

[5] *De Incarn.*, disp. 3, sect. 1.

[6] *E. g.*, Gregory of Valentia (*De Incarn.*, disp. 1, qu. 1, ass. 2) and Cardinal de Lugo (*De Myst. Incarn.*, disp. 1, sect. 1).

[7] De Lugo, *De Myst. Incar.*, disp. 1, sect. 1, n. 9: "*De hoc tamen mysterio angelus proprio lumine adeo parum cognosceret, ut merito dicatur ipsum latuisse atque ideo adinventionem fuisse ipsius Dei et novum aliquid in terra creatum.*"

That human reason could not by itself have arrived at a probable knowledge of the intrinsic possibility of the Incarnation, is admitted by all theologians.

β) Is there Scriptural warrant for the assertion that the Incarnation is a mystery in the strict sense of the term?

The Vatican Council seems to intimate that there is. In defining the dogma that there are absolute mysteries of faith, it quotes a text from St. Paul's First Epistle to the Corinthians (1 Cor. II, 7–9), which refers primarily to the Incarnation. The Apostle expressly speaks of "a wisdom which is hidden in a mystery,[9] which none of the princes of this world knew," in contradistinction to that worldly wisdom which " the Greeks seek after." [10] Now these two kinds of wisdom differ both with regard to their object and in principle. The wisdom of God is the supernatural " spirit of Christ " which " spiritualizes " man, while the natural wisdom of " the disputer of this world " [11] does not rise above the level of the " flesh." [12] Accordingly, too, these different forms of wisdom must have specifically different sources. In matter of fact the " wisdom of the world " is derived from unaided human reason, while the " wisdom of God " has for its author the " Holy Spirit," who by means of external revelation and internal enlightenment unfolds to man " the deep things of God," [13] and " reveals " what " hath never entered into the heart [i. e. intellect] of man." [14] To exclude the notion that the " deep things " of which he speaks are hidden to men only as a matter of fact, but not in principle, the Apostle

---

8 Cfr. Lessius, *De Perfect. Moribusque Divinis*, XII, 5.

9 σοφίαν ἐν μυστηρίῳ.

10 1 Cor. I, 22.

11 1 Cor. I, 20.

12 1 Cor. II, 14 sqq.

13 τὰ βάθη τοῦ Θεοῦ. 1 Cor. II, 10.

14 1 Cor. II, 9, 10.

expressly declares that "the things that are of God no man knoweth but the Spirit of God" who "searcheth all things;" [15] in other words, the mysteries of the Godhead completely transcend the powers of human understanding. As we have already intimated, the Incarnation is a mystery primarily for this reason that it belongs to the free decrees of God which transcend human prescience. [16] The Pauline texts we have just quoted virtually contain the further thought that the interior life of God, and in particular the existence of the Divine Logos, constitutes a supernatural mystery which not even the angelic intellect is able to fathom. [17]

b) The human mind can no more understand the Hypostatic Union than it can fathom the Blessed Trinity; all attempts ever made in this direction have merely accentuated the absolute indemonstrability of the mystery.

It is true that nature offers certain analogies in the shape of substantial syntheses, which aid us to visualize and in a measure to understand the mystery once it is revealed. One such synthesis is, for example, the union of body and soul in man. [18] But it needs only a superficial glance to convince us that there is no real parity between any natural synthesis and the Hypostatic Union. Whatever similarities may be noted are offset by nu-

15 1 Cor. II, 10.

16 Cfr. Eph. I, 9; Col. I, 26 sq.

17 Cfr. Pohle-Preuss, *The Divine Trinity*, pp. 194 sqq.; Al. Schäfer, *Erklärung der beiden Briefe an die Korinther*, pp. 51 sqq., Münster 1903. On the peculiar view which some few exegetes have seen fit to take of the texts quoted above, consult Chr. Pesch, *Praelect. Dogmat.*, Vol. IV, 3rd ed., pp. 39 sq., Freiburg 1909.

18 For other analogues see Lessius, *De Perf. Moribusque Divinis*, XII, 5.

merous and important dissimilarities.[19]   Those who have
spun out these analogies into full-fledged arguments
have notoriously all ended in heresy.   We need but instance Anton Günther and his adherents Baltzer and
Knoodt.[20]   The Christology of Günther savors of Nestorianism, while his teaching on the Trinity is at bottom
but a thinly veiled Tritheism.[21]   Günther's fundamental
fallacy lies in his misconception of the term " person,"
which he wrongly defines as " a self-conscious substance."
Since Christ possessed both a divine and a human consciousness, it was but natural for this nineteenth-century
heretic to ascribe to Him two physical persons, which, he
says, by virtue of a purely " dynamic and formal union "
coalesce into a " *Relationsperson.*" [22]   It was precisely in
this that the heresy of Nestorius consisted — fusing δύο
ὑποστάσεις into ἓν πρόσωπον, and conceiving the union of
the two natures in Christ as a ἕνωσις κατὰ σχέσιν.[23]

c) Though human reason is unable to form an
adequate notion of the nature of the Hypostatic
Union, it finds no difficulty in refuting the objections which various pseudo-philosophers have
raised against the intrinsic possibility of the Incarnation.

a) Priding itself upon its natural powers, the human
intellect from Celsus to Pierre Bayle [24] has contrived

19 Cfr. Janssens, *De Deo-Homine*,
Vol. I, pp. 186 sqq.

20 Cfr. Denzinger-Bannwart, *Enchiridion*, n. 1655.

21 Cfr. Pohle-Preuss, *The Divine
Trinity*, pp. 256 sqq.

22 Günther, *Vorschule zur specu-
lativen Theologie*, 2nd ed., Vol. II,
pp. 283 sqq., Wien 1848.

23 For a fuller exposition and a
thorough refutation of Günther's
system consult Kleutgen, *Theologie
der Vorzeit*, Vol. III, 2nd ed., pp.
60 sqq., Münster 1870.

24 Cfr. the *Dictionnaire Critique*,
s. v. " Pyrrhon."

many "arguments" to show that the Hypostatic Union
is impossible and repugnant to right reason. But none
of them hold water when subjected to careful scrutiny.
For instance: Bayle asserts that if the Divine Logos supplied the human person in Christ, no man can be sure
of his own personality. This conclusion is simply preposterous. Are all human beings so many Christs?
Manifestly not. There is but one Christ.

β) One of the most subtle objections against the dogma
of the Incarnation is that advanced by Celsus, *viz.:* that
a Hypostatic Union of Divinity with humanity would involve a change in the eternal Godhead. Let us briefly
analyze the underlying fallacy of this specious contention.

The dogma of the Hypostatic Union embodies two
separate and distinct truths: (1) The Logos began to
be what He had not been before, namely, true man;
(2) The Logos continued to be what He had been from
all eternity, *viz.:* true God. Does this teaching involve
a mutation?

To begin with, Celsus' objection strikes deeper than the
Incarnation. It involves the general relationship of God
to the universe,— Creation, Preservation, the Divine Con-
cursus, and so forth. God created the world in time,
without Himself undergoing a change from potentiality
to actuality, for He is immutable. The difficulty is considerably enhanced in the case of the Incarnation, because
of the permanent and intrinsic relation which the Logos
bears to the manhood hypostatically assumed by Him.
But the underlying principle is the same. A real change
on the part of the Godhead would occur only in the Monophysite hypothesis, *viz.:* if the two natures were substantially combined, as such, into one nature; in other
words, if the union of the two natures were not hypostatic but merely a natural synthesis. This is not,

however, the meaning of the dogma. A Divine Hypostasis must, even with respect of itself, be conceived as actually infinite in exactly the same manner in which the Divine Nature is infinite. Keeping this in mind, even the unaided human intellect may perceive that the "power of termination" possessed by a Divine Hypostasis must likewise be actually infinite, so much so that it may hypostatically terminate not only in its own Divine Nature, but in some created nature or variety of natures outside itself. Celsus' argument merely proves that the only possible kind of union between Godhead and manhood is the Hypostatic Union. But if this be so, is not the Incarnation altogether inconceivable? No, because the Divine Hypostases are possessed of an infinite capacity *in ipsa ratione hypostaseos.*

On this basis the objection may be solved as follows: In the Incarnation of the Logos God was not drawn down to a mutable creature, but created manhood was elevated to the infinite Hypostasis of the immutable Logos. The change involved in this process consequently does not affect the Λόγος ἄτρεπτος,[25] but falls solely on Christ's hypostatically assumed humanity, which by this unutterable union was endowed with a superior dignity and received the stamp of divine consecration. In the words of St. Augustine, *"Non immutavit homo Deum, sed sic assumptus est, ut commutaretur in melius et ab eo formaretur ineffabiliter excellentius."* [26]

γ) Another objection is indicated by the question: Did the Divine Logos experience an increase of intrinsic

[25] On this term see Newman, *Select Treatises of St. Athanasius,* Vol. II, pp. 383 sq.

[26] This quotation is taken from the great Doctor's work known as *LXXXIII Quaest.,* qu. 73.

perfection by the hypostatic assumption of a created nature?

The absurdity of this question becomes manifest when we recall the fact that the Logos, as a Divine Person, is the Bearer and Possessor of the Divine Nature, which is incapable of being perfected.[27] The Λόγος ἔνσαρκος cannot be more perfect than the Λόγος ἄσαρκος, for the simple reason, among others, that the Second Person of the Blessed Trinity, by assuming human flesh, in no wise changed His identity. God remains the same unchangeably for ever. " *Nihil illi contulit aut detraxit assumpta pro nostra salute humana natura, quam ipse potius unitione suâ glorificavit. Neque minor est Deus Verbum Christo, quia ipse est Christus, neque seipso minor esse potest; et assumptâ carne idem mansit Deus sine dubitatione perfectus*," writes Maxentius.[28]

δ) It is further objected that by assuming manhood the Logos must have experienced an increase of *extrinsic* perfection. This objection is similar to the Pantheistic one, which we have already refuted,[29] that God plus the universe must spell a higher measure of perfection than God minus the universe. Any and every attempt to add divine and creatural perfections must lead to nought. The humanity of Christ and the Divinity of the Logos, if added together, no more result in a higher sum of perfection than the universe plus God. For every creatural perfection, no matter how exalted, is virtually and eminently contained in the perfection of God, and consequently cannot add one jot or tittle to it. Saint Thomas explains this as follows: " *In persona com-*

27 Cfr. Pohle-Preuss, *God: His Knowability, Essence, and Attributes*, pp. 276 sqq.

28 *Dial. contr. Nest.*, l. II.

29 Cfr. Pohle-Preuss, *God: His Knowability, Essence, and Attributes*, 188 sqq.

posita [i. e., Christo] quamvis sint plura bona quam in persona simplici [i. e., Verbo], quia est ibi bonum increatum et bonum creatum, tamen persona composita non est maius bonum quam simplex, quia bonum creatum se habet ad bonum increatum sicut punctum ad lineam, quum nulla sit proportio unius ad alterum. Unde sicut lineae additum punctum non facit maius, ita nec bonum creatum additum in persona bono increato facit melius." [30]

2. THE MUTUAL RELATIONSHIP OF NATURE AND PERSON.—In the Incarnation, as in the Blessed Trinity, the mystery of faith hinges upon the two fundamental notions of "Nature" and "Person," or "Nature" and "Hypostasis," becauses a person is nothing else than a rational hypostasis. For a full explanation of these terms we must refer the reader to our treatise on the Divine Trinity. [31]

a) In that treatise we showed that the notion of "Hypostasis" (and, in the case of rational beings, also that of "Person"), besides "inseity" and "integrity" (*substantia prima integra*), includes, as its chief note, "perseity" (*totietas in se*), i. e., independent subsistence as a being distinct from all other beings. While the concept of "Nature" (substance, essence) corresponds to the question *What?*—that of "Hypostasis" (Person) corresponds to the question *Who?* The Fathers and various councils explain the mutual re-

30 *Com. in Quatuor Libros Sent.,* III, dist. 6, qu. 2, art. 3, ad 1. For a more detailed refutation of these objections consult De Lugo, *De Mysterio Incarn.,* disp. 11, sect. 7; Franzelin, *De Verbo Incarnato,* thes. 33; G. B. Tepe, *Instit. Theol.,* Vol. III, pp. 554 sqq., Paris 1896; Billuart, *De Incarnatione,* disp. 1, art. 1–2.

31 Pohle-Preuss, *The Divine Trinity,* pp. 220 sqq.

lation of these two notions by saying that where several
natures and persons are involved, the persons must be
conceived as *alius et alius,* the natures as *aliud et aliud.*
Thus in the Most Holy Trinity, the Father and the Son
are *alius et alius,* but not *aliud et aliud,* because, though
distinct as Persons, they are absolutely identical in Nature.
In Christ, on the other hand, because of His twofold
nature, we may distinguish *aliud et aliud,* but not *alius
et alius,* because He is only one Person. As St. John
Damascene [32] aptly observes, " *Hypostasis non significat
quid vel quale aliquid est, sed quis est. . . . Oportet vero
scire quod, quae naturâ differunt, aliud et aliud dicuntur,
quae autem distinguuntur numero, vid. hypostases, dicuntur alius et alius. . . . Natura significat quid aliquid sit,
hypostasis vero hunc aliquem [33] vel hoc aliquid.*" [34]

Two conclusions flow from the explanation which we
have given: (1) The heretical principle underlying
Nestorianism, Monophysitism, and the heresy of Günther, namely that " There are as many Hypostases (Persons) as there are natures," must be false from the
philosophical no less than from the theological stand-
point; (2) It is not sufficient, either in philosophy or theology, to draw a purely logical distinction [35] between nature and person.

b) In the Blessed Trinity there is at least a
virtual distinction [36] between person and nature.
In man some hold the distinction may even be
real.[37] There are two opposing theories in regard to this point.

32 *Dial.,* c. 17.
33 τινά.
24 τόδε τι.
35 *Distinctio rationis ratiocinantis.*

36 *Distinctio rationis ratiocinatae
s. cum fundamento in re.*
37 *Distinctio realis.*

a) One of them originated in the sixteenth century, and counts among its adherents such eminent theologians and philosophers as Suarez, Vasquez, De Lugo, Arriaga, and, more recently, Schiffini, Tepe, von der Aa, Fr. Schmid, and Urraburu. These writers maintain that no individual human nature of and by itself possesses personality, *i. e.*, independent subsistence, but there must be superadded to the concrete human nature a peculiar kind of reality in order to constitute it a human person. Thus, for instance, " this particular man " becomes a human person only by the addition of a reality which we may call " being-Peter." In this hypothesis personality is a metaphysical entity separable from nature. But how are we to conceive of that peculiar entity by which a concrete nature is elevated to the rank of an independent personality? On this point the advocates of the theory differ. Peter Hurtado [38] and Quiros ventured the absurd suggestion that personality is a real substance which nature can put on or off like a hat, and which consequently can exist (supported by divine omnipotence) apart from nature. Other divines hold personality to be a " modal reality," [39] which admits of a one-sided but not of a mutual separation between nature and person. *" Per potentiam Dei absolutam sine implicatione posset natura singularis conservari absque ulla personalitate,"* says Gregory of Valentia.[40] These writers base their chief argument upon the consideration that without some such modal reality, detachable from nature, the dogma that Christ's manhood is a perfect human nature but no human person, would be unintelligible. They hold that in becoming man the Logos assumed an impersonal human-

[38] *Metaph.*, disp. 2, sect. 9, n. 50.
[39] *Modus realis, substantialis, suppositalis, forma hypostatica.*
[40] *De Incarn.*, disp. 1, qu. 4, p. 2, opin. 8, obi. 3.

ity — impersonal because devoid of "hypostatic reality" — and communicated to it His own Divine Personality. Thus that which was ἀνυπόστατον became ἐνυπόστατον.[41]

β) A second and more plausible theory is that of Scotus and his school, adopted by Molina, Petavius, Antoine, A. Mayr, Tiphanus, and more recently by Franzelin, Stentrup, Chr. Pesch, and others. These authors hold that the distinction between nature and person in man is not real but virtual, the same concrete object being in one respect nature, and in another, hypostasis or person. The advocates of this theory do not, or at least need not deny that personality in human nature is a real and positive mode, and consequently not a mere negation, as is erroneously held by the Scotists. They merely deny that this positive mode is really distinct and separable from concrete nature. That men are in the habit of circumscribing personality by negative terms (such as, e. g., incommunicability) does not prove that the objective concept of personality is purely negative; just as little as "unity" is a negative concept because we define it as "indivision."

This theory, which is probably the true one, was originally propounded by Theodore Abucara in the eighth century. "Aliudne," he queries, "est substantia [i. e., natura] aliudne hypostasis? Orthodoxus: Aliud et aliud non tamquam res alia et alia, sed quod aliud significat hypostasis et aliud substantia,[42] sicut granum tritici dicitur et est tum semen tum fructus, non tamquam res alia et alia, sed aliud significat semen et aliud fructus."[43] In its application to Christology this theory

---

41 We are not, as was once generally supposed, indebted for this terminology to Leontius of Byzantium (d. about 543); it dates back to the third century. Cfr. Junglas,

Leontius von Byzanz, pp. 148 sqq., Paderborn 1908.

42 Note the virtual distinction,

43 *Opusc.*, 28.

consistently explains the absence of a human person in Christ, not by subtraction, *i. e.,* by the removal of a real and separable mode of subsistence, but by simply adding human nature (without personality) to the superior Hypostasis of the Logos. Because of its importance we shall have to explain this a little more fully.

c) Abstractly, the mutual relationship between Christ's Divinity and His humanity may be conceived in a fourfold manner. (1) Either, person is so united with person that the result is merely one "moral person." This is the error of Nestorius. (2) Or, nature is blended with nature so as to produce a third being intermediate between the two. This is Monophysitism. (3) Or, the human personality, suppressing the Divine Hypostasis of the Logos, is united with the Divine Nature in such wise as to cause Godhead and manhood to subsist in one purely human hypostasis. This heresy is so preposterous that it has never found a defender. (4) Or, lastly, the Divine Person of the Logos, superseding and displacing the human person of Christ, unites itself with His human nature alone. This is the Catholic dogma of the Hypostatic Union.

Why is it that the human nature of Christ, which is like unto ours in everything except sin, is not a human person, but receives its personation from the Logos? This speculative question may be answered as follows:

a) The distinction between nature and person in man being merely virtual, Christ's humanity loses its connatural personality by being assumed into and absorbed by the Divine Logos.

In becoming the property and possession of the Person of the Logos, the manhood of Jesus Christ, by virtue of the Hypostatic Union, loses its *perseitas, i. e.,* its independent existence. Though remaining a *substantia prima et integra* (*i. e.,* a nature), it is no longer a *substantia tota in se* (*i. e.,* an hypostasis), for the reason that it has become a quasi-constitutive element of a higher hypostasis. Tiphanus,[44] Franzelin,[45] and Chr. Pesch[46] base this explanation on sundry Patristic texts. But these texts either accentuate the complete consubstantiality of Christ with man,[47] or lay stress on the Christological axiom: "*Quod assumptum non est, non est sanatum,*"[48] and therefore are not to the point, because the opponents of the peculiar theory we are here considering do not assert that "hypostatic reality" forms a part of human nature; they merely define it as a personifying *modus substantialis,* which by its inmost nature is incapable of being assumed into the Divine Hypostasis of the Logos.[49] A more effective argument for this theory can be drawn from the fact that it had three very ancient defenders in Rusticus Diaconus,[50] Theodore Abucara,[51] and St. Maximus Confessor, and that the

44 *De Hypostasi et Persona,* c. 29.
45 *De Verbo Incarnato,* thes. 31.
46 *Praelect. Dogmat.,* Vol. IV, pp. 55 sqq.
47 *V. supra,* p. 39 sqq.
48 *V.* Soteriology.
49 Cfr. Tepe, *Instit. Theol.,* Vol. III, pp. 498 sqq.
50 This stubborn defender of the

Three Chapters was a deacon of the Roman Church and a nephew of Pope Vigilius. He flourished about the year 550.
51 On Theodore Abucara, who was a contemporary of St. John Damascene, cfr. Hurter, *Nomenclator Literarius Theol. Cathol.,* Vol. I, ed. 3a, col. 647 sq.

opposite doctrine, as one of its chief defenders admits, is a comparatively modern invention.[52]

Theodore Abucara clearly teaches: "*Non satis est compositam esse naturam cum proprietatibus ad generationem hypostasis, sed oportet concurrere ad hoc et non esse partem; quia igitur pars Christi est assumptum corpus animatum* [*i. e., humana natura*], *idcirco non est hypostasis, sed hypostaticum.*"[53]

As regards the later Scholastics, they unanimously maintain that the humanity of Christ would promptly reassume the character of a human person if, and as soon as, it were released from the Hypostatic Union.[54] Not one of them intimates that in this fictitious hypothesis the human nature would require a special and real form of subsistence in order to enable it to become a human person after its elimination from the Logos.

β) The attitude of St. Thomas in this matter is rather uncertain. Both parties to the dispute, *i. e.,* those who assume a real and those who assert a purely virtual distinction between nature and person, appeal with equal confidence to his great authority.

St. Thomas held with Peter Lombard and his master Albertus Magnus that "*Separatio dat utrique partium totalitatem et in continuis dat etiam utrique esse in actu.*

---

[52] ". . . *scholastica disputatione non multis abhinc annis adinventum est.*" P. Vasquez, S. J., *De Incarn.,* disp. 41, c. 4.

[53] *Opusc.,* 28 (Migne, *P. G.,* XCVII, 1578).

[54] This is admittedly the teaching of Peter Lombard, Hugh and Richard of St. Victor, Alexander of Hales, Albertus Magnus, and of Scotus and his school. "*Si Christus deponeret humanitatem,*" says *e. g.* Albert the Great, "*id quod*

deponeret erit substantia rationalis naturae individua, ergo erit persona. Si autem quaeratur, quid conferat ei personalitatem quam prius non habuit, dicendum quod singularitas quam prius non habuit sive incommunicabilitas, ut alii dicunt; nam proprie singularitas facit personam in rationali natura.*" (*Com. in Quatuor Libros Sententiarum,* III, dist. 5, art. 12). Other references in Tiphanus, *De Hypostasi et Persona,* c. 6.

Unde supposito quod [Verbum] hominem deponeret, subsisteret homo ille per se in natura rationali et ex hoc ipso acciperet rationem personae." [55] He further-more lays it down as an axiom that Christ's manhood has no human personality, not on account of some in-herent defect, but in consequence of having superadded to it something which transcends human nature.[56] In those passages of his writings where he speaks of the " destruction of personality " in Christ,[57] St. Thomas seems to employ the term " destruction " in a meta-phorical, not in its strict and literal sense. Thus he argues against the proposition: *"Persona Dei con-sumpsit personam hominis,"* which was falsely attributed to Pope Innocent III:[58] *"Consumptio ibi non importat destructionem alicuius quod prius fuerat, sed impedi-tionem eius quod aliter esse posset. Si enim humana natura non esset assumpta a divina persona, natura hu-mana propriam personalitatem haberet; et pro tanto dicitur persona 'consumpsisse' personam, licet im-proprie, quia persona divina suâ unione impedivit, ne humana natura propriam personalitatem haberet."* [59]

d) It may be objected that Christ's sacred humanity would not be perfect if it lacked the su-

[55] *Comment. in Quatuor Libros Sent.,* III, dist. 5, qu. 3, art. 3.

[56] Cfr. *S. Theol.,* 3a, qu. 4, art. 2, ad 2: *" Naturae assumptae non deest propria personalitas propter defectum alicuius quod ad perfec-tionem humanae naturae pertineat, sed propter additionem alicuius quod est supra humanam naturam, quod est unio ad divinam personam."* Additional texts *apud* Franzelin, *De Verbo Incarnato,* thes. 30.

[57] See the references in Tepe's *Instit. Theol.,* Vol. III, pp. 481 sqq.

[58] Its real author was Faustus of Reji, one of the most influential bishops of Southern Gaul between 450 and 500. The passage occurs in his work *De Spiritu Sancto,* II, 4. On Faustus of Reji and his teaching cfr. Bardenhewer-Shahan, *Patrology,* pp. 600 sqq.

[59] *S. Theol.,* 3a, qu. 4, art. 2, ad 3. For further information on this subtle problem see Franzelin, *De Verbo Incarnato,* thes. 31, Coroll. 1. L. Janssens (*De Deo-Homine, I: Christologia,* pp. 626 sqq.) puts his own construction upon the teaching of the Angelic Doctor.

preme prerogative of personality. But this objection is beside the point. Christ's human nature is a person through the divine personality of the Logos, and it is a far higher prerogative for a created nature to subsist in a Divine Person than in its own personality. *"Natura assumpta in Christo eo ipso est nobilior,"* says St. Bonaventure, *"quod in nobiliori persona stabilitur; unde ordinatio ad dignius, quamvis auferat rationem suppositionis* [*i. e., hypostaseos propriae*], *non tamen aufert dignitatis proprietatem."* [60]

3. WHY THE INCARNATION OF THE LOGOS DOES NOT INVOLVE THE INCARNATION OF THE WHOLE TRINITY.—As there is but a virtual distinction between each Divine Hypostasis and the Divine Essence,[61] and the latter is therefore identical with the Father and the Holy Ghost in precisely the same sense in which it is identical with the Son, it might seem that the Incarnation of the Son necessarily involves the Incarnation of the Father and the Holy Ghost. The subjoined observations will serve to remove this difficulty.

a) It is an article of faith that the substantial and physical union of Godhead and manhood in Christ is strictly hypostatic, *i. e.,* the Godhead is not united with the manhood immediately and formally, as nature with nature, but only in a mediate and indirect manner

---

[60] *Comment. in Quatuor Libros Sententiarum,* III, dist. 5, art. 2, qu. 2, Cfr. St. Thomas, *S. Theol.* 3a, qu. 2, art. 2.

[61] *V. supra,* p. 125.

through the Person of the Logos. Rusticus Diaconus expresses it thus: "*Non Deus Verbum per divinam naturam, sed divina natura per Dei Verbi personam unita dicitur carni.*" [62]   If the relation were reversed, that is to say, if the manhood of Christ were formally united with the nature of the Logos and not with His Person, there would result an impossible commingling of both natures or an equally impossible transformation of the one into the other.   If, therefore, considering the terminus of the Incarnation, we ask: "Which of the Three Divine Persons became man?" the answer is: "Neither the Father nor the Holy Ghost, but solely the Son of God or Logos."   John I, 14: "*Et Verbum caro factum est* — And the Word was made flesh."   The only heretics who ever denied this dogma were the Sabellians and Patripassianists.   All the official creeds and the older ecumenical councils unanimously inculcate it.[63]

Durandus holds that the union of Christ's manhood with the Divine Logos was effected primarily by an absolute attribute common to all three Divine Persons, namely, the absolute self-existence of the Trinity, and only secondarily by the personality of the Logos as such.[64] This theory is out of joint with the dogmatic teaching of the Church.   Were it true, the Incarnation would be primarily an Incarnation of the whole Trinity, and only secondarily of the Son.   The Sixth Council of Toledo (A. D. 675) implicitly condemned this view when it defined: "*Incarnationem quoque huius Filii*

---

62 *Contr. Acephal.*

63 Cfr. St. Thomas, *S. Theol.*, 3a, qu. 3, art. 2: "*Esse assumptionis principium convenit naturae divinae secundum seipsam, quia eius virtute assumptio facta est; sed esse terminum assumptionis non convenit naturae divinae secundum seipsam, sed ratione personae, in qua consideratur: et ideo primo quidem et propriissime persona dicitur assumere.*"

64 *Comment. in Quatuor Libros Sent.*, III, dist. 1, qu. 5, n. 10.

Dei tota Trinitas operasse [*scil. operata esse*] *credenda est* [*scil. efficienter*], *quia inseparabilia sunt opera Trinitatis* [*ad extra*]. *Solus tamen Filius formam servi accepit in singularitate personae* [*i. e., terminative*], *non in unitate divinae naturae, in id quod est proprium Filii, non quod commune Trinitati."* [65]

b) Regarded actively, *i. e.*, as an external operation of God (*opus ad extra*), the Incarnation, though specially appropriated to the Holy Ghost,[66] must have for its efficient cause the entire Trinity or the Divine Essence as such. The Three Divine Persons conjointly created the manhood of Christ, they preserve it in its being and operation, and concur with all its creatural actions. As the Incarnate Word is immanent in the Father and the Holy Ghost by virtue of the Trinitarian Perichoresis,[67] so the Father and the Holy Ghost are in Christ by virtue of the Hypostatic Union. This presence transcends the mode by which the omnipresent God is in all His creatures, and is also superior to the manner of His indwelling in the souls of the just. It is a very special kind of immanence.[68] Cfr. John X, 30 sqq.: *"Ego et Pater unum sumus. . . . Pater in me est et ego in Patre*—I and the Father are one . . . the Father is in me, and I in the Father." John XIV, 9 sq.: *"Qui videt me, videt et Patrem. . . . Non creditis quia ego in Patre et Pater in me est?*—He that seeth me seeth the Father also. . . . Do you not believe that I am in the Father, and the Father in me?"[69]

---

[65] Denzinger-Bannwart, *Enchiridion*, n. 284. Cfr. Tepe, *Instit. Theol.*, Vol. III, pp. 524 sqq.; Billuart, *De Incarn.*, diss. 6, art. 2.

[66] *"Conceptus de Spiritu Sancto."* (On the Divine Appropriations see Pohle-Preuss, *The Divine Trinity*, pp. 244 sqq.)

[67] For an explanation of the Trinitarian Perichoresis cfr. Pohle-Preuss, *The Divine Trinity*, pp. 281 sqq.

[68] Cfr. Pohle-Preuss, *The Divine Trinity*, pp. 281 sqq.

[69] The rather obscure passage of St. Cyril of Alexandria (*In Ioa.*,

c) In this connection theologians are wont to discuss another speculative problem, namely, whether or not the Father or the Holy Ghost might have become man instead of the Son. St. Anselm appears to deny the possibility of such an event, for this reason, among others, that the Incarnation of either one of the other two Persons would lead to inextricable confusion in the use of the name " Son." His argument substantially is that, had the Father become man, He would have been constrained to appear as " *filius hominis,*" which would have been repugnant to His personal character as Father.[70] And the same is true of the Holy Ghost. The Schoolmen preferred to adopt the view of St. Thomas, who says that the Father and the Holy Ghost could have become incarnate as well as the Son, and solves the above-quoted objection as follows: " *Filiatio temporalis, qua Christus dicitur filius hominis, non constituit personam ipsius sicut filiatio aeterna, sed est quiddam consequens nativitatem temporalem: unde si per hunc modum nomen filiationis ad Patrem vel Spiritum Sanctum transferretur, nulla sequeretur confusio personarum.*" [71]

The problem assumes a more complicated aspect if formulated thus: Could the Three Divine Persons together become incarnate in one human nature, in such wise that this human nature would be a three-fold Divine Person, *viz.:* Father, Son, and Holy Ghost?

The question here is not whether the Three Divine Hypostases could become so united in one human nature as to

---

XI): " *carnem absque confusione venisse in unionem cum Verbo et per ipsum cum Patre, relative videlicet, non physice (καὶ δι' αὐτοῦ πρὸς τὸν πατέρα, σχετικῶς δῆλοντε καὶ οὐ φυσικῶς),*" must be interpreted as referring to the Perichore-sis. For a more elaborate treatment of this subject see Franzelin, *De Verbo Incarnato,* thes. 32.

70 *De Fide Trinit. et de Incarn. Verbi,* l. IV.

71 *Summa Theol.,* 3a, qu. 3, art. 5, ad 1.

constitute but one Divine Person. This would entail the Sabellian absurdity that "the Father is the Son." [72] What we wish to ascertain is whether the Three Divine Persons could assume one and the same human nature as three separate and distinct Hypostases. St. Bonaventure thinks that this hypothesis could be "reasonably defended." [73] Not so the later Scotists, who held that the question, thus formulated, involves an intrinsic contradiction. St. Thomas solved the problem on the principle that, "as the Three Divine Persons can without contradiction subsist in one Divine Nature, so they can also subsist in one human nature." [74]

Another still more difficult problem is: Could the Divine Logos either simultaneously or successively assume one or more human natures in addition to the one He already possesses? In other words: Could the Logos become incarnate repeatedly, say, for instance, on different planets? In view of what we have said [75] about the infinite range of a Divine Hypostasis, we are constrained to answer this question in the affirmative. To assert that a Divine Person can assume only one human nature, would be equivalent to denying God's omnipotence and infinity. Therefore the Scholastics teach with St. Thomas: *"Potentia divinae personae est infinita, nec potest limitari ad aliquid creatum. Unde non est dicen-*

---

[72] *"Plures personas assumere unam eandemque naturam* [*in una persona*] *nec est possibile nec est intelligibile,"* says St. Bonaventure (*Comment. in Quatuor Libros Sent.,* III, dist. 1, qu. 3, art. 1).

[73] Cfr. L. Janssens, *De Deo-Homine,* I, pp. 230 sqq.

[74] *S. Theol.,* 3a, qu. 3, art. 6: *"Tres personae possunt subsistere in una natura divina; ergo etiam possunt subsistere in una natura hu-*mana, ita scil. quod sit una natura humana a tribus personis assumpta." Whence it follows: *"Est autem talis divinarum personarum conditio, quod una earum non excludit aliam a communione eiusdem naturae, sed solum a communione eiusdem personae. . . . Sic ergo non est impossibile divinis personis, ut duae vel tres assumant unam humanam naturam."*

[75] *Supra,* pp. 121 sq.

dum quod persona divina ita assumpserit unam naturam humanam, ut non potuerit [simul] assumere aliam. Videretur enim ex hoc sequi quod personalitas divinae naturae esset ita comprehensa per unam naturam humanam, quod ad eius personalitatem alia assumi non possit, quod est impossibile." [76]

4. THE CONTROVERSY REGARDING THE "DOUBLE EXISTENCE" OF CHRIST.—This controversy hinges on the question whether the distinction between an individual substance (or nature) and its existence is real or only logical.

a) Not a few eminent philosophers and theologians hold that the distinction is purely logical, because "reality" and "existence" are merely different terms for the same thing. The Thomists maintain that there is a real distinction. Between the two states designated as "possibility" and "existence," they say, we can conceive a third which is intermediate and may be called "actuality," inasmuch as a possible being transferred from the state of mere possibility to that of actuality is not yet existent, but requires the accession of the *actus existendi,*— a separable entity by which a thing receives its "formal existence." To illustrate the theory by an example: Peter, who is a creature, does not receive his existence through the fact that he is created, *i. e.,* a creature, but by virtue of a supervening *forma existentiae.* It is one of the fundamental axioms of the Thomist school that there are in every creature three really dis-

---

[76] *S. Theol.,* 3a, qu. 3, art. 7. Cfr. L. Janssens, *De Deo-Homine,* I, pp. 221 sqq. On the mode of predication appropriate to such an eventuality cfr. De Lugo, *De Myst. Incarn.,* disp. 13, sect. 3; on the whole subject, Billuart, *De Incarn.,* diss. 6, art. 4.

tinct stages of being, to wit: (1) *Esse essentiae* or physical essence, (2) *esse subsistentiae* or hypostasis, and (3)
esse existentiae or existence, each of which flows successively from the other by way of emanation.

This peculiar theory has given rise to the question:
Is there but one existence in Christ, *i. e.,* that of the
Divine Logos? or are there two existences, a divine and a
human? Cardinal Cajetan, Capreolus, Medina, Billuart,
Gonet, and other Thomists maintain that the sacred humanity of Christ, being deprived of its connatural existence as a human person, derives its existence solely from
the Divine Logos, who displaces and supplies the created
existence of manhood by His Divine Existence in the
same manner in which He displaces and supplies the
missing human personality by His Divine Person.[77]
This view has been adopted by some able theologians
who are not otherwise adherents of the Thomist system
(*e. g.,* the Jesuits Billot and Terrien), and it deserves
to be treated with respect, because it is apt to create
a sublime conception of the Hypostatic Union.[78]

For those who hold that concrete reality and existence
are objectively identical, the question is, of course, meaningless. If a thing exists by the very fact of its being
concretely actual, it is metaphysically impossible to assume that the sacred humanity of Christ is deprived of its

[77] Cfr. Gonet, disp. 8, art. 2, n.
33: "*Dico Verbum non solum subsistentiam, sed etiam existentiam in
humanitate Christi supplere, subin-
deque illam non per existentiam
creatam et sibi propriam, sed dum-
taxat per divinam et increatam existere.*"

[78] E. Commer speaks of it thus:
"*Vere profunda doctrina et mi-
randa, quia vera et propria Christi*

*humanitas optime servatur, dum
ipse Christus et in persona et in
existentia ita pure divinus illustra-
tur, ut omnes eius actiones atque
operae divinum incarnationis my-
sterium probent, quo humana natura
perfecta perfecte quoque Dei facta
atque intime deificata videatur, quod
solum Christum servatorem adoran-
dum decet.*" (*De Iesu Puero Nato,*
p. 10, Vindobonae 1901.)

proper creatural existence, and that this is supplied by the uncreated existence of the Logos.[79]

b) But there is involved in this debate a theological problem which would remain unsolved even were we to admit the Thomistic view that in Christ, *qua* man, existence and reality differ really and objectively. This theological question is, whether or not the sacred manhood of our Lord is *de facto* deprived of its human existence and exists solely by virtue of the divine existence proper to the Logos.   Gregory of Valentia, Toletus, Suarez, Vasquez, Tanner, Franzelin, Stentrup, Chr. Pesch, Tepe, and most theologians of the Scotist persuasion hold that it can be shown on strictly theological grounds that the sacred humanity of Christ in the Hypostatic Union does not exist *per existentiam divinam,* but retains its proper human existence.   They argue as follows:

a) It has been defined by various councils that, apart from a human personality, the sacred humanity of Christ

79 The underlying metaphysical problem is more fully discussed by M. Limbourg, S. J., *De Distinctione Essentiae ab Existentia,* Ratisbonae 1883; Urráburu, S. J., *Ontologia,* pp. 704 sqq., Vallisoleti 1891; Alphons Lehmen, S. J., *Lehrbuch der Philosophie auf aristotelisch-scholastischer Grundlage,* Vol. I, 2nd ed., pp. 334 sqq., Freiburg 1904; A. Rittler, *Wesenheit und Dasein in den Geschöpfen nach der Lehre des hl. Thomas,* Ratisbon 1887; Piccirelli, *De Distinctione inter Actuatam Essentiam Existentiamque Entis Creati Intercedente,* Naples 1906; John Rickaby, S. J., *General Metaphysics* (Stonyhurst Series), pp. 27 sqq., 59 sqq. Fr. Rickaby (*ibid.,* p. 28) gives quotations to show that the problem of essence and existence is not a subtlety peculiar to Scholasticism, but was hotly discussed by authors of various philosophical schools (*e. g.,* Hume, Locke, Bradley).

10

lacks none of the proper attributes of man, [80] and that the union between Godhead and manhood was formally consummated solely in the Person of the Logos.[81] It seems impossible to square the Thomistic theory with these dogmatic definitions. The sacred humanity of our Lord would not be *perfecta humanitas indiminute et sine deminoratione,* were it deprived of its own proper existence, for it would then lack an essential property of human nature; besides, a union consummated in the divine existence would not be purely hypostatic but at the same time an *unio secundum divinam existentiam.*[82] Holding as they do, in common with the theologians of other schools, that the Three Divine Persons do not exist by a "threefold relative existence," but by one absolute existence common to all,[83] the Thomists cannot escape the force of this argument. *"Dico, non dari in divinis tres existentias relativas, realiter inter se et virtualiter ab existentia absoluta essentiae distinctas,"* says, *e. g.,* Gonet.[84] But if the union of Christ's manhood with His Godhead were consummated in the absolute existence of the Triune God, then the entire Trinity would become incarnate,

80 Cfr. *Concilium Chalcedon.* (Denzinger-Bannwart, *Enchiridion,* n. 148): *"Nusquam sublatā naturarum differentiā propter unitionem magisque salvā proprietate utriusque naturae."* *Conc. Lateran. a. 649 sub Martino I* (Denzinger-Bannwart, n. 262): *"Si quis secundum sanctos Patres non confitetur proprie et secundum veritatem naturales proprietates deitatis et humanitatis indiminute in eo [Christo] et sine deminoratione salvatas, condemnatus sit."*

81 Cfr. *Synod. Tolet. XI, a. 675* (Denzinger-Bannwart, *Enchir.,* n. 284): *"In id quod est proprium Filii, non quod commune Trinitati."*

82 Cfr. Ysambert, *De Incarn.,* qu.

17, disp. 1, art. 2: *"Verbum divinum supplere existentiam humanitatis nihil est aliud quam unionem humanitatis cum Verbo fuisse factam in existentia."*

83 That the Father has this absolute existence from Himself, while the Son has it by generation from the Father, and the Holy Ghost by spiration from both the others, is irrelevant to the argument here under consideration.

84 Gonet, Clypeus Theol. Thomist., tr. VI, disp. 3, art. 6, n. 169. Cfr. St. Thomas, *S. Theol.,* 3a, qu. 17, art. 2, ad 3: *"Tres personae non habent nisi unum esse [i. e., existere]."*

and we should no longer have a strictly Hypostatic Union, but a mere natural synthesis. Gonet and Billuart tried to obviate this difficulty by the remark that the Hypostatic Union is consummated in the absolute existence of the Trinity merely *mediate et secundario*. But this is an evasion. All the absolute attributes of God, His wisdom, omnipotence, immensity, etc., could be similarly limited. If the uncreated supplies the created existence, it must supply it in precisely the same manner in which the Divine Personality of the Logos supplies the human personality of the Godman, *i. e.*, primarily and immediately. No other mode is conceivable.

Durandus contended that the sacred humanity of Christ was "primarily and immediately" united with the "absolute subsistence of the Trinity," but only "secondarily and mediately" with the Hypostasis of the Logos.[85] Billuart effectively refuted this theory as follows: "*Si Verbum terminaret naturam humanam formaliter et proxime per subsistentiam communem et absolutam, Pater et Spiritus forent incarnati non minus quam Filius. Atqui falsum consequens. Ergo et antecedens. Prob. sequela. Quod convenit alicui personae Trinitatis ratione alicuius attributi absoluti et communis, convenit toti Trinitati. Sic quia creatio, conservatio, gubernatio, imo et ipsa actio unitiva incarnationis conveniunt uni personae, ratione omnipotentiae conveniunt omnibus.*"[86] By substituting "*existentia*" for "*subsistentia*" in the above argument, it can be effectively turned against Billuart's own position. Billot attempts to solve the difficulty as follows: "*Esse quidem est unum in divinis sicut omnia absoluta, sed tribus distinctis modis relativis habetur, ita ut esse Patris personale qua*

85 *V. supra*, p. 133.   86 *De Incarn.*, diss. 6, art. 2.

tale non sit esse personale Filii nec Spiritus Sancti; est ergo Filius idem esse [i. e., existere] quod Pater et Spiritus Sanctus; sed cum alia relatione." [87] But this explanation, too, is unsatisfactory. For the principle upon which it rests could be applied to the Essence and to all the absolute attributes of God with the same force with which it is applied to His existence. Furthermore it gives rise to an awkward dilemma: Either the concept of the divine relation of Filiation (*filiatio divina*), as such, includes or it does not include existence. If it does *not* include it, the created existence (which is alleged to be lacking) cannot be "supplied" by the divine existence peculiar to the Logos. If the concept of divine Filiation *does* include existence, we are forced to assume "three relative existences," which is repugnant to the common teaching of theologians.[88]

β) The Fathers scarcely anticipated the pivotal point at issue in the Scholastic controversy which we are considering. Like the early councils, however, they laid special emphasis on the doctrine that the Divine Logos assumed a human nature (not person) with all the specific determinations and attributes which human nature possessed before the Fall. Thus St. John of Damascus says: *"Neque enim Deus Verbum quidquam eorum, quae quum nos initio rerum fingeret naturae nostrae inseruit, non assumptum omisit, sed omnia assumpsit, puta corpus et animam intelligentem rationabilemque cum eorum proprietatibus."* [89] One of these properties of human nature is human (*i. e.,* created) existence, and consequently this mode of ex-

---

[87] *De Verbo Incarnato*, p. 98, 4th ed., Rome 1904.

[88] Cfr. Tepe, *Instit. Theol.*, Vol. III, pp. 528 sqq., Paris 1896.

[89] *De Fide Orth.*, III, 6. For additional Patristic texts we must refer the student to Petavius, *De Incarn.*, V, 6.

istence must have formed part of the sacred humanity of Jesus Christ.[90]

Some of the Fathers expressly ascribe a human existence to the sacred manhood of our Lord. Thus St. Cyril of Alexandria [91] draws a clear-cut distinction between the proper (*i. e.*, divine) existence of the Logos,[92] derived by eternal generation from the Father, and His (human) existence in the flesh.[93] Billuart,[94] in his controversy with Suarez and Henno, quotes St. Sophronius against this teaching as follows: "*In illo itaque [Verbo], et non per semetipsam habuit [natura humana] existentiam unam; cum conceptione quippe Verbi haec ad subsistendum prolata sunt.*"[95] But this translation does not render the Greek text accurately. The correct translation, as given by Hardouin,[96] is as follows: "*Simul enim caro, simul Dei Verbi caro . . . in illo enim et non in se [seorsum] obtinuit [caro] existentiam;*[97] *una cum*[98] *conceptione quippe Verbi haec [i. e., corpus et anima = humana natura] producta sunt ad existentiam et unita sunt illi secundum hypostasin eo ipso momento, quo producta sunt ad existentiam realiter veram et indivisam.*" So far from advocating the Thomistic theory, St. Sophronius virtually rejects it by attributing a separate created existence to Christ's manhood.[99]

In the twelfth century the view which we defend was maintained by Euthymius Zigabenus, a Basilian monk, who flourished during the reign of the Emperor Alexius Comnenus (1081–1118). "*Unde de Christo unam hy-*

90 Cfr. Leo I, *Serm.*, 63: "*Nihil assumpto divinum, nihil assumenti deest humanum.*"
91 *Adv. Nestor.*, I (Migne, *P. G.*, LXXVI, 19).
92 τὴν ἰδίαν ὕπαρξιν.
93 σαρκικὴν ὕπαρξιν.

94 *De Incarn.*, diss. 17, art. 2.
95 *Synod. Oecum. VI. Act.*, 11.
96 *Concil.*, t. III, p. 1268.
97 ὕπαρξιν.
98 ἅμα.
99 Cfr. Franzelin, *De Verbo Incarn.*, pp. 305 sqq.

postasin personalem praedicamus," he says, *" eas vero [hypostases], quae existentiam significant, duas affirmare licet, ne alterutram naturam sine existentia esse dicamus; nam hypostasin, quae existentiam significat, in omni natura invenimus, personalem vero non in omni."* [100]

Both parties to this controversy invoke the authority of St. Thomas. In spite of the learned treatise of J. B. Terrien, S. J.,[101] it still remains a matter of dispute whether or not the Angelic Doctor taught that there is a real distinction between essence and existence.[102] It is a most difficult undertaking, at any rate, to put a " Thomistic " construction upon such passages as these: *" Sicut Christus est unum simpliciter propter unitatem suppositi et duo secundum quid propter duas naturas, ita habet unum esse simpliciter propter unum esse aeternum aeterni suppositi. Est autem et aliud esse huius suppositi, non inquantum est aeternum, sed inquantum est temporaliter homo factum, quod esse etsi non sit accidentale, quia homo non praedicatur accidentaliter de Filio Dei, . . . non tamen est esse principale sui suppositi, sed secundarium."* [103] *" Esse humanae naturae non est esse divinae; nec tamen simpliciter dicendum est quod Christus sit duo secundum esse, quia non ex aequo respicit utrumque esse suppositum aeternum."* [104]

100 *Panopl.*, tit. 16. Cfr. Chr. Pesch, *Praelect. Dogm.*, Vol. IV, p. 66, 3rd ed., Freiburg 1909. On Euthymius Zigabenus (more correctly Zigadenus or Zygadenus) cfr. Hurter, *Nomenclator Literarius Theologiae Cath.*, t. II, 2nd ed., col. 12, Innsbruck 1906.

101 *S. Thomae Aquinatis Doctrina Sincera de Unione Hypostatica Verbi cum Humanitate Amplissime Declarata*, Paris 1894.

102 Cfr. A. Lehmen, *Lehrbuch der Philosophie*, Vol. I, 2nd ed., p. 388, Freiburg 1904.

103 *De Unione Verbi*, art. 4.

104 *Op. cit.*, ad 1. Some more texts of the same tenor are quoted by Suarez, *De Incarn.*, disp. 36, sect. 2, and by Franzelin, *De Verbo Incarnato*, thes. 34.

5. The Phrase "Hypostasis Christi Composita."—May we speak of the Hypostasis of our Lord as composite? Tiphanus vehemently denounced this phrase as "dangerous." [105] Nevertheless, it was unhesitatingly employed not only by the later Scholastics but also by the Fathers of the Church and several councils since the fifth century.[106] St. Bonaventure's remark: *"Quoniam verbum compositionis calumniabile est, ideo doctores praesentis temporis sensum . . . retinent, declinantes vocabulum compositionis,"* [107] merely proves that the expression *"Hypostasis Christi composita,"* like St. Cyril's formula *"Una natura Verbi incarnata,"* [108] is open to misconstruction. There is no doubt that it may be used in a perfectly orthodox sense.

The term *Hypostasis Christi* may be taken either in a material or in a formal sense. Materially it is synonymous with " Person of Christ " (*i. e.,* Logos). The Person of the Logos, of course, like the Person of the Father and that of the Holy Ghost, is absolutely simple. In its formal sense *Hypostasis Christi* means *Hypostasis Christus, i. e.,* Christ as such, the Incarnate Word, and in this case it is quite correct to speak of a composite Hypostasis. Tiphanus himself admitted the orthodoxy of the proposition: " *Christus est compositus,"* and consequently was guilty of inconsistency in decrying the phrase " *Hypostasis Christi composita* " as inaccurate.

---

105 *De Hypostasi et Persona,* c. 65–66.

106 Cfr. Franzelin, *De Verbo Incarnato,* thes. 36.

107 *Comment. in Quatuor Libros Sent.,* III, dist. 6, art. 1, qu. 2.

108 *V. supra,* p. 108 sqq.

Composition is the putting together of several parts or ingredients to form one whole. In the case of creatures the ingredients thus combined are " parts " in the strict sense of the word, because they complement and intrinsically perfect one another and the *totum* which they constitute. In this sense, of course, there can be no composition in Christ, who, as the Divine Logos, is incapable of being perfected *ab extra*. Consequently, the humanity of Christ, though perfected and deified by its assumption into the Divine Logos, cannot be conceived strictly as a component part (*compars*) or ingredient of the Logos, or of the *totum* which it forms together with the Logos.[109] For this reason theologians usually designate the sacred humanity of our Redeemer as *quasi-pars* or conceive it *per modum partis, i. e.,* as a component part in a purely figurative sense. Hence the theological axiom: "*Christus est unum ex pluribus, non totum ex partibus.*" [110]

READINGS : — Clemens, *Die spekulative Theologie Anton Günthers,* Köln 1853.—*J. Kleutgen, *Theologie der Vorzeit,* Vol. III, pp. 60 sqq., Münster 1870.— F. Abert, *Die Einheit des Seins in Christus nach der Lehre des hl. Thomas,* Ratisbon 1889.— * F. Schmid, *Quaest. Selectae ex Theol. Dogmat.,* qu. 5, Paderborn 1891.— J. B. Terrien, S. J., *S. Thomae Aquinatis Doctrina Sincera de Unione Hypostatica Verbi cum Humanitate Amplissime Declarata,* Paris 1894.— St. Thomas, *Quaest. Disput., De Unione Verbi* (ed. Paris., 1883, t. II, pp. 532 sqq.)— Wilhelm-Scannell, *A Manual of Catholic Theology,* Vol. II, pp. 91 sqq., 2nd ed., London 1901.

[109] *V. supra,* p. 122 sqq.

[110] Cfr. L. Janssens, *De Deo-Homine,* Vol. I, pp. 147 sqq.; Franzelin, *De Verbo Incarnato,* thes. 36.

SECTION 2

THE INCONFUSION OF THE TWO NATURES IN CHRIST

The " Hypostatic Union " embraces two essential elements: (1) The union of Christ's manhood with the Divine Person of the Logos, and (2) the existence of one Divine Person in two perfect natures, united but unmixed. A commingling of the two natures after the manner of natural compounds would be incompatible with the Hypostatic Union. The Nestorians denied the personal unity of Christ by exaggerating the concept of duality, while the Monophysites went to the opposite extreme of confounding the two natures. The Catholic Church pays due regard to both " unity in duality " and " duality in unity," thus holding the golden mean between these heretical extremes.

ARTICLE 1

THE EXISTENCE OF ONE DIVINE PERSON IN TWO PERFECT NATURES, AS DEFINED AGAINST MONOPHYSITISM

1. THE HERESY OF EUTYCHES VS. THE TEACHING OF THE CHURCH.—Eutyches, an archimandrite (or abbot) of Constantinople, who had nobly defended the unity of Christ at the Council of Ephesus, in 431, sought to strengthen his position by maintaining that Christ had but

UNITY IN DUALITY

one nature ($\mu\acute{o}\nu\eta$ $\phi\acute{v}\sigma\iota s$), because otherwise He could not strictly be one Hypostasis or Person. Eutyches appealed to St. Cyril's famous formulas: $\check{\epsilon}\nu\omega\sigma\iota s$ $\phi\nu\sigma\iota\kappa\acute{\eta}$ [1] and $\mu\acute{\iota}a$ $\phi\acute{v}\sigma\iota s$ $\tau\sigma\check{v}$ $\Lambda\acute{o}\gamma\sigma\nu$ $\sigma\epsilon\sigma a\rho\kappa\omega\mu\acute{\epsilon}\nu\eta$, [2] as favoring his heresy.

a) Eutyches found a powerful protector in Dioscorus, who at that time disgraced the episcopal see of SS. Athanasius and Cyril. At a council held in Ephesus, A. D. 449, and which came to be called the Robber Synod, Eutyches was declared orthodox and the bishops who had crossed him were deposed,— a measure which greatly promoted the spread of the new heresy in Egypt, Palestine, Syria, and Armenia. Though they were unanimous in holding the doctrine of the $\mu\acute{o}\nu\eta$ $\phi\acute{v}\sigma\iota s$, the Monophysites soon split on the question as to how Godhead and manhood are united in Jesus Christ. Some held that the sacred humanity was absorbed and transfused by the Godhead.[3] Others imagined that the two natures were simply welded into one.[4] A third, intermediate faction maintained that the two natures were united in Christ in a manner similar to that in which body and soul are united in man.[5] For an account of the various Monophysitic sects, such as the Acephali, the adherents of Peter the Fuller, called Theopaschitae, the Severians or Phthartolatrae,[6] the Julianists or Aphthartodocetae, the Jacobites,[7] etc., we refer the reader to the

---

[1] *Conc. Ephes.*, can. 3 (Denzinger-Bannwart, *Enchiridion*, n. 115).

[2] *V. supra*, p. 108.

[3] $\check{\epsilon}\nu\omega\sigma\iota s$ $\kappa a\tau\grave{a}$ $\grave{a}\lambda\lambda o\acute{\iota}\omega\sigma\iota\nu$.

[4] $\check{\epsilon}\nu\omega\sigma\iota s$ $\kappa a\tau\grave{a}$ $\sigma\acute{v}\gamma\chi\nu\sigma\iota\nu$.

[5] $\check{\epsilon}\nu\omega\sigma\iota s$ $\kappa a\tau\grave{a}$ $\sigma\acute{v}\nu\theta\epsilon\sigma\iota\nu$.

[6] $\phi\theta a\rho\tau o\lambda\acute{a}\tau\rho a\iota$ = *corrupticolae*.

[7] In spite of the numerous efforts made to convert the Monophysites, this heresy was never completely extirpated. It is still held by the Copts in Egypt and by the Jacobites of Syria and Mesopotamia. The Jacobites were named after Jacobus Baradai (571–578), who, after he had been established as metropolitan of the sect, labored with great success to spread and strengthen Mono-

current manuals of Church history and the respective articles in the *Catholic Encyclopedia.*

b) Catholic orthodoxy found a valiant defender in Pope St. Leo the Great, who in his classic *Epistula Dogmatica ad Flavianum* so clearly defined the Catholic doctrine that the Bishops assembled at Chalcedon, in 451, loudly exclaimed: " Peter hath spoken through the mouth of Leo." [8] The Council of Chalcedon duly emphasized both the hypostatic unity of Christ [9] and the existence of two unmixed [10] natures in one divine Person, by defining that Christ exists in two indivisible and inseparable, but at the same time unchanged and inconfused natures, the indivisible and inseparable unity of Person in no wise destroying the distinction between or the properties peculiar to the two natures.

2. THE TEACHING OF REVELATION.—The Scriptural arguments for Christ's Divinity and humanity, which we have outlined in the first part of this treatise, sufficiently prove the heretical character of Monophysitism as well as Nestorianism.

physitism. (Cfr. Duchesne-Mathew, *The Churches Separated From Rome,* pp. 33 sq., London 1907.) At present the Syrian and Armenian Monophysites have patriarchs at the Zapharan monastery near Bagdad and at Etchmiadzin in the Russian Caucasus. Funk-Cappadelta, *A Man-*

ual of Church History, Vol. I, p. 160.

8 E. H. Blakeney, *The Tome of Pope Leo the Great* (Text and translation on opposite pages, with explanatory notes). London 1923.

9 *Una persona atque subsistentia*
10 *Duae naturae inconfuse, immutabiliter, indivise, inseparabiliter* (ἐν δύο φύσεσιν ἀσυγχύτως, ἀτρέπ-

a) By constantly referring to our Saviour as true God and true man, the New Testament implicitly refutes the heretical conceit that He is the product of a mixture or confusion of natures, for such a being would be neither God nor man.

St. Paul [11] treats the "*forma Dei*" [12] and the "*forma servi*" [13] as separate and distinct, though they are hypostatically united in Christ, "who, being in the form of God, took the form of a servant." [14] Only on the assumption that Godhead and manhood co-exist in two inseparable but at the same time unchanged and inconfused natures in Christ, was He able to say of Himself: [15] "*Ego et Pater unum sumus* — I and the Father are one," *i. e.*, as God, and again: "*Pater maior me est* — The Father is greater than I," *i. e.*, as man.[16] "For," says St. Augustine, "He did not so take the form of a servant as that He should lose the form of God, in which He was equal to the Father. If, then, the form of a servant was so taken that the form of God was not lost, since both in the form of a servant and in the form of God He Himself is the same only-begotten Son of God the Father, in the form of God equal to the Father, in the form of a servant the mediator between God and men, the man Christ Jesus; is there any one who cannot perceive that He Himself in the form of God is also greater than Himself, but yet likewise in the form of a servant less than Himself?" [17] The Johannine

τως, ἀδιαιρέτως, ἀχωρίστως). Cfr.
Ph. Kuhn, *Die Christologie Leos I.*,
Würzburg 1894.

11 Phil. II, 6.
12 μορφὴ Θεοῦ.
13 μορφὴ δούλου.
14 *V. supra*, p. 95.
15 John X, 30.

16 John XIV, 28.

17 "*Neque enim sic accepit formam servi, ut amitteret formam Dei, in qua erat aequalis Patri. Si ergo ita accepta est forma servi, ut non amitteretur forma Dei, quum et in forma servi et in forma Dei idem ipse sit Filius unigenitus Dei Patris,*

passage: "And the Word was made flesh," [18] not only describes the Hypostatic Union of the Divine Logos with human flesh (= human nature), but it also implies that each of the two natures remained perfect in its kind after the union and in spite of it.[19]

b) The Fathers who flourished before the Council of Chalcedon (A. D. 451) believed in the inconfused existence of both natures in Christ as an article of faith.

a) Thus St. Athanasius exclaims: "What hell hath uttered the statement that the body born of Mary is consubstantial [20] with the Godhead of the Logos? or that the Logos was changed into flesh, bone, hair, and into the whole body, and [thus] lost His nature?" [21]   Similarly St. Gregory of Nazianzus: "God came also as a mortal man, combining two natures into one (not: into one nature), the one hidden, the other manifest to men." [22]   St. Ephraem Syrus gives sublime expression to his faith as follows: "*Perfectam habet duplicem naturam, ne duas perdat. Neque enim in una sola natura Deus super terram est visus, neque in altera sola homo in coelos ascendit; verum perfectus ex perfecto, homo ex homine, Deus ex Deo, ex virgine Christus.*" [23] The last of the Greek Fathers, who is at the same time our chief authority concerning their teaching, St. John of Damascus, writes: "If there is but one nature in

in forma Dei aequalis Patri, in forma servi mediator Dei et hominum homo Christus Iesus, quis non intelligat, quod in forma Dei etiam ipse se ipso maior est, in forma autem servi etiam se ipso minor est?" (*De Trinit.*, I, 7, 14.)

18 John I, 14.
19 *V. supra*, p. 93.
20 ὁμοούσιον.
21 *Epist. ad Epictet.*
22 *Carm.*, sect. 2.
23 *Orat. de Marg. Pret.*

Christ, how can He be consubstantial with [His] Father
and mother? The former is God, but the latter [*i. e.,*
Mary] is a human being. But God and man have not
one nature." [24] In the West St. Hilary testifies as
follows: "*Mediator ipse in se ad salutem ecclesiae
constitutus et illo ipso inter Deum et homines mediatoris
sacramento utrumque unus existens, dum ipse ex unitis
in idipsum naturis naturae utriusque res eadem est; ita
tamen ut neutro careret in utroque, ne forte Deus esse
homo nascendo desineret et homo rursum Deus manendo
non esset.*" [25] And St. Ambrose earnestly admonishes
his hearers: "*Servemus distinctionem divinitatis et
carnis* [*i. e., humanitatis*] ; *unus in utroque loquitur Dei
Filius, quia in eodem utraque est natura.*" [26]

β) Not all of the Fathers, however, were so happy
in their choice of terms in treating of this dogma. A
few employed expressions which are open to Monophysitic misconstruction. Such terms are, *e. g.*: κρᾶσις,
μίξις, *mixtura,* etc. Tertullian [27] speaks of Christ as
"*homo Deo mixtus,*" and St. Cyprian says: "*Deus cum
homine miscetur.*" [28] But these are merely incautiously
worded expressions intended to describe the intimate
union of the two natures in one Person. We will quote a
typical passage from St. Augustine, who undoubtedly
held the orthodox faith: "*Sicut in unitate personae
anima unitur corpori, ut homo sit,*" he says, "*ita in unitate
personae Deus unitur homini, ut Christus sit. In illa ergo
persona mixtura est animae et corporis, in hac persona
mixtura est Dei et hominis.*" [29] But he adds by way of

---

24 *De Duab. Volunt.*, 8. Cfr. Petavius, *De Incarn.*, III, 6.

25 *De Trinit.*, IX, n. 3.

26 *De Fide*, II, 9, n. 77. Additional Patristic references in Janssens, *Christologia*, pp. 84 sqq.

27 *De Carne Christi*, c. 15.

28 *De Idol. Van.*; cfr. Petavius,
De Incarn., III, 2; Thomassin, *De
Incarn.*, III, 5.

29 *Ep. ad Volusian.*, III, 11.

warning: *" Si tamen recedat auditor a consuetudine corporum, qua solent duo liquores ita commisceri, ut neuter servet integritatem suam, quamquam et in ipsis corporibus aeri lux incorrupta misceatur."* [30]   In this famous text St. Augustine employs no less than three analogues to illustrate the Hypostatic Union: (1) The union of body and soul in man, (2) the mixture of two liquids, and (3) the mutual interpenetration of air and light. The first two comparisons savor of Monophysitism, for both the union of body and soul and the mixture of liquids are natural compounds. For this reason he supplements them with a third, *viz.:* the mutual interpenetration of air and light, which enter into a most intimate union without losing their specific natures.

The most popular Patristic analogue was the union of body and soul, which Acacius of Constantinople (about 480) chose to bolster his Monophysitic errors. The same ἕνωσις κατὰ σύνθεσιν, he said, which results from the union of body and soul in man,[31] takes place between the Godhead and the manhood of Jesus Christ. But Acacius forgot that comparisons are inadequate and that the Fathers pointed out not only similarities but also important points of difference between the two unions. These points of difference may be reduced to the following heads: (1) Body and soul are mutually related as parts of one whole, in the strict sense of the term, which cannot be said of the Godhead and manhood of Christ.[32] (2) In man the soul stands in a natural relationship to the body, inasmuch as the one postulates the other. In Christ, on the other hand, the mutual relation-

---

30 *Ep. cit.*
31 *V. supra*, p. 148.
32 Cfr. *Fragm. inter Opera S. Athanasii* (Migne, *P. G.*, XXVI, 1233): *" Illic quidem pars hominis sunt anima et corpus, hic vero neque caro pars Verbi neque Verbum pars carnis."*

ship between Godhead and manhood is entirely supernatural.   (3) In man a finite spirit is united to finite flesh,
in Christ an infinite Hypostasis to a finite but complete
nature.[33]   (4) Christ *qua* Godman is both God and man,
whereas man is neither body alone nor soul alone, but a
synthesis of both.[34]

ARTICLE 2

THE EXISTENCE OF TWO WILLS IN CHRIST, AS DEFINED AGAINST MONOTHELITISM

1. MONOTHELITISM AND THE CHURCH.—a)
In order to restore the unity of faith which had
been disturbed by the Monophysitic controversies, Sergius, Patriarch of Constantinople (610–
638, in the days of Mohammedan ascendancy),
with Bishops Theodore of Pharan and Cyrus of
Phasis,[1] pitched upon the formula: Christ has
"one will and one operation." [2]   This phrase,
though not meant to deny the "duality of natures" defined by the Council of Chalcedon, in
matter of fact signalized a revival of Monophysitism and was promptly denounced by the
Palestinian monk Sophronius, who became
Bishop of Jerusalem in 634.   The adherents of
the new doctrine were called Monothelites or
Monergetae.[3]

---

33 Cfr. Rusticus Diaconus, *Contra Acephalos:* " *Anima   compatitur corpori, Deus autem Verbum nequa-quam.*"

34 Cfr. St. Bernard, *De Consider.*, V, 9. On the philosophical ab-surdity of Monophysitism cfr. St. Thomas, *S. Theol.*, 3a, qu. 2, art. 1.

1 Cyrus became Patriarch of Alex-andria in 630.

2 ἐν θέλημα καὶ μία ἐνέργεια.

3 For a good sketch of the rise

Owing to the imprudent and dilatory attitude of Pope Honorius I, who had been deceived by a cleverly worded letter addressed to him by Sergius, the new heresy soon assumed formidable proportions in the Orient. Honorius overemphasized the moral unity of the two wills (= absence of contradiction) as against their physical duality.[4] But he was not at heart a Monothelite heretic;[5] nor did he issue an *ex-cathedra* decision on the subject.

b) Among the first to condemn Monothelitism as a revival of the Monophysite heresy was, as we have already noted, St. Sophronius, Pa-

and spread of the Monothelite heresy see T. Gilmartin, *Manual of Church History,* Vol. I, 3rd ed., pp. 395 sqq., Dublin 1909.

4 Cfr. H. K. Mann, *Lives of the Popes,* Vol. I, Part I, pp. 329 sqq.

5 Funk gives the following considerations to show that Honorius was not at heart a Monothelite. (1) Though in his arguments he constantly, like Sergius, starts with the Hypostatic Union as his premise, yet he never goes as far as the latter, never inferring from this premise the oneness of will or energy. (2) The expression *una voluntas,* which he once uses with approval, is, as the context shows, not to be taken physically, but only morally — it does not mean that Christ has only one will-faculty, but that the will of His untainted human nature agrees (and in this sense is one) with His divine will; it should therefore be taken as a testimony to Honorius' belief in a twofold will. Neither was he at all inclined to accept the doctrine of a single energy, as we may see from

the fragments which remain of his second epistle to Sergius. After having therein condemned as novel, and likely to cause dissent, the doctrines of a single or of a double will, he makes his own the words of the *Epistula Dogmatica* of Leo I, and declares that in Christ's person the two natures work without division and without confusion, each in its proper sphere. (Funk-Cappadelta, *A Manual of Church History,* Vol. I, pp. 165 sq., London 1910). The conduct of Honorius gave rise to many controversies. Cfr. Dom J. Chapman, *The Condemnation of Pope Honorius,* reprinted from the *Dublin Review,* London 1907, and the same writer's article, with bibliography, in Vol. VII of the *Catholic Encyclopedia, s. v.* "Honorius I." Cfr. also Schwane, *Dogmengeschichte der patristischen Zeit,* 2nd ed., §48, Freiburg 1895; Grisar in the *Kirchenlexikon,* Vol. VI, 2nd ed., col. 230 sqq.; L. Janssens, *De Deo-Homine,* Vol. I, pp. 691 sqq.

11

triarch of Jerusalem. Another prominent defender of the orthodox faith against this heresy
was St. Maximus Confessor.[6] Officially the
Catholic truth was first defined by Martin the
First in a council held at the Lateran in 649,
at which the *Ecthesis,* a Monothelite profession
of faith issued by the Emperor Heraclius (638),
together with the *Typus,* a similar edict promulgated by his grandson Constantius II (648), were
solemnly condemned.[7] Pope Agatho (A. D.
680) definitively disposed of the matter by his
"Epistle to the Emperors" (Constantine Pogo-
natus and his brothers Heraclius and Tiberius),
which was read at the Sixth Ecumenical Council[8] of Constantinople (A. D. 680–681) and
hailed by the assembled Fathers as the decision of
St. Peter. This Council drew up a new profession of faith, in which the Creed of Chalcedon
was supplemented by the following phrase:
"We confess, according to the teaching of the
holy Fathers [that there are in Christ] two natural wills[9] and two natural operations, without
division, without change, without separation,
without confusion."[10]

---

6 Died about 662; his name ranks
high in the Patristic annals of the
seventh century. For an account
of his life and writings see Bardenhewer-Shahan, *Patrology,* pp. 576
sqq.

7 Cfr. Denzinger-Bannwart, *Enchiridion,* n. 263 sqq.

8 Sometimes called the Trullan
Council from the domed roof of
the hall in which it was held.

9 δύο   φυσικὰς   θελέσεις   ἤτοι
θελήματα.

10 καὶ   δύο   φυσικὰς   ἐνεργείας
ἀδιαιρέτως, ἀτρέπτως, ἀμερίστως,
ἀσυγχύτως.— The Emperor Philip-

2. THE TEACHING OF REVELATION.—The existence of two wills and two operations in Jesus Christ is clearly taught by Sacred Scripture and the Fathers.

a) The Scriptural argument was first exhaustively developed by Pope Agatho in his *Epistula Dogmatica ad Imperatores*. He quotes these texts among others: Matth. XXVI, 39: *"Pater mi, . . . non sicut ego volo, sed sicut tu* — My Father, . . . not as I will, but as thou wilt." Luke XXII, 42: *"Non mea voluntas, sed tua fiat* — Not my will, but thine be done." The opposition here expressed between the will of Christ and that of His Heavenly Father can not refer to the *divine* will of our Saviour, which is numerically one and really identical with the will of the Father. Consequently it must have reference to His *human* will. The same relation is emphasized in John V, 30: *"Non quaero voluntatem meam, sed voluntatem eius qui misit me* — I seek not my own will, but the will of

picus Bardanes (711–713) again brought Monothelitism to the fore, but his attempt to reintroduce the heresy came to an end with his fall. After this Monothelitism survived only among the Christians of Mount Lebanon (called Maronites from John Maron [+ 701], one of their patriarchs, who was civil as well as ecclesiastical chief of his people and successfully defended their liberty against the Saracens), until, beginning in the twelfth century, at the time of the Crusades, they, too, were gradually united to the Western Church. The opinion which has found favor among them of recent years, that, as a whole, they never professed Monothelitism, is not historically defensible, according to Funk (*A Manual of Church History*, tr. by Cappadelta, Vol. I, p. 165, London 1910).

him that sent me." Another argument for the existence of two wills in Christ is derived by Pope Agatho from those Scriptural passages which accentuate our Lord's obedience to His Heavenly Father.[11] None but a human will, he argued, can exercise the virtue of obedience towards God.

b) Agatho was able to quote abundant Patristic testimony in favor of the doctrine of the two wills and two operations.

a) Thus St. Cyril of Jerusalem draws a sharp distinction both between Godhead and manhood, and between divine and human operation. "Christ was double," he says; "man according to that which was visible, and God according to that which was nowise seen; as man He truly ate as we eat, and as God He fed five thousand people with five loaves of bread; as man He really died, and as God He raised Lazarus from the dead; as man He truly slept in the boat, and as God He walked upon the sea."[12] In the West, Pope Leo the Great, in his *Epistula Dogmatica ad Flavianum*, condemned Monophysitism, and at the same time, as it were in advance, cut the ground from under Monothelitism: "*Sicut enim Deus non mutatur miseratione, ita homo non consumitur dignitate. Agit enim utraque forma cum alterius communione, quod proprium est; Verbo scil. operante quod Verbi est, et carne exequente quod carnis est.*"[13]

11 Cfr. John XIV, 31; "*Sicut mandatum dedit mihi Pater, sic facio.*" Phil. II, 8. On the Logos-teaching of St. Cyril see B. Niederberger, O. S. B., *Die Logoslehre* des hl. Cyrill von Jerusalem, Paderborn 1923.

12 *Catech.*, 4.

13 Denzinger-Bannwart, *Enchiridion*, n. 144.

β) Besides recording their belief in the doctrine of the two wills as part and parcel of the revealed deposit, the Fathers also demonstrated its conformity with right reason and supported it by philosophical arguments.

In the first place they appeal to the metaphysical axiom that, since nature is the principle of operation,[14] a nature cannot be separated from the operation peculiar to it. "No nature is without operation," says Damascene.[15] And Cyril: "Beings whose operation and power [16] are identical, must be of the same species." [17]

In the second place the Fathers point to the epistemological principle that the intellect apprehends the essence of things through their sensible manifestations. In regard to nature and its operations, we first apprehend the operations and from these conclude to the underlying essence.[18] We need only apply this principle to the matter under consideration to see that Monothelitism is purely a revival of Monophysitism. As Pope Agatho puts it, " It is impossible to conceive a nature which does not exercise the operation proper to itself." [19]

---

14 *Natura est principium operationis.*

15 *De Fide Orth.*, III, 13.

16 ἐνέργεια καὶ δύναμις.

17 *Thesaur. Assert.*, 32.

18 " As we perceive the nature of a thing in no other way than by its operations," says St. Sophronius, "a difference of essence always manifests itself by a difference in operation." (*Ep. Syn. ad Sergium*).

19 Cfr. Mansi, *Concil.*, XI, 271. The Pope demonstrates the truth of this proposition by a dilemma: " *Si una est operatio, dicant, si* temporalis an aeterna dicenda est, divina an humana, . . . eadem quae est Patris an alia praeterquam Patris? Si una est eademque [operatio], una est divinitatis et humanitatis Christi communis, quod absurdum est dici. . . . Sin autem (quod veritas continet), dum humana quaedam operatus est Christus, ad solam eius ut Filii personam redigitur, quae non eadem est quae et Patris, secundum aliud profecto et aliud operatus est Christus, ut secundum divinitatem, quae facit Pater, eadem et Filius faciat; similiter secundum humanitatem, quae*

Another axiom adduced by the Fathers against Mono-thelitism is this: *"Numerus voluntatum non sequitur numerum personarum, sed naturarum."* Thus Pope Agatho, quoting the words of St. Maximus: *"Dum tres personae in s. Trinitate dicuntur, necesse est ut et tres voluntates personales et tres personales operationes dicantur, quod absurdum est. . . . Sin autem, quod fidei christianae veritas continet, naturalis voluntas, ubi una natura dicitur Trinitatis, consequenter et una naturalis voluntas et una naturalis operatio intelligenda est. Ubi vero in una persona Christi duas naturas, i. e. divinam et humanam confitemur, sicut duas unius et eiusdem naturas, ita et duas naturales voluntates duasque operationes eius regulariter* [20] *confitemur."* [21] That is to say: Operation follows nature, not person, and hence it is not necessary to assume as many persons as there are operations, and *vice versa.*

c) Two wills would not, as Sergius tried to persuade Pope Honorius, be necessarily opposed to each other. If "duality" [22] were synonymous with "contrariety," [23] Christ could have but one will. Yet the expressions Sergius uses are am-biguous, and may be taken to imply merely that in Christ the human will always remained subject to, and coöperated with the divine. Therefore the Sixth General Council defined: *"Duas natu-rales voluntates non contrarias, absit, iuxta quod impii asseruerunt haeretici, sed sequentem eius humanam voluntatem et non resistentem vel re-*

sunt hominis própria, idem ipse operabatur ut homo" (*l. c.*).

[20] καυουικῶς.

[21] Mansī, *Concil.*, XI, 213.

[22] *Dualitas.*

[23] *Contrarietas.*

luctantem, sed potius et subiectam divinae eius atque omnipotenti voluntati."

Duothelitism (*i. e.,* the doctrine that there are two wills in Christ) is not incompatible with the philosophical principle that actions belong to their respective supposita (*"actiones sunt suppositorum"*). For, although two wills are operative in Christ, both belong to one and the same person, namely, the Divine Logos, who as *principium quod* is possessed of a double *principium quo,* by means of which He exercises two specifically different kinds of operation. Hence the theological axiom: *"Duae operationes, sed unus operans."* [24]

3. THE SO-CALLED THEANDRIC OPERATION OF CHRIST.—The familiar phrase "theandric operation" (θεανδρικὴ ἐνέργεια, *operatio deivirilis*) first occurs in the writings of the Pseudo-Dionysius.[25]

When the Severians, who were moderate Monophysites, at a religious conference held in Constantinople, A. D. 531 or 533, appealed in favor of their doctrine to the writings of Dionysius the Areopagite, the Catholic representative, Hypatius of Ephesus, publicly rejected these writings as spurious.[26] In spite of this protest, however, the works of the Pseudo-Areopagite, owing particularly to St.

---

24 The canon of the VIth Ecumenical Council cited above can be found in Mansi, *l. c.* On the doctrine of Duothelitism see J. H. Newman, *Select Treatises of St. Athanasius,* Vol. II, pp. 331 sqq.

25 *Ep. ad Cai., IV.*

26 Mansi, *Concil.,* VIII, 821. The renewal of this protest, many centuries later, is called " one of the first manifestations of the newly awakened spirit of criticism " by Dr. Bardenhewer. (*Patrology,* translated by Shahan, p. 538.)

Maximus Confessor, who wrote commentaries on them and defended them against the charge of Monophysitism, gradually obtained esteem even among Catholics and exercised a far-reaching influence on theological science.[27] The phrase " theandric operation " became current chiefly in consequence of a canon adopted by the Lateran Council held under Martin I, in 649.[28]

a) For a better understanding of the term "theandric operation" it will be useful to consult the commentary on the writings of the Pseudo-Areopagite by St. Maximus Confessor, who conjointly with St. Sophronius was the chief champion of Catholic orthodoxy against Monothelitism. "Christ acted solely as God," he explains, "when, though absent, he cured the ruler's son; He acted solely as man, though He was God, when He ate and was troubled; He acted both as God and as man when He miraculously gave sight to the man born blind by spreading clay upon his eyes, when He cured by mere contact the woman who was troubled with an issue of blood —and these [last-mentioned] operations are properly called theandric." [29]

Accordingly we must distinguish in Christ

27 Cfr. Bardenhewer-Shahan, *Patrology*, p. 537 sq.

28 Denzinger-Bannwart, *Enchiridion*, n. 268: " *Si quis secundum scelerosos haereticos deivirilem operationem, quod Graeci dicunt θεανδρικήν, unam operationem insipienter suscipit, non autem duplicem esse confitetur secundum sanctos Patres, hoc est divinam et humanam, aut ipsam deivirilis . . . novam vocabuli dictionem unius esse designativam, sed non utriusque mirificae et gloriosae unitionis demonstrativam, condemnatus sit.*"

29 θεανδρικαί. Maximus Confessor, *In Ep. IV Dionys. Areop.*

three different and distinct operations: (1) purely divine,[30] such as, for instance, the omnipotent fiat which He pronounced on the son of the ruler; (2) purely human,[31] such as eating and sorrowing; and (3) mixed,[32] partly divine and partly human, such as, e. g., the cure, by physical contact, of the man born blind and the woman troubled with an issue of blood. Christ's purely divine operations by their very nature are not theandric, since He performs them in His capacity as Second Person of the Divine Trinity conjointly with the Father and the Holy Ghost. Only those acts of our Lord can be called theandric which He performs partly as God and partly as man, or merely as man.[33]

b) In its strict and proper sense the term "theandric" is applied to those divine operations only which are wrought with the coöperation of our Lord's human nature, such as, for example, the raising of Lazarus to life by means of the cry: "Lazarus, come forth!" [34] But it would be heretical to conceive this "mixed" or "theandric" operation of the Godman monergetically as a compound neither divine nor human. Christ's divine *energia* proceeds solely from His divine nature, His human *energia* solely from

[30] ἐνέργεια θεοπρεπής.
[31] ἐνέργεια ἀνθρωποπρεπής.
[32] ἐνέργεια θεανδρική κατ᾽ ἐξοχήν.

[33] Cfr. J. H. Newman, *Select Treatises of St. Athanasius*, Vol. II, pp. 412 sqq.
[34] John XI, 43.

His human nature, though both belong to the Person of the Logos hypostatically and precisely in the same manner as the two natures themselves.[35]

St. John of Damascus says: "*Non divisas operationes dicimus aut divisim operantes, sed unite utramque cum alterius communione, quae propria ipsi sunt, operantem.*"[36] As it is the Person of the Logos alone who operates as *principium quod* through the Divine Nature, common to all Three Persons of the Blessed Trinity as *principium quo,* none other than the Son of God or Logos can be regarded as the "hegemonic principle" (τὸ ἡγεμονικόν) of this "mixed" operation.[37]

c) It would, however, be a mistake to except such purely human acts and emotions as hunger, thirst, exhaustion, pain, suffering, and death, from the theandric operation of the Godman and to restrict the latter term solely to those "mixed" or composite acts in the performance of which His Godhead and manhood coöperated. In a wider sense our Saviour's purely human actions and emotions, too, are truly theandric.

[35] Cfr. Newman, *l. c.*

[36] *De Fide Orthod.,* III, 19.

[37] St. Augustine aptly exemplifies this truth as follows: "*Quis neget, non Patrem, non Spiritum Sanctum, sed Filium ambulasse super aquas? Solius enim Filii caro est, cuius carnis illi pedes aquis impositi et per aquas ducti sunt. Absit autem, ut hoc sine Patre fecisse credatur, quum de suis operationibus universaliter dicat: Pater autem in me manens facit opera sua; ut sine Spiritu S., quum similiter opus sit Filii, quod eiiciebat daemonia. Illius quippe carnis ad solum Filium pertinentis lingua erat, qua imperabatur daemonibus ut exirent et tamen dicit: In Spiritu S. eiicio daemonia.*" Contr. Serm. Arianor., c. 15. Cfr. Petavius, *De Incarn.,* VIII, 10; Stentrup, *Christologia,* thes. 51.

For it is the Godman who performs them, not a mere man. By virtue of the Hypostatic Union the purely human actions and affections of the Godman are at the same time and in a true sense actions and affections of the Divine Logos, who, as the "hegemonic principle," dominates and controls the purely human element and through the mediation of His manhood as *principium quo* performs human deeds and suffers human affections quite as truly as He performs divine deeds through His God-head. Thus and thus only was it possible for the Son of God to redeem the human race by His passion and death. The limitation implied in the last sentence will explain why we must conceive this special divine co-operation as connected with His human actions and affections only in so far as they bear an intrinsic relation to the atonement. For, as Rusticus Diaconus observes: "*Deus Verbum et in humanitate existens in coelo ubique consuetas operationes implevit, licet quasdam et inaestimabiles etiam per corpus. Quid enim differebat ad operationes eius ab initio, utrum non haberet an haberet humanitatem, dum per humanitatem non plueret, non tonaret, non astra moveret et si, licet simpliciter dicere, non amplius per eam sit operatus nisi sola, quae noviter propter nostram sunt facta salvationem, pro qua et inhumanatus est.*" [38] It is in this same sense that the Sixth Ecumenical Council defines: [39] "*iuxta quam rationem et duas naturales voluntates et operationes confitemur, ad salutem humani generis* [40] *convenienter in eo concurrentes.*"

---

[38] *Contr. Aceph.* (Migne, *P. L.*, LXVII, 1191).

[39] Denzinger-Bannwart, *Enchiridion*, n. 291.

[40] πρὸς σωτηρίαν τοῦ ἀνθρωπίνου γένους.

SECTION 3

THE INSEPARABILITY OF THE TWO NATURES IN CHRIST

The inseparability of the two natures, while not an essential mark, is an integral property of the Hypostatic Union.

A separation between the two natures is conceivable only in one of three ways: (1) Christ's manhood might have existed prior to its union with the Godhead and become united with it at a later period of its existence; (2) the sacred manhood might have dissociated itself temporarily from the Logos in the past; (3) the Logos might dissociate Himself from His manhood at some future time. All three of these suppositions are inadmissible, as we will show in three distinct theses.

Thesis I: The Hypostatic Union of the Logos with His manhood began at the moment of Christ's conception.

This proposition embodies an article of faith.

Proof. At a Council held in Constantinople (A. D. 543) against the unorthodox teachings of

Origen,[1] the proposition that Christ's human nature existed prior to the Incarnation was condemned as heretical. The Sixth Ecumenical Council expressly defined: *"In incarnatione Verbi non fuit deitas copulata carni prius animatae aut prius praefactae vel animae praeexistenti coniuncta, . . . sed cum ipso Verbo [caro et anima] existentiam habuerunt: . . . simul quippe caro, simul Dei Verbi caro; simul caro animata rationalis, simul Dei Verbi caro animata rationalis."* [2]

a) That this teaching has a solid foundation in Scripture can be shown from Rom. I, 3: *"Factus ex semine David,"* and Gal. IV, 4: *"Factum ex muliere."* These texts not only assert that Christ was true man, but that He became man through His conception by the Virgin Mary, that is to say, in the instant of His conception. If the conception of the man Christ and the Incarnation of the Divine Logos had not been absolutely simultaneous, but separate and independent events, Mary would not be really and truly the Mother of God.[3] She would indeed have given birth to the Son of God, but she would

---

[1] The researches of Fr. Diekamp (*Die origenistischen Streitigkeiten im 6. Jahrhundert und das V. Allgemeine Konzil,* pp. 46 sqq., Münster 1899) have established the fact that this Council enjoyed ecumenical authority. Cfr. Denzinger-Bannwart, *Enchiridion,* n. 204; Nicephorus Callistus, *Hist. Eccl.,* XVII, 28.

[2] *Acta,* art. 11.

[3] θεοτόκος. Cfr. Newman, *Select Orations of St. Athanasius,* Vol. II, 210 sqq.

not have conceived Him; the Hypostatic Union would have occurred some time between the conception and the birth of Jesus.

b) St. Cyril was well aware of this, for he remarked against Nestorius: "The Blessed Virgin did not conceive a mere man, upon whom the Logos subsequently descended; but He subjected Himself to a carnal birth by a union which had its inception in the maternal womb." [4] The dogma was most clearly and trenchantly formulated by Pope St. Leo the Great in the following terms: *"Natura quippe nostra non sic assumpta est, ut prius creata post assumeretur, sed ut ipsâ assumptione crearetur."* [5]

Thesis II: The Logos never even for an instant dissociated Himself from His manhood.

This thesis may be characterized as *"doctrina catholica."*

Proof. The Sixth Ecumenical Council declared that the two wills and two operations in Christ are united inseparably ($ἀχωρίστως$). Since this Council did not expressly mean to define the inseparability of the two natures, but had in view the inseparable personal unity of our Lord, it may be objected that a dogmatic argu-

---

4 *Ep. ad Nestor.*, 1.

5 *Ep.*, 35, c. 3. Cfr. St. Fulgentius, *De Incarn.*, 4: *" Quam carnem non conceptam accepit uni-* *genitus Deus, sed in ea est Deus altissimâ humilitate conceptus."* See also Petavius, *De Incarn.*, IV, 11; Suarez, *De Incarn.*, disp. 16.

ment based upon its definition would not be conclusive in support of our present thesis.   This objection cannot, however, be urged against the following canon of the Eleventh Council of Toledo
(675): ". . . *quas [duas naturas] ita in se una
Christi persona univit, ut nec divinitas ab humanitate nec humanitas a divinitate possit aliquando
seiungi.*"   The Ethiopian liturgy contains the
sentence: "I believe that the Godhead has never,
even for an hour or for a moment, been separated
from the manhood."

a) The only juncture at which a temporary
cessation of the Hypostatic Union could possibly
have occurred, was the *triduum mortis, i. e.,* the
time that elapsed between the death of Christ
and His Resurrection.   But we have it on the
authority of the Apostles' Creed that the dissolution of the human nature of our Lord did
not in matter of fact entail the cessation of the
Hypostatic Union.   "He was buried, and descended into hell," *i. e.,* His body was buried, but
His soul descended into hell.   The death of Christ
did not consist in a separation of His manhood
from His Godhead, but in the dissolution of His
human nature, *i. e.,* the separation of body from
soul, both of which, though temporarily dissociated, remained the true body and soul of the Son
of God.   From our Lord's exclamation on the
Cross: "My God, why hast thou forsaken me!"

certain heretics argued that the Hypostatic Union was interrupted during His Passion and death. But this conclusion is absolutely unwarranted. Hugh of St. Victor in conformity with the teaching of the Fathers explains the passage as follows: "God merely withdrew His protection, He did not sever the union." [6]

b) Did the blood shed by our Lord during His sacred Passion remain hypostatically united with the Godhead during the *triduum mortis?* This is a somewhat more difficult question, which demands an extended explanation.

a) Though not of faith, it is theologically certain that in Christ's *living* body, both before His death and after the Resurrection, His sacred Blood was united to the Logos hypostatically, not merely in a mediate manner, as were, for instance, His hair, nails, etc. [7] Whether and how far a man's blood is informed by his soul is a question in regard to which physicians, physiologists, and philosophers have not yet reached an agreement. Many hold that the blood is merely an inanimate medium by which the tissues of the body are nourished and relieved of effete matter. [8] Putting this controversy aside, it is theologically certain that the Hypostatic Union is not limited to the sphere informed by the soul, but comprises

[6] "*Deus subtraxit protectionem, sed non separavit unionem.*" *De Sacram.*, II, 1, 10. On certain difficult Patristic passages cfr. Petavius, *De Incarn.*, XII, 19.

[7] Suarez contended against Durandus and some of the earlier Schoolmen: "*Sanguis Christi Do-mini proxime et immediate fuit unitus Verbo Dei. Haec conclusio est hoc tempore ita certa, ut contraria non possit sine errore defendi.*" (*De Incarn.*, disp. 15, sect. 6, n. 2.)

[8] Cfr. Urráburu, *Psychol.*, pp. 800 sqq., Vallisoleti 1897.

all those factors which constitute the proper essence and
integrity of human nature. It would be wrong, therefore, to argue that since, according to one theory at least,
the spiritual soul immediately informs only the spinal and
sympathetic nerves, the nervous system alone in Christ
was immediately (*secundum hypostasin*) united with the
Logos, all other parts of His body only mediately (*in
hypostasi*). Whatever physiological theory one may
prefer to adopt, the hypostatic (*i. e.*, immediate) union
of the Logos with His living blood can be demonstrated
independently of the question whether or not the soul
of Christ animated this blood from within. Holy
Scripture tells us that we were redeemed " with the
Precious Blood of Christ," [9] and it is this same Precious
Blood which is proposed to our adoration in the consecrated chalice during Mass.[10] Pope Clement VI expressly declares [11] that, because of its union with the Divine Word, a single drop of the Precious Blood of our
Lord would have sufficed to redeem the world. St.
Thomas voices the opinion of the medieval Schoolmen
when he says: " *Manifestum est quod sanguis in pas-
sione effusus, qui maxime fuit salubris, fuit divinitati
unitus; et ideo oportuit quod in resurrectione iungeretur
aliis humanitatis partibus.*" [12]

β) It is not easy to demonstrate that, like His soul
or His inanimate body, the blood which our Saviour
shed on the Cross remained hypostatically united with
the Logos during the three days that elapsed between

9 Cfr. 1 Pet. I, 18 sq.; 1 John
I, 7; Heb. IX, 12 sqq.; Apoc. VII,
14.
10 See the dogmatic treatise on
the Holy Eucharist.
11 *Extrav. Com.*, l. V, tit. 9, c. 2:
" *Non guttam sanguinis modicam,*
12

*quae tamen propter unionem ad
Verbum pro redemptione totius humani generis suffecisset, sed copiose
velut quoddam effluvium noscitur
effudisse.*"
12 *Quodlib.*, V, art. 5.

His death and Resurrection.   In the fifteenth century a
violent controversy broke out over this question between
members of the Dominican and the Franciscan Orders.
Pope Pius II, in 1464, after listening to a formal debate
which lasted three days, commanded both parties to
cease quarrelling and reserved the final decision to the
Holy See.[13]   No such decision was ever published.   Since
the Council of Trent the opinion of the Dominicans has
become the prevailing one among theologians.   It is to
the effect that during the *triduum mortis* the Logos remained hypostatically united at least with that portion
of His Precious Blood which He re-assumed after the
Resurrection.   The contradictory opinion of the Fran-
ciscans no longer has any prominent defenders outside
of Scotist circles.[14]   Some older theologians [15] held that
the Blood of Christ was never at any time united with
the Divine Logos *secundum hypostasin,* so that, had the
Apostles during the *triduum mortis* consecrated bread
and wine, it would have become mere blood, but not the
blood of the Godman.   This view is altogether obsolete
and untenable.   The dogmatic definition of the Triden-
tine Council: *"Ipsum autem corpus sub specie vini et
sanguinem sub specie panis animamque sub utraque
[specie existere non quidem vi verborum, sed] vi naturalis illius connexionis et concomitantiae, qua partes
Christi Domini . . . inter se copulantur,"* [16] plainly intimates that " body " and " blood " stand on the same level,
and consequently either both are united with the Divine
Logos, or neither of them is.   It follows that since the
bloodless corpse of our Redeemer was still truly the body

---

13 Cfr. Denzinger-Bannwart, *Enchiridion,* n. 718.

14 Its last notable champion was
Fr. Collius (*De Sanguine Christi,*
Mediol. 1612).

15 *E. g.,* Alphonsus Tostatus
(+ 1455) and Gabriel Biel (+
1495).

16 Denzinger-Bannwart, *Enchiridion,* n. 876.

of the Logos, the blood that had flown from it was not dissociated from the Hypostatic Union.

γ) Jerusalem, Beyrout, Rome, Mantua, Boulogne, Bruges, Weingarten, Reichenau, Stans, Neury Saint-Sepulchre, and a number of other places claim, or at one time claimed, to possess authentic relics of the Precious Blood of our Divine Saviour.[17] If these relics were genuine blood shed by our Lord during His sacred Passion, this would merely prove that some particles of Christ's body were not re-assumed but permanently eliminated from the Godhead. They may be venerated like particles of the holy Cross, but it would be idolatry to give them divine worship.[18] This principle applies *a fortiori* to blood which is believed to have flown miraculously from consecrated hosts or images of Christ. St. Thomas inclines to the opinion that all the alleged relics of the Precious Blood preserved in different churches throughout Christendom belong to this class. "*Sanguis autem ille, qui in quibusdam ecclesiis pro reliquiis conservatur, non fluxit ex latere Christi, sed miraculose dicitur effluxisse de quadam imagine Christi percussa.*"[19] This fluid is not the blood of Christ at all, because the glorified Saviour "no longer dies," and consequently sheds no more blood. For the rest it is well to be cautious in accepting such medieval legends. The phenomenon of "bleeding hosts" may be caused by a certain rare *micrococcus,* called *prodigiosus,*[20] the action of which is described thus by one of our leading

---

17 Cfr. the *Catholic Fortnightly Review,* Vol. XVI (1909), No. 10, pp. 296 sqq.

18 Cfr. Benedict XIV, *De Festis,* §374. See A. Jox, *Die Reliquien des kostbaren Blutes unseres göttlichen Heilandes,* Luxemburg 1880.

On the different kinds of worship (*latria, dulia, hyperdulia,* etc.) see Pohle-Preuss, *Mariology.*

19 *S. Theol.,* 3a, qu. 4, art. 2.

20 Also *Monas prodigiosa Ehrenberg.*

bacteriologists: "Starchy substances, such as boiled potatoes, bread, rice, hosts, etc., show moist, blood-red spots, which sometimes spread rapidly. The sudden appearance of such spots on articles of daily use has given rise to all sorts of curious superstitions." [21]

δ) The theological axiom: "*Quod semel Verbum assumpsit, nunquam dimisit*" applies absolutely only to the soul of our Divine Redeemer; in regard of His body, including His Precious Blood, it has but relative value. The blood which Christ shed at the circumcision, and when He was scourged, and during His agony on Mount Olivet, unquestionably left the union with His Godhead for ever. This applies in an even greater measure to the secretions incident to the ordinary anabolic and catabolic processes of nature, *e. g.*, tears, perspiration, sputum.[22]

Thesis III: The Logos will never dissociate Himself from His manhood.

This proposition embodies an article of faith.

Proof. While the so-called Seleucians heretically taught that Christ had "transplanted His sacred humanity to the sun," [23] Marcellus of Ancyra,[24] and his disciple Photinus of Sirmium,[25]

21 A. de Bary, *Vorlesungen über Bakterien*, p. 11, Leipsic 1885. Cfr. the article "Hostien" in Burg's *Kontrovers-Lexikon*, pp. 414 sqq., Essen-Ruhr, 1905.

22 Cfr. Tepe, *Instit. Theol.*, Vol. III, pp. 541 sqq., Paris 1896; Chr. 3rd ed., pp. 80 sqq., 95 sqq., Friburgi Pesch, *Praelect. Dogmat.*, Vol. IV, 1909; L. Janssens, *De Deo-Homine*, Vol. I, pp. 294 sqq., Friburgi 1901.

23 Cfr. Ps. XVIII, 6: "*In sole posuit tabernaculum suum.*"

24 Died about 374. Cfr. Newman, *Select Orations of St. Athanasius*, Vol. II, pp. 196 sqq.; Bardenhewer-Shahan, *Patrology*, pp. 241 sq. What remains of Marcellus' writings is to be found in Chr. H. G. Rettberg, *Marcelliana*, Göttingen 1794.

25 Died about 376. His numerous writings have all perished. Cfr. Th. Zahn, *Marcellus von Ancyra*, pp. 189 sqq., Gotha 1867.

maintained that the Saviour would not dispossess
Himself of His body until after the resurrection
of the flesh. The Second General Council of
Constantinople (A. D. 381) rejected this heresy
by adding to the Nicene Creed the phrase: "Of
whose kingdom there shall be no end." [26]

a) The perpetual inseparability of our Lord's
two natures is implied in the Scriptural teaching (1) that Christ is eternal and (2) that He
is forever our High Priest and King. The eternal existence of Christ (not to be confounded
with the eternity of the Divine Logos) is taught
in Heb. XIII, 8: *"Iesus Christus heri et hodie,
ipse et in saecula* — Jesus Christ, yesterday, and
to-day, and the same for ever." That the Apostle in this passage means the Godman, *i. e.,* the
synthesis of Logos and manhood, is evidenced by
his teaching in regard to Christ's eternal priesthood. Cfr. Heb. VII, 24: *"Hic* [*scil. Christus*]
*eo quod maneat in aeternum, sempiternum habet
sacerdotium* — But this one [Christ] for that
he continueth for ever, hath an everlasting priesthood." He is also called Eternal King. Cfr. Luke
I, 33: *"Et regni eius non erit finis* — And of
his kingdom there shall be no end." God Himself "hath sworn" that the priesthood "according
to the order of Melchisedech" shall never come

---

[26] οὗ τῆς βασιλείας οὐκ ἔσται τέλος. Cfr. Denzinger-Bannwart,
Enchiridion, n. 86.

to an end.[27] It is equally certain that the kingdom of Christ, *i. e.,* the triumphant Church which is His mystical body, together with its High Priest and King, will endure for ever.

b) The unanimity of the holy Fathers in regard to this dogma makes it unnecessary for us to elaborate the argument from Tradition. In his controversy with Marcellus of Ancyra St. Cyril of Jerusalem denounces the new heresy as "another dragon's head lately arisen in Galatia," and he concludes his exposition of the orthodox belief with the injunction: "This hold fast, this believe; but what heresy has brought forth, that reject; for thou hast been most clearly instructed regarding the kingdom of Christ which will never end." [28] St. Chrysostom writes trenchantly: "[Christ] put on our flesh, not to put it off again, but to keep it for ever." [29]

READINGS: — Assemani, *Bibliotheca Orientalis,* t. II, dissert. De Monophysitis, Romae 1721.— Ph. Kuhn, *Die Christologie Leos I. des Grossen in systematischer Darstellung,* Würzburg 1894.— Hefele, *Konziliengeschichte,* 2nd ed., Vols. II and III, Freiburg 1875–1877.— Chr. Walch, *Historie der Ketzereien,* Vols. IV to VIII, Leipsic 1878.— J. A. Dorner, *History of the Development of the Doctrine of the Person of Christ,* 5 vols., Edinburgh 1861–63.— Wilhelm-Scannell, *A Manual of Catholic Theology,* Vol. II, pp. 74 sqq., 82 sqq., 2nd ed., London 1901.— Funk-Cappadelta, *A Manual of Church History,* Vol. I, pp. 157 sqq., 163 sqq., London 1910.— J. H. Newman, *Select Treatises of St. Athanasius,*

27 Cfr. Ps. CIX, 4.
28 *Catech.,* 15, n. 27.
29 *Hom. in Ioa.,* 11. Cfr. Peta-
vius, *De Incar.,* XII, 18; Suarez, *De Myst. Vit. Christi,* disp. 51, sect. 1.

Vol. II, pp. 331 sqq., 412 sqq.— Freddi-Sullivan, *Jesus Christ the Word Incarnate, Considerations Gathered from the Works of the Angelic Doctor, St. Thomas Aquinas,* pp. 169 sqq., 195 sqq., St. Louis 1904.— W. H. Hutton, *The Church of the Sixth Century,* London 1897.

CHAPTER II

THE EFFECTS OF THE HYPOSTATIC UNION

The effects of the Hypostatic Union, in their concrete manifestation, are called attributes of Christ. They may be considered in relation (1) to the Person of our Redeemer, or (2) to His Divine Nature, or (3) to His human nature.

The attributes of Christ's Divine Nature manifestly coincide with the divine attributes in general, and as such are treated in the first two volumes of this series of dogmatic text-books.[1]

In the following two Sections we shall consider: (1) The attributes of Christ's Divine Person and (2) those of His Human Nature.

GENERAL READINGS: — Oswald, *Christologie,* §§ 7–9, 2nd ed., Paderborn 1887.—* Scheeben, *Dogmatik,* Vol. III, §§ 223–253, Freiburg 1882 (summarized in Wilhelm-Scannell, *A Manual of Catholic Theology,* Vol. II, pp. 108 sqq., 2nd ed., London 1901). —* Franzelin, *De Verbo Incarnato,* thes. 37–45, Romae 1881.— Heinrich-Gutberlet, *Dogmatische Theologie,* Vol. VII, Mainz 1896.— Th. H. Simar, *Lehrbuch der Dogmatik,* 4th ed., Vol. I, pp. 465 sqq., Freiburg 1899.— W. Humphrey, S. J., *The One Mediator,* pp. 238 sqq., London *s. a.*— Freddi-Sullivan, S. J., *Jesus Christ the Word Incarnate,* St. Louis 1904.

1 Pohle-Preuss, *God: His Knowability, Essence, and Attributes,* St. Louis 1911, and *The Divine Trinity, ibid.* 1912.

SECTION 1

THE ATTRIBUTES OF CHRIST ACCORDING TO HIS DIVINITY

ARTICLE I

THE PERICHORESIS OF THE TWO NATURES IN CHRIST

1. DEFINITION OF PERICHORESIS.—The notion of Perichoresis (περιχώρησις or συμπεριχώρησις, in Latin *circumincessio,* later *circuminsessio*) embraces two essential elements: (a) Duality in unity and (b) Unity in duality. The former is the material, the latter the formal element.

In other words: The mutually in-existing substances must be (1) really distinct and (2) substantially one. Without a real distinction there would be no Perichoresis but absolute identity; without substantial unity the two substances would merely co-exist side by side.

The specific nature of Perichoresis depends entirely on the manner in which the elements are combined in one *unum substantiale.* Trinitarian differs essentially from Christological Perichoresis, is its exact counterpart in fact, because the mutual relations of nature and person in the Blessed Trinity and in Christ are precisely con-

trary.[2] "As in the Trinity, three Persons exist in one
nature, so in the Word Incarnate, two natures exist
in one Person, and therefore the Fathers applied the
term Perichoresis to both mysteries. But as Trinitarian
Perichoresis proceeds, so to speak, from the statical possession of a common nature, so in the mystery of the
Incarnation Perichoresis is based upon the Hypostatic
Union, *i. e.,* that powerful magnet by which the human
nature is drawn into substantial communion with the
Godhead. This latter Perichoresis reaches its climax in
the effective interpenetration of both natures in Christ's
theandric operation."[3] In Christ, therefore, the bond
which unites Godhead and manhood is the Divine Person
of the Logos, who possesses at once two natures intimately united, indwelling in each other by virtue of the
Hypostatic Union.[4]

Considered in relation to the Hypostatic Union, Perichoresis is its counterpart rather than an effect flowing
therefrom. For, as Oswald truly observes, "The Sym-
perichoresis of the two natures, effected by personal
unity, is merely the reverse side of that personal unity
by which it is effected; the two complement each other
and together constitute the perfect expression of the
hypostatic or physical union."[5] According to our human mode of conception, the Hypostatic Union precedes
Perichoresis as a condition precedes that which it conditions, and therefore we conceive the latter as an effect
of the former.

In Christology, therefore, Perichoresis may be
defined as "the mutual in-existence of the two

2 *V. supra,* pp. 3 sq.
3 L. Janssens, *De Deo-Homine,*
Vol. I, p. 684, Freiburg 1901.
4 Cfr. St. Gregory of Nazianzus,
Ep. 101 ad Cledon.: καὶ περιχωρου-
σῶν τῶν φύσεων εἰς ἀλλήλας τῷ
λόγῳ τῆς συμφυΐας.
5 Oswald, *Christologie,* p. 160, 2nd
ed., Paderborn 1887.

unmixed natures (the divine and the human) by
reason of their hypostatic union with the Person
of the Logos."

2. THE POWER OF PERICHORESIS.—In conformity with our previous teaching in regard to
the immutability of the Logos,[6] we claim that the
power which unifies and binds together the two
natures in Perichoresis cannot proceed from the
humanity of Christ; it must originate in the
Divine Logos, who, despite His own impene-
trability, in a manner ineffable and mysterious,
seizes, penetrates, and immerses Himself in the
human nature, and thus becomes ὁ Θεὸς λόγος
ἐνανθρωπήσας — the God-Word Incarnate.

a) Leporius describes this process somewhat technically as follows: "*Deus qui capax est, non capabilis,
penetrans, non penetrabilis, implens, non implebilis, qui
ubique simul totus et ubique diffusus per infusionem
potentiae suae misericorditer naturae mixtus est humanae,
non humana natura naturae est mixta divinae. Caro
igitur proficit in Verbum, non Verbum proficit in carnem,
et tamen verissime Verbum caro factum est.*"[7] Perichoresis is therefore not a mutual interpenetration (*com-
penetratio mutua*); it must rather be defined as a mutual in-existence (*inexistentia mutua*) of the two natures
in Christ. Human nature, being a created substance, cannot be immersed in the Logos in the same way in which
the immutable Logos immerses itself in it. St. John of

6 *V. supra*, pp. 121 sq.
7 *Libell. Emend.*, n. 4. On the
monk Leporius and his *Libellus
Emendationis* cfr. Hurter, *Nomen-*
clator Literar. Theologiae Catholicae,
Vol. I, 3rd ed., col. 287, Innsbruck
1903.

Damascus puts it thus: "The penetration does not proceed from the flesh, but from the Godhead. For it is impossible that the flesh should permeate the Godhead; but by penetrating into the flesh, the Divine Nature has endowed the flesh with an inexplicable penetration of itself, which is called unition."[8]

b) In view of this dissimilarity, there can be no doubt as to what the holy Fathers mean when they speak of a "*deificatio humanitatis*" and refer to the flesh of Christ as "*vivifica*." The term *deificatio* ($\theta\epsilon\iota\omega\sigma\iota\varsigma$) does not signify apotheosis in the Monophysitic sense. It is rather to be taken as indicating merely the deification of Christ's manhood through the medium of Perichoresis or the Hypostatic Union. St. John Damascene says: "From the time that God the Word became flesh, He is as we are in everything except sin, and of our nature without confusion. He has deified our flesh for ever through the mutual interpenetration of His Godhead and His flesh without confusion."[9] Consequently the $\theta\epsilon\iota\omega\sigma\iota\varsigma$ is not based on $\sigma\upsilon\gamma\chi\upsilon\sigma\iota\varsigma$, but on the $\pi\epsilon\rho\iota\chi\omega\rho\eta\sigma\iota\varsigma$ of the two natures resulting from their Hypostatic Union. To deification thus defined there corresponds as a practical correlative the "vivifying power of Christ's flesh," because His humanity (which is what is meant by flesh), represents a "second nature" hypostatically incorporated with and intimately possessed by the Divine Logos, which (second nature) as *instrumentum coniunctum,* produces truly theandric effects.[10] "*Si quis non confite*

---

8 *De Fide Orthodoxa*, III, 19: "*Commeatio non ex carne, sed ex divinitate facta est. Impossibile est enim carnem permeare divinitatem; sed divina natura quum per carnem semet immeavit, dedit etiam carni*

inexplicabilem in se ipsam immeationem, quam unitionem vocant."

9 *Or. de Imagin.*, I, 21.

10 *V. supra*, pp. 162 sqq.

tur," says the Council of Ephesus (431), *" carnem Domini vivificatricem esse et propriam ipsius Verbi Dei Patris sed velut alterius praeter ipsum coniuncti eidem per dignitatem aut quasi divinam habentis habitationem, ac non potius vivificatricem esse, quia facta est propria Verbi cuncta vivificare valentis,*[11] *anathema sit."* [12]

3. THE IMPORT OF PERICHORESIS.—The doctrine of Perichoresis contains the most effective and trenchant refutation of all Christological as well as Trinitarian heresies. It categorically excludes Nestorianism and Adoptionism, which assert that the two natures co-exist side by side, and it disproves Monophysitism and Monothelitism, because the mutual in-existence of the two natures necessarily supposes their respective integrity. Thus there can be no exaggeration of the notion of unity, which would result in real confusion. Perichoresis represents the golden mean between heretical extremes and is equally effective against Nestorius and Eutyches. Implying as it does the truth that there are in Christ two natures, a divine and a human, it strikes effectively at all those heresies which deny either the Divinity or the humanity of our Lord and Saviour. Pope Leo the Great gives apt expression to this thought when he says: *"Tota enim est in*

11 σάρκα ζωοποιόν . . . ὅτι γέγονε ἰδία τοῦ Λόγου τοῦ τὰ πάντα ζωογονεῖν ἰσχύοντος.

12 Denzinger-Bannwart, *Enchiridion,* n. 123. Cfr. Petavius, *De Incarn.,* X, 1 sqq.

maiestate humilitas, tota in humilitate maiestas, nec infert unitas confusionem, nec dirimit proprietas unitatem." [13]

ARTICLE 2

THE COMMUNICATION OF IDIOMS

1. DEFINITION OF THE TERM.—What is technically known as the Communication of Idioms may be defined as "a mutual exchange of divine and human properties in virtue of the Hypostatic Union." Though practically identical with Perichoresis, the Communication of Idioms may more appropriately be regarded as an effect thereof. For if the Divine Person of the Logos is both God and man, it is inevitable that His Godhead and His manhood should interchange their respective properties, and this is precisely what is meant by *communicatio proprietatum s. idiomatum* (ἀντίδοσις τῶν ἰδιωμάτων ἢ ἰδιοτήτων). We thus have a transfer of predicates or attributes from one nature to the other, as, *e. g.,* "God has suffered," or "The man is God." Since, however, "interchange" and "predication" are not synonymous terms, it will be better, for the sake of clearness, to distinguish between the (ontological) interchange of idioms and the (logical) predication of the several kinds of attributes.

13 *Serm. de Pass.,* 3, c. 1.

a) *Communicatio idiomatum* means the actual transfer of divine attributes to the man Jesus and of human attributes to the Divine Logos. The extent and mode of this transfer depend on the manner in which Godhead and manhood are united in Christ. After a fashion even Nestorianism and Monophysitism admitted a Communication of Idioms, but their theory, made to conform with the heretical system of which it is a corollary, differs essentially from the approved Catholic doctrine. Communication of Idioms in the Catholic sense is based on this principle: "In Christ God is man and man is God; but Godhead and manhood are by no means identical." In the words of the Council of Ephesus: *"Una persona composita Christus totus est Deus et totus est homo; totus est Deus etiam cum humanitate, sed non secundum humanitatem Deus, et totus est homo cum divinitate, sed non secundum divinitatem homo*—One composite person, Christ, is all God and all man; He is all God even with His manhood, but not according to His manhood; and He is all man with His Godhead, but not according to His Godhead." [1]

It is wrong to say, therefore, as some theologians do, that the doctrines of Perichoresis and Communication of Idioms represent a mere Scholastic logomachy. They constitute a touchstone of orthodoxy in all questions re-

1 Cfr. Hardouin, *Concil.*, I, 1640.

garding the union between the Godhead and human nature. Perichoresis is merely the reverse side of the Hypostatic Union, while the ἀντίδοσις τῶν ἰδιωμάτων represents a necessary and important corollary of that dogma. These two doctrines enable the theologian to conclude *a posteriori* from the one to the other, and from the effect to the cause, *i. e.*, the Hypostatic Union itself. It is by means of this method that we have demonstrated the Hypostatic Union from Sacred Scripture, Tradition, and the Creeds, and by this same method Nestorius was convicted of heresy in his teaching on the Communication of Idioms.

b) By Predication of Idioms we understand the *communicatio idiomatum* expressed in terms of thought or speech. Needless to say, a term must correspond to the thing which it is intended to designate. Formulated in logical terms the ontological law underlying the *communicatio idiomatum* gives us the following rule of predication: "Whatever is predicated of the Divine Person of Christ according to His Divine Nature, can and must be predicated of the same Divine Person also in His human nature, and *vice versa;* but the predicates proper to the Divine Nature must not be assigned to the human nature, and *vice versa.*"

The first part of this rule is based upon the unity of the one Divine Person in two natures; the second, upon the fact that the two natures co-exist separately and inconfused in one Person. " *Christus est una persona et hypostasis in utraque natura, divina scil. et humana,*" says St. Thomas, " *unde potest utriusque naturae nomine*

*designari; et quocunque nomine significetur, potest prae-
dicari de eo id quod est utriusque naturae, quia utrique
non supponitur nisi una hypostasis. Et per hunc modum
possumus dicere, quod " homo creavit stellas" et quod
" Dominus gloriae est crucifixus"; et tamen non creavit
stellas secundum quod homo, sed secundum quod Deus:
nec crucifixus est secundum quod Deus, sed inquantum
homo."* [2]* This rule is merely an application of the general principles of logic. Of sugar, for instance, we
can say in concrete terms: " The white is sweet" and
" The sweet is white," because the unity of the underlying *suppositum* produces an objective identity between
its attributes. But we cannot say that "whiteness is
sweetness," because the two qualities thus denoted are
separate and distinct entities and their concepts cannot
be interchanged. Reduced to its simplest terms, therefore,
the Christological law of predication reads: *"Mutua
idiomatum praedicatio valet tantummodo in concreto, non
valet in abstracto."* We can say of Christ, for instance,
" God is man," or " Man is God," but we cannot say,
" Divinity is humanity," or " Humanity is Divinity."
For according to a general rule of logic, concrete terms
alone demonstrate or " suppose " the hypostasis or person, while abstract terms always demonstrate or suppose
the nature of a being.[3]

2. SPECIAL RULES FOR THE PREDICATION OF
IDIOMS.—The *communicatio idiomatum* is not
always accurately predicated.

a) The only correct predicates are those based
upon the orthodox doctrine that there is in Christ

2 *Lect. in 1 Cor.*, 2, II.
3 Cfr. St. Thomas, *S. Theol.*, 3a, qu. 16, art. 4.

13

but one Person, and that this one (Divine) Person possesses two inconfused natures.

a) Human predicates can be applied to the Divine Hypostasis only *in concreto*. It is only by concrete terms that a subject is designated as the bearer of its predicates, and the rules of logic permit us to affirm the objective identity of subject and predicate. We may, therefore, say: "God is man," "The Logos is the Son of Mary," "Christ was weary"; for in making these statements we simply assert that one and the same person exercises two distinct natural functions.

β) If, however, the Λόγος ἔνσαρκος is to be expressly designated according to either one of His two natures, the respective predicates, even if concrete, must in each case be in accord with their proper subject. The reason is quite obvious. The subject in every such case is not taken formally as a person, but as a person constituted in this or that determined nature. It is correct, therefore, to say: "Jesus as God is the creator of the universe," "The Logos as man suffered and died;" but it is false to say: "Christ as man created the world," or "Christ as God was crucified." The two last-mentioned propositions require a negative particle to make them true ("Christ as God was *not* crucified," "Christ as man did *not* create the world"), though in this negative form they again become false if the apposition is removed, *e. g.,* "The Son of God was not crucified."

γ) Of abstract predicates those only can be applied to the Divine Hypostasis which connote a divine attribute, *e. g.,* "Christ is the Godhead," "The man Jesus is omnipotence itself." The reason is that the Hypostasis of the Logos is really identical with the Divine Nature and all its attributes. This rule does not, however, apply to abstract terms that express a purely human quality, because the Godhead is not and cannot be identical with manhood. Hence it would be false to say that " The Logos is the human nature," or " Christ is mortality."

b) Predicates which deny the unity of Person or involve a confusion of the two natures in Christ [4] are necessarily false.

α) Any predicate which would either formally exclude the Divine Person or include a (non-existing) human person, would give rise to false and heretical inferences; for example: " The Son of Mary is not the same as the Son of the Father," or " Christ is a mere man." To this category belongs the Adoptionist thesis: " The man Jesus is not the natural, but an adopted son of God."

β) Whenever divine and human attributes are expressed by means of abstract terms, these terms may not, under pain of heresy, be interchanged (e. g., " The Godhead is the manhood," " Mortality is omnipotence "), because abstract terms logically " suppose " the nature of a being, and the two natures in Christ are distinct and inconfused.

γ) Purely human abstract terms must not be predicated of the Godhead,[5] because the Divine Person and the human nature of Christ are in no wise identical. Hence it would be wrong to say: " The Logos is manhood " (instead of: " The Logos is man "). This rule also applies to those concrete human attributes which by their very nature cannot be predicated of the Divine Hypostasis, e. g., body and soul as essential components

4 The first-mentioned error is that of Nestorius, the second that of the Monophysites.

5 The case is, of course, different with such abstract terms as denote divine attributes.

of human nature. Not even during the *triduum mortis* would it have been correct to say: "The Son of God is a corpse," or "The Logos is a soul," because, though concrete, the terms body and soul apply solely to the human nature in its essential constituents.

δ) No human *concretum,* and *a fortiori* no human *abstractum,* can be predicated of a divine *abstractum.* Hence it would be inaccurate to say: "The Godhead is the Son of Mary," or "Omnipotence was crucified," or, still worse, "Divine wisdom is passibility." There is but one exception to this rule, namely if the abstract term is employed by the speaker or writer — as it was sometimes employed by the Fathers — in lieu of a concrete, *e. g.,* "*Deitas* [= *is qui habet deitatem*] *nata est ex Virgine.*" In the famous hymn attributed to St. Ambrose a concrete is substituted for an abstract term: "*Tu ad liberandum suscepturus hominem* [= *naturam humanam s. humanitatem*] *non horruisti Virginis uterum.*"

ε) Lastly, such attributes as are based on the supposition that the Incarnation has not yet taken place, may be predicated of the Logos, but not of Christ. Hence it is incorrect to say: "Christ was made man," instead of: "The Son of God (or Logos) was made man." This is a rule which is often violated by catechists and preachers; fortunately, however, disregard of it does not involve heresy.

c) Ambiguous predicates are those which, being couched in indefinite terms, admit of both an orthodox and a heretical interpretation. Predicates of this sort have always been popular with heretics, because they afford a comfortable hiding place to those who covertly attack the Catholic faith.

When such ambiguous predicates occur in the writings of the Fathers the presumption is always in favor of orthodoxy.   Preachers, catechists, and all who write on theological subjects should, however, bear in mind that they are bound to express the Catholic doctrine in correct, unmistakable, and unequivocal terms.   Thus, instead of saying: " Christ is a creature," it is preferable to use the phrase: " Christ according to His manhood is a creature," thus positively excluding Arianism.   In view of Nestorianism certain expressions which were employed by the Fathers before the rise of that heresy have been officially proscribed and must now be avoided; e. g., homo deifer (ἄνθρωπος θεοφόρος), homo divinus s. dominicus (ἄνθρωπος θεῖος ἢ κυριακός), etc.   St. Augustine in his *Retractationes* recanted the phrase " homo dominicus " which he had employed in his earlier writings.[6]   The Council of Ephesus decreed: " *Si quis audeat dicere hominem Christum Theophorum, id est Deum ferentem* [7] *ac non potius Deum esse veraciter* [8] *dixerit . . . anathema sit.*" [9]

3. SOME FAMOUS AMPHIBOLOGIES.—In the history of Christology three phrases have become famous: (a) *"Christus est servus Dei"* (δοῦλος Θεοῦ); (2) *"Unus de SS. Trinitate crucifixus est;"* and (c) *"Christus secundum humanitatem est omnipraesens."*   The first two of these locutions admit of an orthodox interpretation, but the

6 " *Nunc mallem me non dixisse.*"
7 θεοφόρον ἄνθρωπον.
8 Θεὸν εἶναι κατὰ ἀλήθειαν.
9 *Conc. Ephesin.,* can. 5; cfr. Denzinger-Bannwart, *Enchiridion,* n. 117.

last is inadmissible because based on the Lutheran error of Ubiquitarianism.

a) While it is true that St. Paul speaks only of the " form of a servant," [10] and nowhere directly refers to our Saviour as " servant of God," [11] the prophet Isaias expressly described the coming Messias as עֶבֶד יְהוָה (= *servus Dei*). The Adoptionists seized upon this phrase to support their false theory that, side by side with the divine υἱότης, there exists in Christ a creatural δουλεία, which ceases only in virtue of a gracious υἱοθεσία or adoption on the part of God. Against this heretical teaching Pope Hadrian wrote in his decree approving the Council of Frankfort (A. D. 793): "*Adoptivum eum Filium, quasi purum hominem, calamitati humanae subiectum, et quod pudet dicere, servum eum impii et ingrati tantis beneficiis liberatorem nostrum non pertimescitis venenosâ fauce susurrare, . . . etsi in umbra prophetiae dictus est servus propter servilis formae conditionem, quam sumpsit ex Virgine.*" [12] This dogmatic definition clearly states under what conditions it is permissible to speak of Christ as "*servus Dei.*" The word "*servus*" may be taken hypostatically in the sense of "*Hypostasis Christi est serva,*" in contrary opposition to "*Filius naturalis Dei,*" who, as such, cannot be a servant of His Father, with whom He is consubstantial. In this sense the use of the term is heretical. If, however, "*servus Dei*" be taken substantively in the sense of "*Christus est servus Dei ratione naturae servae,*" in so far as, in His human nature, He owes obedience to the Father, of whom He Himself says:

---

10 "*Forma servi* (μορφὴ δού-λου)."

11 "*Servus Dei* (δοῦλος Θεοῦ)."

12 Denzinger-Bannwart, *Enchiridion*, n. 310.

" The Father is greater than I," the term is Scriptural and thoroughly orthodox.[13]

b) The formula: *" Unus de SS. Trinitate crucifixus est"* is also quite orthodox in itself, but was used in a heretical sense in the fifth century by Peter the Fuller, Bishop of Antioch and leader of the Theopaschitae. Peter held that the Godhead as such was crucified. In this sense the phrase was condemned by Pope Felix III (483–492). A. D. 519 the so-called Scythian monks, headed by John Maxentius, in their intemperate zeal for the purity of the faith against the Nestorians and Monophysites, vehemently demanded that the proposition: " One of the Trinity suffered in the flesh," be made a shibboleth of orthodoxy and incorporated into the Creed of Chalcedon. Already at Constantinople the papal legates had declared that the Creed of Ephesus and Chalcedon was sufficiently explicit against the two heresies. August 13, 520, Pope Hormisdas wrote to Possessor, an African bishop resident at Constantinople, severely rebuking the quarrelsome spirit of the Scythian monks.[14] The hesitating attitude of Pope Hormisdas towards these fanatical monks did not mean that the Church condemned the formula in question, for not long after (A. D. 553) the Fifth General Council of Constantinople declared that " Whoever does not profess that our Lord Jesus Christ, who was crucified in the flesh, is true God and the Lord of glory, and one of the Blessed Trinity, let him be anathema." [15]

13 Cfr. Suarez, *De Incarn.*, disp. 44; Petavius, *De Incarn.*, VII, 7; De Lugo, *De Mysterio Incarn.*, disp. 28, sect. 3.

14 Cfr. Bardenhewer-Shahan, *Patrology*, p. 548.

15 " *Si quis non confitetur, Dominum nostrum Iesum Christum, qui crucifixus est carne, Deum esse verum, et Dominum gloriae, et unum de Sancta Trinitate (καὶ ἕνα τῆς ἁγίας τριάδος), talis a. s.*" (Can. 10. apud Denzinger-Bannwart, *Enchiridion*, n. 222). On the affair of Pope

That the Theopaschitae interpreted the formula in a
Monophysitic sense, is evident from the fact that they
added "*qui crucifixus es pro nobis*" to the ancient doxology, thereby insinuating that they believed the thrice
holy Trinity, *i. e.,* the Godhead itself, to have been crucified for us. The Church has ever abhorred this Theo-
paschitic heresy, as appears from the *Professio Fidei
Orientalibus Praescripta* drawn up by Urban VIII and
Benedict XIV, which says: "*Per quam definitionem
[Concilii Chalcedonensis] damnatur impia haeresis illo-
rum, qui Trisagio ab angelis tradito et in praefata Chalce-
donensi synodo decantato: 'Sanctus Deus, sanctus fortis,
sanctus immortalis, miserere nobis' addebant: 'qui crucifixus es pro nobis,' atque adeo divinam naturam trium personarum passibilem asserebant et mortalem.*" [16] Even
thus illegitimately expanded, the doxology could still be
interpreted in an orthodox sense, provided it were understood as relating to Christ alone and not to the whole
Trinity; for Christ, being true God, is "holy, strong, and
immortal," and "was crucified for us" in the flesh. But
the Church has always regarded this hymn as a profession
of faith in the Blessed Trinity.[17]

c) The Lutheran doctrine of Ubiquitarianism originated in a wrong application of the *communicatio idiomatum.* Luther wished to defend his teaching on the Holy
Eucharist against Zwingli without having recourse to the
Catholic dogma of transubstantiation. He was not satisfied with saying, in conformity with the rules govern-
ing the Communication of Idioms, that "Christ is omnipresent," but falsified this true proposition by making it

Hormisdas and the Scythian monks
see H. Grisar, S. J., *History of
Rome and the Popes,* Vol. II, pp.
302 sqq., London 1912.

16 Denzinger-Bannwart, *Enchiridion,* n. 1463.

17 Cfr. Is. VI, 3; Apoc. IV, 8.
See Franzelin, *De Verbo Incarnato,*
p. 348, Rome 1910.

read: "Christ, as man, *i. e.,* according to His human nature, is omnipresent;" nay, he went so far as to assert that "the body of Christ is omnipresent." The early Lutheran divines treated this ludicrous theory as an article of faith and expounded it with a wealth of subtle distinctions; but in process of time its absurdity became so glaringly apparent that Ubiquitarianism was gradually dropped.[18]

Belief in the omnipresence of Christ's human nature, particularly His material body, is repugnant to common sense and to the teaching of Revelation. Holy Scripture treats the local circumscription (*ubicatio localis*) of the body of Christ both during His earthly pilgrimage[19] and after His glorious Resurrection,[20] as a matter of course. The mysteries of our Saviour's life which are proposed to us as articles of faith in the Apostles' Creed (such as, *e. g.,* His conception, His birth, His death, His burial, His descent into hell, His resurrection, etc.), would be utterly meaningless in the Ubiquist hypothesis. "*Unus idemque homo,*" says St. Fulgentius, "*localis ex homine, qui est Deus immensus ex Patre.*"[21] And the Second Council of Nicaea (A. D. 787) defines: "*Si quis Christum Deum nostrum circumscriptum[22] non confitetur secundum humanitatem,[23] anathema sit.*"[24]

READINGS: —* St. Thomas, *S. Theol.,* 3a, qu. 16, art. 1–12.— Billuart, *Summa S. Thomae, Tr. de Incarnatione,* diss. 16.—L. Janssens, *De Deo-Homine,* Vol. I, pp. 570 sqq., Friburgi 1901.—

18 Cfr. G. Esser in the *Kirchenlexikon,* 2nd ed. Vol. XII, *s. v.* "Ubiquitätslehre."

19 Cfr. Matth. XXVI, 11; John XI, 14–21, XVI, 28.

20 Cfr. Matth. XXVIII, 5 sq.; Mark XVI, 6; Luke XXIV, 51; Acts I, 11, III, 21; Heb. VIII, 1.

21 *Ad Trasam.,* II, 17.

22 περιγραπτόν.

23 κατὰ τὸ ἀνθρώπινον.

24 Denzinger-Bannwart, n. 30. For a detailed refutation of Ubiquitarianism see Bellarmine, *De Christo,* l. III, c. 9–20; L. Janssens, *De Deo-Homine,* Vol. I, pp. 611 sqq.; Tepe, *Instit. Theol.,* Vol. III, pp. 551 sqq.

The teaching of the Fathers is fully expounded by Petavius, *De Incarnatione*, IV, 15-16, and * Stentrup, *Christologia*, thes. 37 sqq., Oeniponte 1882.— Cfr. also Wilhelm-Scannell, *A Manual of Catholic Theology*, Vol. II, pp. 108 sqq., 2nd ed., London 1901.

ARTICLE 3

THE DIVINE SONSHIP OF CHRIST AS DEFINED AGAINST ADOPTIONISM

1. ADOPTIONISM AND THE CHURCH.—a) Towards the close of the eighth century, Archbishop Elipandus, of Toledo, and his disciple Felix, Bishop of Urgel in Catalonia, taught that there is a twofold filiation in Christ, and that, as man, He is not the natural, but only an adopted Son of God. The Adoptionists appealed to Holy Scripture, to the writings of Isidore of Sevilla, and to certain ambiguous phrases in the Mozarabic liturgy in support of their false teaching.

b) Contemporary theologians of the stamp of Beatus of Astorga, Agobard of Lyons, Paulinus of Aquileja, Richbod of Treves, and especially Alcuin, soon perceived that the doctrine of a twofold filiation involved the heresy of a double personality in Christ, and that, consequently, Adoptionism was merely a new form of Nestorianism. Pope Hadrian the First took the same view. In a dogmatic epistle (A. D. 785) he warned the Spanish bishops against the poisonous doctrines of Elipandus and his followers, "who do not blush to affirm that the Son of God is an adopted son,—a blasphemy which no other heretic has dared to enunciate, except the perfidious Nestorius, who claimed that the Son of God is a mere man." [1]   Adoptionism was solemnly condemned at a council held "by Apostolic authority" in Frankfort, A. D. 794.[2]

2. ADOPTIONISM REFUTED FROM DIVINE REVELATION. — Since Adoptionism is little more than a thinly veiled Nestorianism, it is scarcely necessary to enter into its refutation after what we have said against the latter heresy.[3]

Felix and Elipandus succeeded in veiling the heretical implications of their teaching by a dialectic device, which logic enables us to expose by means of the so-called supposition of terms.   " Even where we are dealing with one and the same univocal term, there are various ways in which it may be construed.   The same term may stand for something different." [4]   Thus, in the proposition: " Christ as man is the true and natural Son of God," the phrase " as man " may be construed as meaning " Christ according to His humanity," [5] or " Christ regarded as this particular man." [6]   In the last-mentioned case " this particular man " is identical with the Divine

1 Cfr. Denzinger-Bannwart, *Enchiridion*, n. 299.

2 Denzinger-Bannwart, n. 311 sqq. Cfr. H. K. Mann, *The Lives of the Popes in the Early Middle Ages*, Vol. I, Part II, pp. 439 sqq., London 1902. On the Neo-Adoptionism of Abélard and the qualified Adoptionism of certain later theologians see J. F. Sollier, art. " Adoptionism " in the *Catholic Encyclopedia*,

Vol. I. Cfr. also the *Kirchenlexikon*, 2nd ed., Vol. I, 242 sqq.

3 *Supra*, pp. 89 sqq.

4 G. H. Joyce, S. J., *Principles of Logic*, pp. 37 sq., London 1908.

5 = *secundum humanitatem.* This is what logicians call the *sensus formalis reduplicativus.*

6 = *ut hic homo.* This is technically called the *sensus specificativus.*

Hypostasis of the Logos, and thus understood the proposition is unexceptionable. But to assert, as the Adoptionists did, that "Christ [regarded as this particular
man] is the Son of God not by generation, but by adoption, not by nature, but by grace,"[7] is to assert the existence of two persons in Christ and to deny the Hypostatic
Union of the two natures. Hence the dogmatic principle: "Christ, regarded as this particular man, is not
an adoptive but the natural Son of God,"[8] is merely
an application of the doctrine of the Communication of
Idioms.

a) Adoptionism is unscriptural. The Bible
nowhere refers to Jesus as the adopted Son of
God, but consistently calls Him the true, the only-
begotten, and the only Son of God in the strict
sense of these terms.

When, *e. g.*, St. John speaks of "the only-begotten Son
of God who is in the bosom of the Father,"[9] he evidently
refers to Jesus. St. Paul, too, in teaching: God
"spared not even his own Son, but delivered him up for
us all,"[10] plainly says that the Person who was delivered
up was God's own (*i. e.*, natural) Son. And when
Jesus after His baptism emerged from the Jordan, the
voice of the Father spoke from heaven: "This is my
beloved Son, in whom I am well pleased."[11]

The Adoptionists appealed to Rom. I, 4: "Who was
predestinated the Son of God (ὁρισθέντος υἱοῦ Θεοῦ)."
He who is predestined to be the Son of God, they ar-

7 "*Christum* [*ut hunc hominem*]
*non genere esse Filium Dei, sed
adoptione, non naturâ, sed gratiâ.*"
Cfr. Denzinger-Bannwart, *Enchiridion*, n. 311.

8 "*Christus, ut hic homo, est
Filius Dei naturalis, non adoptivus.*"
9 John I, 18.
10 Rom. VIII, 32.
11 Matth. III, 17.

gued, cannot be the natural Son of God, but a son
by grace only, *i. e.*, by adoption. The majority of the
Greek Fathers,[12] however, do not interpret ὁρίζειν in the
sense of "predestine" (προορίζειν), but in the sense of
"show," "prove," "demonstrate," and they translate the
Pauline text as follows: "The Son of God was shown
(demonstrated, proved) to be such by His resurrection."
This interpretation is borne out by the context.[13]   But
even if we accept the word *"praedestinatus,"* which is
supported by the authority of the Vulgate, the Latin
Fathers, Irenæus, and Epiphanius, as a correct translation of ὁρισθέντος, Rom. I, 4 furnishes no argument
in favor of Adoptionism. The obvious meaning of the
text would then be: "The man Jesus was predestined
by the Hypostatic Union to be the natural Son of God."
Or, as St. Augustine puts it: "Jesus was predestined,
so that He who was to be the Son of David according
to the flesh, should yet be in power the Son of God."[14]
The notion that the only-begotten Son of God was predestined to be an adoptive son of His Father, is positively repugnant to the Christological teaching of St.
Paul.[15]

b) The earlier Fathers had implicitly rejected
Adoptionism in their teaching on the Hypostatic
Union.

a) Many relevant Patristic texts have been collected by
Alcuin in his *Liber adversus Haeresin Felicis.*[16]   St.

---

12 *E. g.*, St. Chrysostom, *Hom. in
Rom.*, II, n. 2.
13 Cfr. the commentary of Estius
upon this passage; also Suarez, *De
Incarn.*, disp. 50, sect. 2.
14 *"Praedestinatus est ergo Iesus,
ut qui futurus erat secundum car-*

*nem filius David, esset tamen in
virtute Filius Dei." (De Praedest.
Sanctor.*, XV, n. 31.)
15 Cfr. Pohle-Preuss, *The Divine
Trinity*, pp. 56 sqq.
16 Reprinted in Migne, *P. L.*, CI,
87 sqq.

Augustine appeals to the Bible. "Read, therefore, the Scriptures," he says, "nowhere will you find it said that Christ is a Son by adoption." [17] St. John of Damascus says in a recently discovered treatise against the Nestorians: "We confess, therefore, in regard to our Lord Jesus Christ, who is one of the Holy Trinity [that He has] two natures, each perfect according to its own definition and concept, lest we introduce a change or commixture, but only one hypostasis, lest we allow a duality of persons and a fourth person to slip into the Trinity. For the nature constitutes [not causally, but formally] another [being], while the hypostasis determines another [one and a] person." Professor Fr. Diekamp of Münster, to whom we are indebted for our knowledge of this treatise, comments on it as follows: "Damascene's purpose is to demonstrate the unity of the Divine Hypostasis. He begins by introducing one argument on which all others depend, namely, that the assumption of two hypostases in Christ would necessarily entail the assumption of a twofold sonship and of a fourth person in the Godhead." [18]

β) The only Patristic objection that can be urged against our dogma is drawn from the writings of St. Hilary. "*Potestatis dignitas non amittitur,*" he

17 *Contr. Secund. Manich.*, 5: "*Lege itaque Scripturas, nusquam invenies de Christo dictum, quod adoptione sit filius.*" Cfr. also his *Tract. in Ioa.*, VII, 4: "*Oportebat ergo ut ille baptizaret, qui est Filius Dei unicus, non adoptatus. Adoptati Filii ministri sunt unici; unicus habet potestatem, adoptati ministerium.*"

18 Here is the passage in the original Greek: "Ὁμολογοῦμεν τοιγαροῦν ἐπὶ τοῦ Κυρίου ἡμῶν Ἰησοῦ Χριστοῦ, τοῦ ἑνὸς τῆς ἁγίας τριάδος, δύο μὲν φύσεις, ἑκάστην τελείαν κατὰ τὸν ἑαυτῆς ὅρον τε καὶ λόγον, ἵνα μὴ τροπὴν ἢ σύγχυσιν εἰσάγωμεν, μίαν δὲ τὴν ὑπόστασιν, ἵνα μὴ δυάδα υἱῶν καὶ τέταρτον τῇ τριάδι παρεισενέγκωμεν πρόσωπον. ἡ μέν γὰρ φύσις ἄλλο ποιεῖ, ἡ δὲ ὑπόστασις ἄλλον καὶ πρόσωπον ἀφορίζει." Cfr. *Theologische Quartalschrift* (Tübingen), 1901, pp. 561 sqq. On the subject-matter of this paragraph the student may consult Petavius, *De Incarn.*, VII, 2 sqq.

says, "*dum carnis humilitas adoptatur.*" [19]   But, as St. Thomas points out, *adoptatur* in this passage can only refer to the union of Christ's human nature with the Person of the Divine Logos.[20]   This interpretation is in perfect accord with another passage from the same work where St. Hilary says: "*Multi nos filii Dei, sed non talis hic Filius; hic enim et verus et proprius est Filius, origine, non adoptione, veritate, non nuncupatione, nativitate, non creatione.*" [21]   It is indeed true that the Mozarabic liturgy contains such expressions as "*adoptio Christi*" and refers to Jesus as "*homo adoptivus*"; but it nowhere employs the term "*filius adoptivus,*" and the context shows that *adoptare* is used for *assumere, homo adoptivus* being therefore equivalent to *homo assumptus, i. e. incarnatus.*

3. THEOLOGICAL CONTROVERSIES.—The fundamental fallacy of Adoptionism is brought into clearer light by the Scholastic controversies which arose over two cognate questions, namely: (1) Is there room for a second filiation based on grace besides the natural sonship of Christ resulting from the Hypostatic Union? and (2) Is the Divine Sonship of Jesus Christ based on more than one title?

a) Durandus [22] and numerous Scotist theologians [23] admit that Jesus, as this specific man, was the natural

---

19 *De Trinit.*, II, 27. Other recensions have *adoratur* instead of *adoptatur.*

20 *S. Theol.*, 3a, qu. 23, art. 4, ad 4: "*Impropria est locutio, et accipitur ibi adoptatio pro unione humanae naturae ad personam Filii.*"

21 *De Trinit.*, III, 11.

22 *Comment. in Quatuor Libros Sent.*, III, dist. 4, qu. 1.

23 Scotus himself seems to have

and not merely an adopted Son of God,[24] but contend that there was room for a second filiation, parallel to the first, and resulting from grace. It is the essential function of sanctifying grace, they argued, to elevate him in whom it indwells to the state of adoptive sonship. But sanctifying grace indwelled in the human soul of Christ. Consequently, Christ, as man, is not only the natural Son of the Father, but also an adoptive Son of the Trinity. This view, while not identical with the Adoptionist heresy of Felix and Elipandus,[25] is false and dangerous. The same arguments which Pope Hadrian the First and the Council of Frankfort marshalled against Adoptionism can be effectively urged against Durandus' theory of Christ's adoptive sonship. Adoption is commonly defined with St. Thomas as "an act of grace by which a stranger is constituted or installed as son and heir." [26]   Therefore, " Christ cannot be called the adopted Son of God, except it be supposed that he is not one Person with the Logos, or that the Logos, by assuming human nature, lost His natural Sonship and became something foreign to God." [27] He who is by nature the Son of God, cannot become an adopted son by grace, because He already possesses more than the rights and privileges which adoption confers. Hence the Council of Frankfort says: *" Adoptivus dici non potest nisi is qui alienus est ab eo, a quo dicitur adoptatus,"* [28] *i. e.,* Adoption presupposes that the person to be adopted is not

been guilty of inconsistency in his treatment of this question.

[24] They were ignorant of the decision of the Council of Frankfort, but held its doctrine.

[25] As Vasquez asserts in his Commentary on the *Summa Theologica* of St. Thomas, p. 3, disp. 89.

[26] *" Adoptio est personae extraneae in filium et haeredem gratuita assumptio."* S. Theol., 3a, qu. 23, art. 1.

[27] Wilhelm-Scannell, *A Manual of Catholic Theology,* Vol. II, p. 128.

[28] Cfr. Hardouin, *Concil.,* IV, 875.

a son but a stranger to the adopting Father. It follows that Christ possessed sanctifying grace, which elevates men to the dignity of "children of God," merely as an ornament,[29] because, in the words of Suarez, He "was incapable of being adopted." [30] This idea is emphasized by the Council of Frankfort: "*Unde in Dei Filium non cadit nomen adoptionis, quia semper verus Filius, semper Dominus, ac per hoc et post assumptum hominem veri Filii vocabulum non amisit, qui numquam verus desiit esse Filius.*" [31]

Holy Scripture and the Fathers never predicate adoptive sonship of Christ. On the contrary, they accentuate the fact that, whereas men are children of God by law (*i. e.,* by adoption), Christ is the natural Son of God in the true and strict sense of the term.[32]

b) Suarez [33] and Vasquez [34] take a different view. They reject the idea of adoptive filiation and contend that as Christ's eternal γέννησις is inadequate to explain His Divine Sonship, there must be a secondary reason why, as man, He is the natural Son of God. This secondary reason, according to their theory, which they base on Heb. I, 2, is the state of grace proper to Christ, as man, by virtue of the Hypostatic Union. It is this state of grace which entails the "divine heritage." This supplementary divine filiation does not, however, rest on generation in the strict sense of the term, and hence Suarez and Vasquez are

---

29 *Ornatus.*

30 *De Incarn.,* disp. 49, sect. 2, n. 5.

31 See Hardouin, *Concil.,* IV, 877. Cfr. also De Lugo, *De Myst. Incarn.,* disp. 31, sect. 1.

32 Thus Cyril of Alexandria, *In Ioa.,* I, 12 (Migne, *P. G.,* LXXIII, 153): υἱοὶ δὲ ἡμεῖς κεκλήμεθα Θεοῦ κατὰ θέσιν καὶ κατὰ μίμησιν· κατὰ φύσιν ἄρα καὶ κατὰ ἀλήθειαν αὐτὸς — We have been called sons of God by adoption and imitation, but He [is the Son of God] in nature and truth." Cfr. Billuart, *De Incarn.,* diss. 21, art. 2, § 3.

33 *De Incarn.,* disp. 49, sect. 1 sq.

34 *Comment. in S. Th.,* III, disp. 89, c. 14.

constrained to admit two preposterous and indemonstrable corollaries: (1) that, side by side with natural filiation in Christ there exists another, which is figurative or analogical; and (2) that the man Jesus is the natural Son not only of the Father, but of the whole Blessed Trinity. Vasquez appeals to Pope Hadrian's remark that the exclamation " This is my beloved Son " proceeded from the whole Trinity, and not from the Father alone, and that it was addressed to Christ as man rather than as God. But Hadrian does not say that the Trinity addressed Christ as its Son; he merely says that it addressed Him as " Son of the Father," and was well pleased in Him as such. The idea of a secondary natural filiation based on Christ's humanity is as foreign to the Fathers as the notion of adoptive sonship which it entails. A secondary natural filiation in the strict sense can have its ontological cause only in generation by the Father; in a figurative and analogical sense it is equivalent to that adoptive sonship which is based upon human sanctity and divine inheritance, and which Suarez and Vasquez reject. If the concept of Christ's natural (divine) sonship be founded on something besides the relation of generation between Father and Son, the difficulties become labyrinthine. If the eternal γέννησις were not the only source of natural sonship in the Godhead, the Holy Ghost, too, might be called the natural Son of God, and Christ, as man, would be the natural son of the Holy Ghost, nay of the Logos, and consequently His own Son. To escape such absurdities it is necessary to hold that natural divine sonship is based solely on eternal generation and not on the fact that " Christ as man is sanctified and has a title to the divine inheritance." [35]   St. Thomas says: " Christus est Filius Dei secundum perfectam ra-

[35] Suarez, *l. c.,* sect. 2, n. 30.

tionem filiationis; unde quamvis secundum humanam na-
turam sit creatus et iustificatus, non tamen debet dici Fi-
lius Dei neque ratione creationis neque ratione iustifica-
tionis, sed solum ratione generationis aeternae, secundum
quam est Filius solius Patris.   Et ideo nullo modo debet
dici Christus Filius Spiritus S. nec etiam totius Trini-
tatis." [36]

The weakest point of the theory is the corollary, expressly admitted by Suarez, that Christ, as man, would
have to be called " the natural Son of the Trinity."   This
preposterous idea is opposed to the teaching of St. Augustine,[37] and especially to that of St. Fulgentius, who
says : *" Proinde non solum Iesum Christum filium Trini-*
tatis omnino non dicimus, sed etiam sic confitemur Iesum
Christum solius Dei Patris Filium, ut eum nullatenus
separemus.   Magnae quippe impietatis est, alium putare
Christum, alium Iesum Christum, quum unus sit utique
Dei et hominis Filius Iesus Christus, Filius scil. solius Pa-
tris, non totius utique Trinitatis." [38]   In vain do Suarez
and Vasquez urge that if the Father or the Holy Ghost
would become incarnate, either would thereby become
Son of God, *i. e.,* Son of the entire Trinity.   " Such a
man," retorts De Lugo, " would not be an adoptive son,
because he would not be a stranger, nor a natural son, because not produced by natural generation."   In virtue of
the Communication of Idioms the incarnate Father would
yet be none other than the Father, and the Holy Ghost
none other than the Holy Ghost, though in His human
nature each would appear as " Son of Man." [39]

36 *S. Theol.,* 3a, qu. 32, art. 3.
37 *Enchir.,* c. 38 sqq.
38 *Fragm. c. Fabian.,* c. 32.

39 De Lugo, *De Myst. Incarn.,*
disp. 31, sect. 3.

READINGS: — De Lugo, *De Mysterio Incarnationis,* disp. 31, sect. 1 sqq.— Enhuber, *Dissert. de Haeresi Adoptianorum* (Migne, *P. L.,* CI).— J. Bach, *Dogmengeschichte des Mittelalters,* Vol. I, pp. 102 sqq., Wien 1873.—* Hefele, *Konziliengeschichte,* 2nd ed., Vol. III, pp. 630 sqq., Freiburg 1877.— J. A. Ketterer, *Karl der Grosse und die Kirche,* München 1898.— K. Giannoni, *Paulinus II., Patriarch von Aquileja,* Wien 1896.— E. H. Limborgh, *Alcuinus als Bestrijder van het Adoptianisme,* Groningen 1901.— Alzog-Pabisch-Byrne, *Manual of Universal Church History,* Vol. II, pp. 174 sqq., Cincinnati 1899.— T. Gilmartin, *Manual of Church History,* Vol. I, 3rd ed., Dublin 1909.— Wilhelm-Scannell, *A Manual of Catholic Theology,* Vol. II, 2nd ed., pp. 126 sqq., London 1901.— H. K. Mann, *The Lives of the Popes in the Early Middle Ages,* Vol. I, Part II, pp. 439 sqq., London 1902.

THE ATTRIBUTES OF CHRIST ACCORDING TO HIS
HUMANITY

In consequence of the Hypostatic Union, Jesus Christ was more than an ordinary man. The divine element in Him, not as an inherent form (*forma inhaerens*) but *per modum effectus,* overflowed into His sacred humanity and conferred upon it an altogether unique dignity. (1) His will was distinguished by extraordinary ethical perfection or holiness; (2) His intellect commanded an unusual wealth of human knowledge; (3) His entire manhood with all its essential and integral constituents was and is worthy of divine adoration.

ARTICLE 1

THE ETHICAL PERFECTION OF CHRIST'S HUMAN WILL, OR
HIS HOLINESS

All that we have said in a previous treatise[1] of the ethical goodness or sanctity of God, applies to Christ in so far as He is God. In the present Article we are concerned only with the *human* holiness of our Lord, that

1 *God: His Knowability, Essence, and Attributes,* St. Louis 1911,
pp. 251 sqq.

is to say, the holiness of His created soul, or, more specifically, of one particular faculty of that soul, namely, His will. The formality of holiness, *i. e.,* the character wherein exactly it consists, is "exemption from sin combined with rectitude of moral conduct."[2] Bearing this definition in mind, we proceed to prove the holiness of Christ's humanity in a systematic series of theses, in which we shall bring out (1) the negative element of holiness, *i. e.,* sinlessness, and (2) its positive element, *i. e.,* moral purity.

Thesis I: Christ, as man, was exempt from original sin and concupiscence.

This thesis is of faith in both its parts.

Proof. Christ's freedom from original sin is defined in the *Decretum pro Iacobitis* of Pope Eugene IV (1439): *"Qui sine peccato conceptus, natus et mortuus humani generis hostem peccata nostra delendo solus suâ morte prostravit."*[3]

Freedom from original sin implies freedom from all the evil consequences thereof, especially from concupiscence (*fomes peccati*). *"Si quis defendit Theodorum impiissimum Mopsuestenum, qui dixit, alium esse Deum Verbum et alium Christum a passionibus animae et concupiscentiis carnis molestias patientem, talis anathema sit,"* says the Fifth General Council of Constantinople.[4]

---

2 *Ibid.*
3 Cfr. Denzinger-Bannwart, *Enchiridion,* n. 711.

4 Held A. D. 553. Cfr. Denzinger-Bannwart, *Enchiridion,* n. 224.

a) That Christ was actually and by right free from original sin appears from all those Scriptural texts which in general terms aver His sinlessness and impeccability, or specially emphasize the fact that He appeared in the flesh for the purpose of expiating the inherited guilt which weighed upon the human race. Had He been tainted by original sin, He would not have been the "lamb unspotted and undefiled," [5] nor would He have been able to take away "the sin of the world," [6] for the sin of the world is original sin, and it is impossible to assume that He who was destined to take away original sin was tainted by it Himself. For this reason St. Paul, who repeatedly ascribes to the Godman genuine "flesh," (*i. e.*, a human nature), never calls this flesh "sinful." Cfr. Rom. VIII, 3: "God sending his own Son, in the likeness of sinful flesh and of sin, hath condemned sin in the flesh." In drawing a parallel [7] between Adam, the first man, who was "of the earth, earthly," [8] and Christ, the second Adam, who was "from heaven, heavenly," [9] the Apostle virtually excludes original sin from the Godman; else the parallel would be absolutely meaningless.

[5] 1 Pet. I, 19: ἀμνὸς ἄμωμος καὶ ἄσπιλος. Cfr. Wilhelm-Scannell, *Manual,* Vol. II, pp. 132 sq.

[6] John I, 29: τὴν ἁμαρτίαν τοῦ κόσμου.

[7] 1 Cor. XV, 47. On this parallel see F. Prat, *La Théologie de Saint Paul,* Vol. II, pp. 261 sqq.

[8] ἄνθρωπος ἐκ γῆς χοϊκός.

[9] ἄνθρωπος ἐξ οὐρανοῦ.

The Fathers regarded Christ's freedom from original sin as a self-evident corollary flowing from His divine dignity and the origin of His human nature. As man no less than as God Christ is the natural Son of God, and to assert that He was conceived in original sin would be equivalent to affirming that the Divine Logos was tainted by sin. " God alone is without sin," says Tertullian, " and the only man without sin is Christ, because Christ is God." [10]   Another argument may be formulated thus: Original sin can be transmitted in no other way than by natural, *i. e.,* sexual generation. But Christ was conceived by the Holy Ghost and born of a virgin. Consequently He can not be tainted by original sin.[11]

b) If Christ was conceived without original sin, He must have been exempt from concupiscence (*fomes peccati*). This conclusion is so patent that even the heretics (Apollinarists and Monothelites, for instance) who denied Him intellect (νοῦς) and a human will (θέλησις), did not venture to charge Him with moral imperfection.

" If any one believe that the flesh of Christ lusted against the spirit," exclaims St. Augustine, " let him be anathema." [12]   The temptations of Christ recorded in

---

10 " *Solus Deus sine peccato, et solus homo sine peccato Christus, quia et Deus Christus.*" (*De Anima,* 41.)

11 " *Non enim in iniquitate conceptus est, quia non de mortalitate conceptus est. Nec eum in peccatis mater eius in utero aluit, quem virgo concepit, virgo peperit: quia fide concepit, fide suscepit. Ergo* ecce Agnus Dei. Non habet iste traducem de Adam; carnem tantum suscepit de Adam, peccatum non assumpsit. Qui non assumpsit de nostra massa peccatum, ipse est qui tollit nostrum peccatum.*" (St. Augustine, *Tr. in Ioa.,* IV, c. 1.)

12 " *Quisquis credit, carnem Christi contra spiritum concupivisse, anathema sit.*" (*Op. Imperf.,* IV,

Sacred Scripture were external occasions or suggestions
which did not elicit consent or delectation, but were
promptly repulsed ("Begone, Satan!"). "God who, by
becoming incarnate in the womb of the Virgin, had entered this world without sin, tolerated no contradiction in
Himself. While it was possible, therefore, for Him to
be tempted by suggestion, no sinful delectation ever entered His soul." [13]

Thesis II: Christ was free from all personal sin.

The truth embodied in this thesis is an article
of faith.

Proof. The actual sinlessness of our Lord
(*impeccantia*) is unquestionably an article of
faith. *"Si quis dicit,"* says the Council of Ephesus, *"et pro se obtulisse semetipsum oblationem
et non potius pro nobis solis—non enim eguit
oblatione, qui peccatum omnino nescivit,—anathema sit —* If any one assert that Christ sacrificed Himself for Himself, and not for us alone,
—for He who was absolutely free from sin had
no need of sacrifice—let him be anathema." [14]
The Council of Chalcedon calls Him "like unto
us in all things except sin." [15]

47.) Other Patristic texts in Petavius, *De Incarn.*, XI, 11.

13 St. Gregory the Great, *Hom.
in Ev.*, XVI (Migne, *P. L.*,
LXXVI, 1135). Cfr. also St.
Thomas, *S. Theol.*, 3a, qu. 15, art.
2; Suarez, *De Incarn.*, disp. 34,
sect. 2; De Lugo, *De Myst. Incarn.*,
disp. 26, sect. 4.

14 *Conc. Ephes.* (A. D. 431), can.
10. Cfr. Denzinger-Bannwart, *Enchiridion*, n. 122.

15 *" Per omnia nobis similem
absque peccato."* *Conc. Chalced.*
(A. D. 451). Cfr. Denzinger-Bannwart, n. 148.

Even without these plain ecclesiastical definitions the sinlessness of Christ would have to be received as a revealed dogma, because it is expressly taught in Holy Scripture. The prophet Isaias says of the coming Messiah: "He hath done no iniquity, neither was there deceit in his mouth," [16] and the Archangel Gabriel declares to the Virgin Mary: *"Quod nascetur ex te sanctum* [17] *vocabitur Filius Dei* — The Holy which shall be born of thee shall be called the Son of God." [18] St. Paul declares that Christ "knew no sin," and says [19] that, though He was "tempted in all things like as we are," [20] He yet remained "without sin." [21] In another place he describes our Lord as "holy, innocent, undefiled, separated from sinners." [22] No man ever dared to challenge his accusers as Jesus did according to the testimony of the fourth Evangelist. John VIII, 46: *"Quis ex vobis arguet me de peccato?* — Which of you shall convince me of sin?" His whole life was so pure that thousands have attained to sainthood by following Him. In fact, there is no other way of being delivered from blindness of heart than by "endeavoring to conform one's life wholly to the life of Christ." [23]

---

[16] Is. LIII, 9. Cfr. 1 Pet. II, 22: "Who did no sin, neither was there guile found in his mouth."

[17] τὸ γεννώμενον ἐκ σοῦ ἅγιον.

[18] Luke I, 35.

[19] Heb. IV, 15.

[20] καθ' ὁμοιότητα = similiter ac nos.

[21] χωρὶς ἁμαρτίας.

[22] "Sanctus, innocens, impollutus, segregatus a peccatoribus." (Heb. VII, 26.)

[23] Thomas à Kempis, *The Imita-*

Thesis III: Christ as man, was incapable of sinning.

This proposition is *fidei proxima*.

Proof. In our Second Thesis we proved Christ's sinlessness (*impeccantia*). We now proceed to demonstrate His impeccability (*impeccabilitas*), which the Vatican Council intended to define as an article of faith.[24]

Theologians are not fully agreed as to the true conception of Christ's "impeccability." We may distinguish three leading opinions. (1) The shallowest one, least in harmony with Catholic belief, is that held by Anton Günther, who, in order to safeguard Christ's free-will, maintained that He was impeccable because God foresaw from all eternity that He would never actually sin.[25] (2) Durandus, Scotus, and the Nominalists contended that our Lord's impeccability was founded, not on an intrinsic quality of His will, but on an extrinsic disposition of Divine Providence by which His will, which was in itself capable of committing sin, was prevented from yielding to temptation. This is what is called the theory of external impeccability.[26] Because of its consonance with the Scotistic doctrine of the impeccability of the Elect in Heaven,[27] this rather unsatisfactory theory is ex-

---

tion of Christ, Ch. 1. On the "Spiritual Sense of the Imitation" see Brother Azarias, *Phases of Thought and Criticism*, pp. 89 sqq., New York 1896. For the argument from Tradition the reader is referred to the Patristic texts quoted below in support of Thesis III.

24 Cfr. *Schema Constit. Vat. (Col-*

lectio Lacensis, VII, 560): "*Non solum non peccavit, sed nec peccare potuit.*"

25 This is called *impeccabilitas consequens*.

26 *Impeccabilitas externa*.

27 *Impeccabilitas beatorum*. Cfr. the dogmatic treatise on Eschatology.

pressly secured against theological censure by a decree of Paul V. (3) The third opinion is that of Peter Lombard,[28] adopted by St. Thomas,[29] and championed by his entire school as well as by all Jesuit theologians. It holds that Christ is impeccable by virtue of an intrinsic quality of the will resulting from the Hypostatic Union of the two natures. This is called *impeccabilitas interna.*

a) The Bible does not expressly teach the impeccability of our Divine Saviour, but the texts we have quoted in support of His sinlessness go far towards proving that He was incapable of sinning. The Fathers and the early councils of the Church unanimously uphold the impeccability of our Divine Redeemer and trace it to the Hypostatic Union.

St. Cyril of Alexandria, *e. g.,* says: " All those who maintain that Christ was able to commit sin — I know not how — are foolish and destitute of reason."[30] St. Augustine teaches that the Hypostatic Union makes it impossible for Christ to sin. "It was by this [the grace of God]," he says, "that a man, without any antecedent merit, was at the very moment of His existence as man so united in one person with the Word of God, that the very person who was Son of man was at the same time Son of God, and the very person who was Son of God was at the same time Son of man; and by the adoption of His human nature into the divine, the grace itself became in a way so natural to the man as to leave no room for the entrance of sin."[31] Similarly St. Leo

---

28 *Lib. Sent.,* III, dist. 12.
29 *S. Theol.,* 3a, qu. 15, art. 1.
30 *Anthropom.,* c. 23.

31 *Enchiridion* c. 40: ". . . *ut idem ipse esset Filius Dei qui filius hominis et filius hominis qui Filius*

the Great: "For we should not be able to vanquish the author of sin and death, were it not for the fact that our nature was assumed and appropriated by Him whom sin cannot sully and death cannot claim." [32] Fulgentius' teaching on this point is distinguished by extraordinary clearness. "The Godhead cannot be overcome," he says, "therefore also the humanity of Christ remained without sin, because it was assumed into the Godhead, which of its very nature is incapable of committing sin." [33] In conformity with the teaching of the Fathers the Sixth Ecumenical Council (680) defined: "*Sicut enim eius caro Dei Verbi dicitur et est, ita et naturalis carnis eius voluntas propria Dei Verbi* [34] *dicitur et est; . . . humana eius voluntas deificata* [35] *non est perempta, salvata est autem magis secundum deiloquum Gregorium dicentem: 'Nam illius velle, quod in Salvatore intelligitur, non est contrarium Deo, deificatum totum.'*" [36]

b) The theological reasons for Christ's impeccability are trenchantly set forth by St. Thomas as follows: "*Simpliciter loquendo Christus nunquam potuit peccare. Potest enim considerari ut viator vel ut comprehensor [scil. per visionem*

Dei: ac sic in naturae humanae susceptione fieret quodammodo ipsa gratia illi homini naturalis, quae nullum peccatum possit admittere." (Cfr. St. Augustine, *De Corr. et Grat.*, XI, 30; *De Praedest. Sanctor.*, XV, 30).

32 *Ep. Dogmat. ad Flavian.*, c. 2: "*Non enim superare possemus peccati et mortis auctorem, nisi naturam nostram ille susciperet et suam faceret, quam nec peccatum contaminare nec mors potuit detinere.*"

33 *Ad Trasam.*, III, 29: "*Deitas non potest superari; propterea utique etiam Christi humanitas sine peccato permansit, quia eam in unitate personae divinitas accepit, quae naturaliter peccare non novit.*"

34 θέλημα ἴδιον τοῦ Θεοῦ Λόγου.
35 θέλημα θεωθέν.

36 Cfr. Denzinger-Bannwart, *Enchiridion*, n. 291. Other proofs can be found in Petavius, *De Incarn.*, XI, 11; Vasquez, *Comment. in S. Th.*, III, disp. 61, c. 3; Suarez, *De Incarn.*, disp. 35, sect. 2.

beatificam] vel ut Deus. Ut viator quidem dux videtur esse dirigens nos secundum viam rectam; . . . secundum quod fuit comprehensor, mens eius totaliter est coniuncta fini. . . . Secundum autem quod fuit Deus, et anima et corpus eius fuerunt organum deitatis, . . . unde peccatum non poterat attingere ad eius animam, sicut nec Deus potest peccare." [37] Accordingly, the impeccability of Christ is based on these three grounds: (1) His mission as leader of the human race, (2) the fact that He always enjoyed the beatific vision, and (3) the Hypostatic Union of the two natures. Of these grounds the last is no doubt the strongest, in fact it is the only decisive one among the three. On this account the Fathers laid particular stress on the consideration that it would be just as reasonable to assume that the Godhead is capable of sinning as that the Logos should permit His human nature, which, in consequence of the Hypostatic Union, is entirely His own, to be tainted by even the slightest sin.

Durandus tried to weaken the force of this conclusion by objecting that sin is no more repugnant to the infinite holiness of the Logos than death is repugnant to His eternity. But it is contrary to Christian sentiment to say that the Logos, by virtue of the Communication of Idioms, is fully as capable of committing sin as

37 *Com. in Quatuor Libros Sent.,* III, dist. 12, qu. 2, art. 1.

He is of suffering and dying.   Passibility is no disgrace, but sin is.   Being a mere *malum poenae,* passibility may even, for the purposes of salvation, become a *bonum,* and as such be assumed into and sanctified by the Hypostatic Union.   Sin, on the other hand, being a *malum culpae,* is absolutely and under all circumstances repugnant to the holiness of God.   Hence there is no parity between death and sin.[38]

c) But if Christ could not sin, how can He be said to have had a free will?   And how was it possible for Him to take upon Himself suffering and death voluntarily in expiation of our sins? This is a serious difficulty; indeed De Lugo does not hesitate to call it one of the gravest problems of theology.[39]

Despite our inability fully to reconcile these two truths, we must uphold our Lord's free will as staunchly as the reality of His human nature.   Cfr. John X, 18: *"Sed ego pono eam* [*scil. animam*] *a meipso, et po-testatem habeo* [40] *ponendi eam* [*scil. moriendi*] *et potesta-tem habeo iterum sumendi eam: hoc mandatum* [41] *accepi a Patre meo* — But I lay it [*i. e.,* my life] down of my-self, and I have power to lay it down [*i. e.,* to die] ; and I have power to take it up again.   This commandment have I   received of my Father." [42]   St. Augustine teaches: "The spirit of the Mediator showed how it was through no punishment of sin that He came to the

38 Cfr. Tepe, *Instit. Theol.,* Vol. III, pp. 582 sqq.; Janssens, *De Deo-Homine,* I, pp. 666 sqq.; Franzelin, *De Verbo Incarnato,* thes. 43.

39 " *Una ex gravissimis theolo-giae.*"   (*De Myst. Incarn.,* disp. 26, sect. 2.)

40 ἐξουσίαν ἔχω.

41 ἐντολήν.

42 Cfr. Is. LIII, 7.

death of the flesh, because He did not leave it against His will, but because He willed, when He willed, as He willed." [43]

The difficulty of reconciling these two dogmas is well brought out by the following dilemma: In suffering for us, Christ, as man, either acted of His own free choice or not. If He was *not* free, His Passion lacked meritoriousness and therefore had no power to redeem us. If He *was* free, He was able to rebel against the commandment (*mandatum*) of the Father, *i. e.*, to sin. Consequently, it is necessary to deny either His free-will or His impeccability.

The Scholastics have suggested a variety of theories to escape this dilemma. Francis Amicus, S. J.,[44] enumerates no less than eleven different solutions, of which the eleventh can be formulated in seven different ways. In spite of this *embarras de richesse* no really satisfactory solution of the difficulty has yet been found. We shall briefly review the more probable suggestions.

a) One of the first attempts to solve the difficulty was made by Francis De Lugo (d. 1660). Though at first considered " singular," it subsequently obtained considerable renown through the authority of Petavius, Pallavicini, Velasquez, Riva, and others. De Lugo held that neither the free-will of Christ nor the meritoriousness of His passion and death was affected by the " commandment of the Father," because this commandment was not a " precept " [45] binding strictly under pain of sin, but purely a paternal " wish," [46] which the Son accepted of His own free choice, and which by this acceptance,

---

43 " *Demonstravit spiritus Mediatoris, quam nulla poena peccati usque ad mortem carnis accesserit, quia non eam deseruit invitus, sed quia voluit, quando voluit, quomodo* voluit." (*De Trinit.*, IV, 13, 16.)

44 Died 1651.

45 *Praeceptum.*

46 *Beneplacitum.*

with the consent of the Father, from a conditional became an absolute mode of redemption.[47]

This view seems to have been shared by St. Anselm.[48] What are we to think of it? The rules of sound exegesis will hardly permit us to regard the *mandatum Patris* as a mere *beneplacitum,* because throughout the New Testament *mandatum* (ἐντολή) is employed as a technical term to describe a strict precept.[49] Moreover, in enforcing the duty of obedience to God's commands, Christ never once makes an exception in His own favor. On the contrary, He expressly declares: "*Si praecepta mea* [50] *servaveritis, manebitis in dilectione mea, sicut et ego Patris mei praecepta* [51] *servavi, et maneo in eius dilectione* — If you keep my commandments, you shall abide in my love, as I also have kept my Father's commandments, and do abide in his love." [52] Our Divine Saviour Himself religiously practiced the virtue of obedience. Cfr. Phil. II, 8: "He humbled himself, becoming obedient unto death, even to the death of the cross." Obedience, in the words of St. Thomas, "is a special virtue, and its special object is a precept, tacit or expressed." [53] For these and other reasons De Lugo's theory is combated by the Thomists,[54]

---

47 "*Praeceptum illud et mandatum, quod Christo Pater edidisse dicitur, . . . non absolutum imperium videtur fuisse, sed simplex significatio consilii ac voluntatis suae, qua multa illi proponebat Pater ad humanam recuperandam salutem remedia: ex quibus quod vellet eligeret, adeo ut, quidquid ex omnibus capesseret, id sibi gratum esse ac placere monstraret.*" (Petavius, *De Incarn.,* IX, 8, 6.)

48 "*Non enim illi homini Pater, ut moreretur, cogendo praecepit, sed ille, quod Patri placiturum et homi-* nibus profuturum intellexit, hoc sponte fecit." (*Medit. de Redempt.,* XI.)

49 Cfr. Matth. V, 19, XXII, 36; John X, 18, XII, 49.

50 τὰς ἐντολάς μου.

51 τοῦ πατρός μου τὰς ἐντολάς.

52 John XV, 10.

53 "*Obedientia est specialis virtus et eius speciale obiectum est praeceptum tacitum vel expressum.*" (*S. Theol.,* 2a 2ae, qu. 104, art. 2.)

54 Cfr. Billuart, *De Incarn.,* diss. 18, art. 4, § 1.

15

the Scotists, and many Jesuit theologians, *e. g.,* Suarez, Vasquez, Gregory of Valentia, Toletus, John De Lugo,[55] Chr. Pesch, and Tepe.

β) A second theory for solving the difficulty was excogitated by Ysambert,[56] and adopted by Gregory of Valentia, Vasquez, and Lessius. Cardinal Franzelin regards it as equally probable with the one already discussed.[57] It may be summarized as follows: The Father (or the Blessed Trinity) enjoined upon the Son a rigorous precept to die, but the manner of its execution (time, place, motives, circumstances, etc.) was left to the Redeemer's own free decision. In other words: the "commandment" of the Father regarded only the substance of the atonement but left all accidental circumstances to the free determination of the Son. Or, in the technical language of the Schoolmen: While Christ's death was of strict precept *in genere,* not so its execution *in individuo.* But does not this theory unduly restrict the free will of our Blessed Redeemer by limiting it to the mode and circumstances of the divine command? Ysambert and his followers met this objection by asserting that the innumerable circumstances surrounding its execution were so intimately bound up with the command itself that substance and accidents were really inseparable. Did not the holy martyrs, too, die freely for the faith, though they were condemned to death? Under the circumstances they could not have escaped martyrdom, yet it is accounted to them as a meritorious deed and they are rewarded for it. This explanation has the advantage that it does not do violence

[55] Cardinal John De Lugo was a brother of P. Francis De Lugo. Both were eminent theologians and members of the Society of Jesus.

[56] *Comment. in S. Theol.,* III, qu. 18, disp. 2, art. 6.

[57] *De Verbo Incarnato,* thes. 44.

to the Biblical term *mandatum* (ἐντολή). Nevertheless it
is not altogether convincing. To assert that our Lord enjoyed freedom of choice only with regard to the concrete circumstances of His death, is tantamount to ad-
mitting that He was not free to die or not to die. But
Holy Scripture bases the value and meritoriousness of
His death upon the *substantia mortis* as well as upon its
modus.[58] Consequently this theory does not do full justice to the sense of Scripture. In the words of De Lugo:
"*Videtur non tribuendum Christo ad laudem, quod mortuus fuerit simpliciter et absolute . . . nec redemisse
homines, quia mortuus, sed quia tunc vel libentius vel ex
tali motivo mortuus fuerit.*"[59] In spite of these objections, however, Ysambert's theory is not altogether devoid
of probability.

γ) A third theory destined to reconcile free-will and
impeccability in Christ is that of the early Schoolmen. They held that the human will of our Divine
Saviour, though physically able to commit sin, attained
impeccability by a continuous series of actual graces
and was determined to a free though infallibly certain
acceptation of the decree involving His death by one
special grace of particular strength and effectiveness.
Impeccability thus conceived, *i. e.*, in consonance with
free-will, is called "confirmation in grace" (*confirmatio
in gratia*). We may suppose it to have been the happy
lot of the Blessed Virgin also. St. Bonaventure explains the process thus: "*Determinatio potentiae ad
unum potest esse dupliciter, vid. per necessitatem naturae et per confirmationem gratiae. Si sit per necessitatem naturae, tunc tollit arbitrii libertatem ac per hoc
tollit dignitatem meriti. Si autem sit determinatio per*

<hr>

[58] Cfr. Is. LIII, 10; Phil. II, 8;   [59] *De Mysterio Incarn.*, disp. 26,
Heb. XII, 2.   sect. 7.

*confirmationem gratiae, quum talis confirmatio simul stet
cum libera voluntate, sic non tollit ab ipso opere boni-
tatem moris, quum sit voluntarium, ac per hoc nec quali-
tatem meriti. In Christo autem fuit liberum arbitrium
determinatum ad unum non per necessitatem naturae,
sed per confirmationem gratiae."* [60] Among the later
Scholastics this particular theory was adopted by Molina,[61]
Suarez,[62] Lessius, and Tanner. Its leading defenders at
the present time are Cardinal Billot [63] and Chr. Pesch.[64]
Though it is sufficiently plausible, most other theologians
reject this theory, (1) because it were preposterous to admit that it was physically possible for Christ, who was the
Divine Logos, to commit sin, and (2) because to explain Christ's impeccability otherwise than by the Hypostatic Union and the beatific vision, is equivalent to
basing it on an inferior principle which might be applied to any saint. Against the former objection some
advocates of this theory contend that, as the physical liberty of committing sin is an essential attribute of every
rational creature, it cannot be a reprehensible defect, and
therefore is not repugnant to the Hypostatic Union,
provided, of course, that the necessary measures be
taken to prevent the power to sin from ever effectuating
a sinful act under any circumstances. Of such necessary measures, they add, "confirmation in grace" is the
first and most effective. But this explanation is hardly
tenable. It is far easier to refute the second objection.
"Confirmation in grace" is really nothing else than a
necessary effect of the Hypostatic Union, which postulates with metaphysical necessity that the human will of

60 *Comment. in Quatuor Libros Sent.*, III, dist. 18, art. 1, qu. 2, ad 1.

61 *Concord.*, disp. 53, membr. 4.

62 *De Incarn.*, disp. 37, sect. 3.

63 *De Verbo Incarn.*, thes. 28.

64 *Praelect. Dogmat.*, Vol. IV, pp. 180 sqq.

Christ be endowed with intrinsic impeccability by all moral means at the command of an omnipotent God.[65]

δ) There is a fourth theory which tries to harmonize the dogma of our Lord's free-will with that of His impeccability by asserting that He could have obtained from His Heavenly Father at any time a revocation of, or a dispensation from the rigorous mandate which commanded Him to die for the salvation of mankind. This theory is based mainly on Matth. XXVI, 53: *"An putas quia non possum rogare Patrem meum et exhibebit mihi modo plus quam duodecim legiones angelorum?* — Thinkest thou that I cannot ask my Father, and he will give me presently more than twelve legions of angels?"* Though Pallavicini boasts of having publicly combated this opinion of his famous master De Lugo during the latter's life-time in Rome, it has yet found many adherents, among them Maurus Hurtado, Carleton, Mayr, Legrand, and more recently Tepe.[66] We are inclined to think that it effectively safeguards both the free-will and the impeccability of Christ. A precept remains in force so long as the lawgiver does not dispense from it. On the other hand, to employ De Lugo's own words, *"non potest maior libertas excogitari, quam ita acceptare mortem, ut posset non solum tunc, sed nunquam eam acceptare, . . . quia licet haberet praeceptum, poterat Christus impetrare facile ablationem praecepti."* [67]

---

[65] For a refutation of the difficulties arising from the Saviour's impeccability as a result of the beatific vision, see Chr. Pesch, *Praelect. Dogmat.*, Vol. IV, pp. 187 sqq. As regards the nature and properties of the efficacious graces which condition, and ultimately effect, the state of "confirmation in grace," they are differently explained by the Thomists and the Molinists. We shall discuss this question more fully in our treatise on Grace. Cfr. also Billuart, *De Incar.*, diss. 18, art. 4, § 2; Gonet, *De Div. Verbi Incarn.*, disp. 21, art. 3, n. 85; Bellarmine, *De Iustific.*, V, 11.

[66] *Instit. Theolog.*, Vol. III, pp. 599 sqq.

[67] *De Myst. Incarn.*, disp. 26, sect. 8, n. 103.

To this theory Velasquez, Chr. Pesch, and others oppose the following dilemma: " Either the *mandatum mortis* was an unconditional or it was a conditional command; if it was unconditional, no dispensation was possible; if it was conditional, no dispensation was needed." But, as De Lugo [68] triumphantly shows against Velasquez, this argument proves too much and therefore proves nothing. *Positive* precepts, whether given to a community (as, *e. g.,* monogamy) or to an individual (as, *e. g.,* the command to Abraham to sacrifice his son), are never essentially irrevocable or indispensable. [69]

Thesis IV: The human nature of Christ, in virtue of the Hypostatic Union, was and is substantially sanctified by the increate holiness of the Divine Logos.

This thesis is held by nearly all theological schools.

Proof. By substantial sanctity we do not understand sanctifying grace, [70] but that peculiar holiness which was effected in the human soul of Christ by its incorporation with the Divine Logos in the Hypostatic Union. The only school of theologians who demur to this thesis are the Scotists. They assert that the holiness of Christ was accidental, *i. e.,* solely due to sanctifying grace. [71] Because of this Scotistic opposition our thesis cannot be qualified as a theological conclusion,

68 *Op. cit.,* sect. 9.

69 For a refutation of certain other objections raised against this theory we must refer the student to G. B. Tepe, *Institutiones Theol.,*

Vol. III, pp. 599 sqq.

70 *Sanctitas accidentalis.*

71 Cfr., *e. g.,* Fr. Henno, *Theol. Dogmat.,* disp. 14, qu. 1, art. 1 sq.

but is merely *communis* in the technical sense of
the term.

Under the rules which govern the Communication of
Idioms,[72] the "increate sanctity" of the Logos appears
to be as intransferable as His immensity or omnipotence.
Why, then, do Catholic theologians, who reject the
Lutheran doctrine of ubiquity,[73] make an exception in
favor of the attribute of sanctity? We shall try to
explain this seeming inconsistency.

It is true that the divine sanctity of the Logos is no
more capable of being transferred to a mere creature
than any other divine attribute. On the other hand, however, the manhood united with the Logos, by the very
fact of becoming "the second nature" of one of the
Three Divine Persons, must be infinitely pleasing to
God, and, consequently, infinitely holy, even in the hypothesis that it were not endowed with sanctifying grace.
By virtue of the Hypostatic Union the man Jesus is the
natural Son of God,[74] in whom the Father must be
infinitely well pleased. But He could not possibly be
well pleased in one who lacked holiness.[75] Consequently,
the man Jesus, irrespective of His being or not being endowed with sanctifying grace, is substantially holy by
virtue of His Hypostatic Union with the Logos, who is
substantial sanctity. Thus holiness is the only divine attribute which is substantially communicable to a creature.

---

72 *V. supra*, pp. 187 sqq.

73 *V. supra*, pp. 194 sq.

74 *V. supra*, pp. 196 sqq.

75 "*Alia vero coniunctio est hominis ad Deum non solum per affectum aut inhabitationem [= acci-
dentaliter], sed etiam per unitatem
hypostasis seu personae, ut scil. una
et eadem hypostasis seu persona sit*

*Deus et homo. Et haec quidem
coniunctio hominis ad Deum est
propria Iesu Christi . . . et gratis-
simum Deo facit, ita quod de ipso
singulariter dicatur: Hic est Filius
meus dilectus, in quo mihi com-
placui.*" (St. Thomas Aquinas,
Comp. Theol., c. 222.)

But does not such a substantial communication of a divine attribute entail Monophysitic or Pantheistic assumptions? It does not. First, because sanctity in a human being involves only an ethical relation towards God, and, secondly, whereas the infinite sanctity of the Logos is held to be communicable to the creature, it is not held to be communicable in an infinite manner. For, as Suarez justly observes, "the grace of union is infinite in its kind and renders human nature infinitely pleasing [to God], though not in an equal measure with Divinity. Divinity is pleasing in itself, humanity merely by its union with Divinity, and consequently Divinity is infinite in the strict sense of the term, whereas humanity is infinite only under a certain respect." [76]

a) That Jesus, as man, was substantially sanctified by his Hypostatic Union with the Divine Logos can be demonstrated from Sacred Scripture. Cfr. Luke I, 35: "*Quod nascetur ex te sanctum, vocabitur Filius Dei* — The Holy which shall be born of thee [Mary], shall be called the Son of God." Here Christ's divine sonship is given as the ontological reason why He was sanctified in the womb of His mother. It follows that the man Jesus was holy because he was the Son of God. Now, divine sonship depends upon the Hypostatic Union as an indispensable condition. Consequently, the Hypostatic Union

[76] "*Gratia unionis est in suo genere infinita et reddit humanitatem infinite gratam, licet non aeque atque est grata divinitas ipsa; quia haec est grata per essentiam, illa per unionem, unde illa est infinita simpliciter, haec secundum quid.*" (Suarez, *De Incarn.*, disp. 22, sect. 1, n. 22.) Cfr. Chr. Pesch, *Praelect. Dogmat.*, Vol. IV, pp. 140 sq.

alone was sufficient to sanctify the humanity of Christ.

St. Paul, referring to the Messianic Psalm XLIV, verse 8, compares Christ's substantial sanctity with the anointment of His humanity with Divinity: *"Propterea unxit te Deus, Deus tuus,*[77] *oleo exultationis prae participibus tuis* — Therefore God, thy God, hath anointed thee with the oil of gladness above thy fellows." [78] Origen comments on this text as follows: " Just as the substance of an ointment is something different from its odor, so Christ is different from His fellows (*i. e.*, the prophets and Apostles). And as a receptacle containing the substance of an ointment can nowise assume an evil smell, whereas those who go too far away from its odor can contract an evil smell (*i. e.*, by sin), so it was utterly impossible for Christ, as the vessel in which the substance of the ointment was contained, to contract the odor of sin." This interpretation of the forty-fourth Psalm is quite common. Thus St. Ambrose writes: *"Deus est qui ungit, et Deus qui secundum carnem ungitur Dei Filius. Denique quos habet unctionis suae Christus nisi in carne participes? Vides igitur quia Deus a Deo unctus est; sed in assumptione naturae unctus humanae Dei Filius designatur."* [79] The same thought is expressed somewhat more tersely by St. Gregory of Nazianzus: " God the Father anointed Christ with the oil of joy above all His fellows, when He united the human nature with the Godhead, in order to make them both into one." [80]

The argument for our thesis may be effectively condensed into the formula: *Unio hypostatica = unctio substantialis = sanctificatio substantialis.*

---

[77] ἔχρισέ σε ὁ Θεός, ὁ Θεός σου.
[78] Heb. I, 9.
[79] Orig., *De Princ.*, II, 6; Ambr.,
De Fide ad Gratian., I, 3 (Migne, P. L., XVI, 556).
[80] *Orat.*, V, *sub fin.*

b) The name "Christ," though used in a figurative sense, admirably describes the essential constitution of the Godman. Χριστός is derived from χρίειν, "to anoint," and designates our Lord as the Anointed, *unctus,* in a special and pre-eminent sense.

Describing as it does not merely the Son of God, nor yet merely the Son of man, but the Godman (θεάνθρωπος) as such, "Christ" is truly a proper and personal name. In the Old Testament priests,[81] kings,[82] and prophets,[83] were consecrated with holy oil, and thereby became accidentally "anointed of the Lord." Christ, who unites in His Person the three offices of priest, king, and prophet, is alone of all men anointed with an anointment formally substantial, because the invisible ointment of the Divinity, namely, the Divine Substance itself, permeates and perfects His human nature in virtue of the Hypostatic Union.

The Fathers are unanimous in interpreting the name "Christ" in this personal sense. "We call 'Christ' a personal name," says, *e. g.,* St. John of Damascus, "because it is not assumed one-sidedly, but designates a twofold nature. For He Himself anointed Himself: as God, He anointed His body with His Divinity; as man, He received anointment, since He is both God and man."[84] The human nature thus substantially anointed with Divinity must needs be substantially holy. For, as Nazianzen puts it, "[*Filius*] *dicitur Christus propter divinitatem; haec enim est unctio humanitatis, non sanctificans operatione, ut in aliis Christis, sed totius ungentis*

81 Cfr. Lev. IV, 3.
82 Cfr. Is. XLV, 1; Ps. CIV, 15.
83 Cfr. 3 Kings XIX, 15 sqq.
84 *De Fide Orthodoxa,* III, 3 (Migne, *P. G.,* XCIV, 990).

praesentiâ, cuius effectus est, ut qui ungit dicatur homo et ut quod ungitur faciat Deum." [85]   Or, in the words of St. Augustine: *" In quo [scil. Verbo] et ipse Filius hominis sanctificatus est ab initio creationis suae, quando Verbum factum est caro, quia una persona facta est Verbum et homo. Tunc ergo sanctificavit se in se, hoc est, hominem se in Verbo se, quia unus Christus Verbum et homo, sanctificans hominem in Verbo."* [86]

c) The Hypostatic Union does not, however, communicate to the soul of Christ formally and substantially that " love which God has for Himself," and which is a vital immanent act of the Divine Trinity and constitutes the innermost essence of divine holiness.[87]   God's intrinsic essence is as incommunicable to creatures as the vital act by which He knows Himself.[88]   What is substantially and formally communicable is the so-called objective holiness of God, *viz.:* the dignity, majesty, and adorableness of the Logos, which mediately effects the moral sanctity of the man Jesus, making him not only *sacrum* (ἱερόν), but *sanctum* (ἅγιον).[89]   On this ineffable and infinite dignity of the Godman is based both the adorability of Christ's humanity and the infinite meritoriousness of all the free acts which His soul inspired.

Does the sanctity of Christ's human nature consist formally in the Personality of the Logos, or in His Divinity, or in both?   This is a subtle problem, concern-

85 *Or.*, 30, n. 21 (Migne, *P. G.*, XXXVI, 132).

86 *Tract. in Ioa.*, 108, n. 3.   Cfr. Petavius, *De Incarn.*, XI, 8 sq.   On the meaning of the name Christ cfr. Scheeben, *Dogmatik*, Vol. II, § 222, Freiburg 1878; L. Janssens, *De Deo-Homine*, Vol. I, pp. 637 sqq., Friburgi 1901; Ph. Friedrich, *Der Christus-Name im Lichte der* *alt- und neutestamentlichen Theologie*, Köln 1905.

87 Cfr. Pohle-Preuss, *God: His Knowability, Essence, and Attributes*, pp. 423 sqq.

88 Cfr. Pohle-Preuss, *op. cit.*, pp. 113 sqq.

89 Cfr. Scheeben, *Dogmatik*, Vol. II, p. 160.

ing which theologians are not agreed. The more common opinion (St. Thomas, Suarez, and De Lugo) is that the substantial sanctity of Christ's manhood is formally communicated to it by the *Personality* of the Logos, which incorporates itself immediately and formally with His humanity in the Hypostatic Union. Others maintain that since the Person of the Logos is the possessor and bearer of His Divine Nature, the *Divinity* of the Logos must be regarded at least as the mediate *forma sanctificans* of His humanity. A third theory assumes that the Godhead, abstracted from its bearer, *i. e.,* the Logos, is the immediate and formal *forma sanctificans*. But this absurd and impossible hypothesis involves the danger of degrading the Hypostatic Union to the level of a mere natural synthesis. Vasquez no doubt felt this, for he refrained from pushing his thesis *" Formam sanctificantem esse ipsam deitatem "* [90] to its last conclusions. He based it on such Patristic expressions as *" deificatio "* and *" unctio humanitatis per divinitatem,"* which Scheeben [91] interprets as follows: The phrases " Deification " and " Anointment of humanity with Divinity " describe the divine nature or substance of the Logos in the sense of St. Cyril, *i. e.,* the divinely spiritual nature of the Logos as the formal principle of sanctification, without separating Personality and Nature, which are so intimately united in the Logos that both together penetrate and perfect His human nature.[92]

Thesis V: Besides the substantial sanctity resulting from the " grace of union," the human soul of our Lord also possessed an accidental holiness which,

though not actually infinite, was by far the most perfect created in the present economy.

This proposition is theologically certain.

Proof.   By accidental or created (in contradistinction to substantial) holiness we understand primarily the state of sanctifying grace.[93]

Being a creature, the soul of Christ was incapable of an actually infinite sanctity; yet, by virtue of the Hypostatic Union, it was endowed with a superabundance of grace, greater than any other conceivable in the present economy.

Theologians are at variance as to the degree of certainty to be attributed to our present thesis.   Suarez holds it to embody an article of faith, or at least a doctrine which it is morally certain that the Church acknowledges as divinely revealed (*fidei proximum*), while Vasquez, Petavius, and De Lugo[94] regard it merely as a theologically certain deduction.   All agree in attributing the moral necessity of the existence of superabundant grace in Christ, not to a positive decree of God, nor to the merits of Christ's human soul, but to the Hypostatic Union.   The soul of our Lord, in consequence of its personal union with the Logos, was endowed with the greatest measure of grace which in the present economy God can bestow on any creature.   Though in its last analysis due to the "grace of union," and therefore supernatural in character, the plenitude of grace with which the soul of Christ was endowed was connatural to, *i. e.*, a moral postulate of His nature.

---

[93] *Gratia habitualis sive sanctificans.* It will be treated in the seventh volume of this series of dogmatic text-books, on *Grace, Actual and Habitual.*

[94] *De Myst. Incarn.*, disp. 16, sect. 5, n. 91.

a) The Scriptural argument for our thesis is mainly based on John I, 14 sqq.: *"Et Verbum caro factum est et habitavit in nobis . . . plenum gratiae et veritatis. . . . Et de plenitudine eius nos omnes accepimus et gratiam pro gratia* [95]— And the Word was made flesh, and dwelt among us . . . full of grace and truth . . . and of his fulness we all have received, and grace for grace."

The "Word Incarnate," *i. e.*, the Godman, is here described as "full of grace" [96] in specifically the same sense in which we are said to have received from His fulness "grace for grace." In other words, there is no qualitative difference between the grace of the Giver and the grace of those who receive — the two are absolutely homogeneous. Now, the grace which man receives from his Redeemer is primarily sanctifying grace or justification. Consequently the soul of Christ must have been endowed with this same grace, and with such a fulness [97] thereof that all who were redeemed by Him, severally and together (including the Blessed Virgin, who was so singularly endowed), can participate in, without ever exhausting it. [98] It will not do to say that John I, 14 could, without straining, be applied to the mere *gratia unionis, i. e.*, substantial sanctification. The *gratia unionis* is not homogeneous with the *gratia iustificatorum,* and consequently cannot be the immediate fount from which the justified draw. Whenever the Bible speaks

---

[95] καὶ ἐκ τοῦ πληρώματος αὐτοῦ ἡμεῖς πάντες ἐλάβομεν, καὶ χάριν ἀντὶ χάριτος.

[96] *Plenus gratiae,* πλήρης χάριτος.

[97] Plenitudo, πλήρωμα.

[98] Cfr. Maldonatus' exposition of the text, John I, 14.

of a plenitude of grace, it always means *created* grace,[99] whereas it defines the "grace of union," which results in substantial holiness, as "the fulness of the Godhead." Cfr. Col. II, 9: "*Quia in ipso inhabitat omnis plenitudo divinitatis* [100] *corporaliter* — For in Him dwelleth all the fulness of the Godhead corporeally." Then there are a number of Scriptural texts in which Christ, as man, is said to be "anointed with Divinity" (= *gratia unionis*), and also "with the Holy Ghost" (= *gratia sanctificans*), the latter anointment evidently presupposing the former. Isaias says of the future Messias: "*Egredietur virga de radice Iesse . . . et requiescet super eum Spiritus Domini, Spiritus sapientiae et intellectus, etc.*— And there shall come forth a rod out of the root of Jesse . . . and the Spirit of the Lord shall rest upon him: the spirit of wisdom, etc." [101] With this passage compare another by the same prophet: "*Spiritus Domini super me, eo quod unxerit Dominus me* — The spirit of the Lord is upon me, because the Lord hath anointed me," [102] and Acts X, 38: "*Quomodo unxit eum Deus Spiritu Sancto* [103] *et virtute* — How God anointed him with the Holy Ghost, and with power." Whenever Scripture says of an ordinary mortal that "he was anointed with the Holy Ghost," or "the Holy Ghost rests upon him," the meaning is that the person in question was endowed with supernatural graces, of which the chief is sanctifying grace, both on its own account and because it is the condition and foun-

99 Cfr. Luke I, 28: "And the angel being come in, said unto her [Mary]: Hail, full of grace." Acts VI, 8: "And Stephen, full of grace and fortitude, did great wonders and signs among the people."

100 πᾶν τὸ πλήρωμα τῆς θεότητος.
101 Is. XI, 1 sqq.
102 Is. LXI, 1 sqq.
103 ὡς ἔχρισεν αὐτὸν ὁ Θεὸς πνεύματι ἁγίῳ.

dation of the " seven gifts of the Holy Ghost." Since the Bible employs the same terms in respect of our Divine Saviour,[104] the soul of Christ cannot be conceived as devoid of sanctifying grace. In other words, our Lord possessed created or accidental in addition to substantial holiness.

b) Among the numerous Patristic texts which theologians are accustomed to quote in support of this thesis, we can admit as really convincing only those that draw a clear-cut distinction between created holiness and the " grace of union," and expressly attribute both to the soul of our Lord.

St. Cyril of Alexandria says: " Christ sanctifies Himself, since as God He is holy by nature, but according to His humanity He is sanctified together with us, in that . . . He does not hesitate to call us His brethren."[105] St. Chrysostom asserts both the existence and the superabundance of sanctifying grace in our Divine Redeemer. " The full measure of grace," he says, " has been poured out over that Temple [i. e., Christ]. For He doth not dispense grace according to measure. We have received of His fulness, but that Temple hath received the complete measure of grace. This is what Isaias meant when he said: [The Spirit of the Lord] shall rest upon him, etc. In Him is all grace, in men but a small measure, a drop of that grace."[106] St. Augus-

104 Cfr., e. g., Luke IV, 18: " Spiritus Domini super me, propter quod unxit me — The Spirit of the Lord is upon me, wherefore he hath anointed me."

105 Dial. De SS. Trinit., 6 (Migne, P. G., LXXV, 1018).

106 In Ps., 44, 2. The passage in Isaias referred to by Chrysostom is XI, 2.

tine beautifully expounds the Scriptural texts which
we have adduced above as follows: "The Lord Jesus
Christ Himself not only *gave* the Holy Spirit as God,
but also *received* it as man, and therefore He is said
to be full of grace [107] and of the Holy Spirit.[108] And
in the Acts of the Apostles it is still more plainly written
of Him, 'Because God anointed Him with the Holy
Spirit.' [109] Certainly not with visible oil, but with the
gift of grace, which is signified by the visible ointment
wherewith the Church anoints the baptized." [110]

St. Thomas Aquinas says: "*Necesse est ponere in
Christo gratiam habitualem propter tria: primo quidem
propter unionem animae illius ad Verbum Dei, . . .
secundo propter nobilitatem illius animae, . . . tertio
propter habitudinem ipsius Christi ad genus humanum.
Christus enim, inquantum homo, est mediator Dei et hominum, ut dicitur 1 Tim. 2; et ideo oportebat quod haberet
gratiam etiam in alios redundantem secundum illud Io. 1,
16: De plenitudine eius omnes accepimus, et gratiam
pro gratia.*" [111] Of these three reasons the first, which is
based on the Hypostatic Union, is the most important:
"*Ex ipsa igitur unione naturae humanae ad Deum in
unitate consequens est, ut anima Christi donis gratiarum
habitualibus prae ceteris fuerit plena; et sic habitualis
gratia in Christo non est dispositio ad unionem, sed magis
unionis effectus.*" [112]

[107] John I, 14.
[108] Luke XI, 52, IV, 1.
[109] Acts X, 38.
[110] Aug., *De Trinit.*, XV, 26, 46: "*Dominus ipse Iesus Spiritum S. non solum dedit ut Deus, sed etiam accepit ut homo; propterea dictus est plenus gratiâ (Io. 1, 14) et Spiritu Sancto (Luc. 11, 52; 4, 1). Et manifestius de illo scriptum est in Actibus Apostolorum: quoniam*

unxit eum Deus Spiritu Sancto (Act. 10, 38). Non utique oleo visibili, sed dono gratiae, quod visibili significatur unguento, quo baptizatos ungit Ecclesia." Other Patristic texts quoted by Petavius, *De Incarn.*, XI, 6.

[111] *S. Theol.*, 3a, qu. 7, art. 1.
[112] *Comp. Theol.*, c. 214. For a more elaborate treatment see Suarez, *De Incarn.*, disp. 18, sect. 2.

16

c) In this connection theologians are wont to discuss the following questions: (α) When was the fulness of sanctifying grace infused into the human soul of Christ? and (β) Was that soul also endowed with other supernatural prerogatives, such as the theological virtues? The former question is suggested by Luke II, 52: "And Jesus advanced in wisdom, and age, and grace with God and men." The latter arises from a comparison between Christ and justified man. (γ) A third question, the most important of all, has to do with the so-called "grace of headship" (*gratia capitis*).

α) All theologians are agreed that, as the fulness of sanctifying grace was included in the "grace of union," the accidental sanctification of the soul of Christ must have exactly coincided with the moment of the Hypostatic Union, *i. e.,* with the instant of His conception.[113]

From this teaching not even St. Bonaventure dissents, though he holds the peculiar view that for the soul of our Divine Lord the state of grace was a " preparation " or *debita dispositio* for, rather than an effect of, the Hypostatic Union. No matter whether it be regarded as a preparation or an effect, unless we admit that the " fulness of grace " was from the very beginning a relatively infinite entity incapable of increase, we shall be compelled to assent to the absurd conclusion that the Hypostatic Union exercised a stronger influence over

the soul of Christ in later life than at the moment of
His conception. These considerations furnish us with
a key to the proper interpretation of Luke II, 52: *"Et
Iesus proficiebat* [114] *sapientiâ et aetate et gratiâ* [115] *apud
Deum et homines* — And Jesus advanced in wisdom,
and age, and grace with God and men." He who from
the very beginning possessed the fulness of created grace
could not advance in interior holiness. Christ was
equally holy as a babe and as an adult man. The exercise of virtue, therefore, could not merit for Him an increase of sanctifying grace, as is the case with us, but
merely greater extrinsic glory for Himself and additional favors for us. The Fathers and theologians explain His advance in wisdom and grace not as an increase in, but merely as an outward manifestation of
sanctifying grace.[116] But why does Sacred Scripture
say that He advanced in wisdom and grace, as He advanced in age, *with God?* [117] Because the works of wisdom which he performed, and His diligent co-operation
with actual grace, by means of which His holiness gradually became manifest to His fellow-men, were meritorious and pleasing in the eyes of God.

β) In the ordinary process of justification the
infusion of sanctifying grace is accompanied
by other supernatural prerogatives, *viz.:* the

---

114 προέκοπτεν.

115 χάριτι.

116 προκοπὴ κατὰ φανέρωσιν.
Cfr. St. Thomas, *S. Theol.*, 3a, qu.
7, art. 12, ad 3: "*Aliquis potest
proficere dupliciter. Uno modo secundum ipsos habitus sapientiae et
gratiae augmentatos; et sic Christus
in eis non proficiebat. Alio modo
secundum effectus, inquantum scil.*

*aliquis sapientiora et virtuosiora
opera facit; et sic Christus proficiebat sapientiâ et gratiâ, sicut et aetate, quia secundum processum aetatis perfectiora opera faciebat, ut
se verum hominem demonstraret, et
in his quae sunt ad Deum, et in
his quae sunt ad homines.*"

117 παρὰ Θεῷ.

three theological and the so-called moral virtues, together with the seven gifts of the Holy Ghost. Now, it would be wrong to hold that the human soul of Christ enjoyed the state of grace in the same sense as we do, only in a more perfect manner. The soul of our Blessed Redeemer, by virtue of the Hypostatic Union of the two natures, is in a class altogether by itself.

Of the theological virtues Christ doubtless possessed charity. Not so faith and hope. There was no room in His soul for the theological virtue of faith, because He already enjoyed the beatific vision. *"Christus a primo instanti suae conceptionis plene vidit Deum per essentiam,"* says St. Thomas, *" et per hanc visionem beatificam etiam omnia supernaturalia clarissime perspexit, unde in eo fides esse non potuit."* [118] Nor could He exercise the virtue of hope, because the actual enjoyment of the beatific vision renders theological hope useless, nay impossible. One cannot hope to attain what one already possesses. Only with respect of such gifts of grace as He did not yet possess, *e. g.,* His glorification by means of the Resurrection and Ascension, was Christ able, after a fashion, to exercise hope.[119]

Of the infused moral virtues Christ cannot possibly have practiced repentance (*poenitentia*), because it supposes forgiveness of sins. Our Divine Lord had no sins to be wiped out by contrition and penance. He was absolutely sinless and impeccable in His human as well as in His divine nature. As regards the other moral virtues,

---

118 *S. Theol.,* 3a, qu. 7, art. 3.
119 Cfr. St. Thomas, *S. Theol.,* 3a, qu. 7, art. 4.

it is the common opinion of theologians that Jesus
possessed them all, both natural and supernatural.
Though inferior in character to the supernatural, the
natural virtues, too, were His, because they serve to perfect human nature, and no ideal man is conceivable without them.

It is of faith that the soul of Christ was endowed
with the seven gifts of the Holy Ghost, though, of
course, " godliness " in Him was not a servile fear (*timor
servilis*) but that filial reverence (*timor filialis*) which a
good son bears towards his father. Cfr. Is. XI, 2 sq.:
"*Et requiescet super eum spiritus Domini: spiritus sapientiae et intellectus, spiritus consilii et fortitudinis,
spiritus scientiae et pietatis, et replebit eum spiritus
timoris Domini* — And the Spirit of the Lord shall rest
upon him: the spirit of wisdom, and of understanding,
the spirit of counsel, and of fortitude, the spirit of
knowledge, and of godliness; and he shall be filled with
the spirit of the fear of the Lord." [120]

γ) Through the Hypostatic Union Christ not
only received for Himself personally the plenitude of all graces but likewise the *gratia capitis,
i. e.,* the natural and supernatural headship of all
creatures.

Christ is " full of grace and truth," and " of His
fulness we have all received." [121] Thus from the *gratia
unionis* spontaneously flows the *gratia capitis,* in virtue
of which our Lord is the natural and supernatural Head

[120] On the *gratiae gratis datae* of
Christ compare St. Thomas, *S.
Theol.,* 3a, qu. 7, art. 7–8. On the
entire subject of this thesis cfr.
L. Janssens, *De Deo-Homine,* Vol.
I, pp. 341 sqq.
[121] John I, 14, 16.

of fallen men, of the angels, in fact of all rational creatures, nay even of inanimate nature.[122]   Where there is a head there must be members to constitute an organism. St. Thomas [123] distinguishes a twofold relationship between the head and the body, *distinctio* and *conformitas*. Under the first-mentioned aspect the head is distinguished from the members of the body (1) by its dignity as the sole possessor of the five senses; [124] (2) by its government as the ruler of the whole organism,[125] and (3) by the vital influence it exercises over the entire body.[126]   The conformity of the head with the body manifests itself (1) by the unity of its nature [127] with that of the body, because head and members are homogeneous; (2) by the unity of order [128] which connects the members with the head and regulates their respective functions; (3) by the unity of continuity,[129] in so far as the head is perfectly joined to its members.   Both series of relations are organically interrelated and point each to the other. The dignity of the head supposes the existence of homogeneous members from among which it stands out. Again the head could not rule over the body were it not that the members are wisely ordained towards one another.   Lastly, the exercise of the head's influence depends on the existence of organic continuity by which the vital fluids are enabled to circulate freely through the organs.   This allegory is based upon Sacred Scripture. Let us apply it to the Godman.

122 For a discussion of the subtle problem how the *gratia capitis* is related to the *gratia unionis*, and whether or not it is objectively identical with habitual grace, we must refer the reader to Billuart, *De Incarn.*, diss. 9, art. 4, and to St. Thomas, *S. Th.*, 3a, qu. 8, art. 5.

123 *De Verit.*, qu. 29, art. 4.
124 *Dignitas.*
125 *Gubernatio.*
126 *Causalitas.*
127 *Unitas naturae.*
128 *Unitas ordinis.*
129 *Unitas continuitatis.*

1. As God, Christ is the Lord rather than the Head of His creatures. As man, He is first and above all the Head of His Church, which, in the words of Suarez,[130] consists of men and is partly militant here on earth, partly triumphant in Heaven. This is an article of faith clearly expressed in many passages of Holy Scripture, especially in the Epistles of St. Paul. Cfr. Eph. I, 22 sq.: "*Et omnia subiecit sub pedibus eius, et ipsum dedit caput supra omnem ecclesiam,*[131] *quae est corpus ipsius*[132]— And he hath subjected all things under his feet, and hath made him head over all the Church, which is his body." Col. I, 18: "*Et ipse est caput corporis ecclesiae,*[133] *qui est principium, primogenitus ex mortuis, ut sit in omnibus ipse primatum tenens* — And he is the head of the body, the church, who is the beginning, the first-born from the dead; that in all things he may hold the primacy." Christ is the mystic Head of the human race and of His Church in a threefold manner. (1) As the most perfect man who can possibly exist, He excels all His fellowmen by His infinite dignity,[134] and consequently is the Head of humankind in a higher sense even than Adam.[135] (2) In virtue of the Hypostatic Union Christ is by His very nature the King of kings and Lord of lords,[136] the Ruler of all men. (3) Lastly He is pre-eminently our Head, because of the supernatural influence[137] which He exer-

130 *Comment. in S. Theol. S. Thomae Aquinatis*, III, disp. 23, sect. 1, n. 2, ed. Vives, t. XVII, 647, Paris 1859: "*Christus est caput totius Ecclesiae, quae ex hominibus constat, sive in terra militantis sive in coelo regnantis.*"

131 κεφαλὴν ὑπὲρ πάντα τῇ ἐκκλησίᾳ.

132 τὸ σῶμα αὐτοῦ.

133 ἡ κεφαλὴ τοῦ σώματος τῆς ἐκκλησίας.

134 *Dignitas.*

135 Cfr. Rom. V, 14 sqq.

136 *Gubernatio.* Cfr. Eph. I, 20 sqq.; 1 Cor. XV, 21 sqq.

137 *Causalitas.*

cises over those who are actually or potentially united
with Him as members of His mystic body.[138]

To ascertain the extension of the true Church it is
necessary to distinguish, as theologians commonly do,
between actual and potential membership. Unquestionably all those human beings are in vital communion
with Christ as their mystic Head, who are actually
united with Him either by the heavenly light of glory,[139]
or by sanctifying grace, or at least by internal faith.
The Godman Jesus Christ is truly the head and fountain
of all graces for the elect in Heaven, for the poor souls
in Purgatory, and for all just men as well as all believing
sinners on earth. These four classes together constitute
the Church. The elect in Heaven behold Him in His
transfigured humanity, which to the faithful on earth remains hidden under the species of bread and wine.[140]
He operates in all through faith or charity, thus binding
together the members of the militant with those of the
suffering and the triumphant Church into one mystic
body, called " Communion of Saints." [141]

So far theologians are quite unanimous. But they
differ when it comes to determining the line which di-
vides the actual members of the Church from those who
are merely potential Christians. Apostates and overt
heretics can not be actual members of the Church, because they have voluntarily severed the arteries which

138 Cfr. John I, 16, XV, 1 sqq.,
XVII, 21 sqq.; Eph. IV, 11 sqq.;
1 Cor. X, 16 sq., XII, 12 sq. Cfr.
Conc. Trident., Sess. VI, cap. 16
(Denzinger-Bannwart, *Enchiridion*,
n. 809): " *Quum enim ille ipse
Iesus tamquam caput in membra et
tamquam vitis in palmites in ipsos
iustificatos iugiter virtutem influat,
etc.*"

139 On the *lumen gloriae* see
Pohle-Preuss, *God: His Knowability,
Essence, and Attributes,* pp. 101 sqq.

140 Cfr. John VI, 57; 1 Cor. X,
16 sq.

141 On the Communion of Saints
see J. P. Kirsch, *The Doctrine of
the Communion of Saints in the Ancient Church* (tr. by J. R. M'Kee),
London 1911.

connected them with the mystic Head. But what about covert heretics? Can they be considered actual members of the Church? Suarez says no; Bellarmine replies in the affirmative.[142] With regard to the heathen, theologians are pretty generally agreed that they belong to the Church potentially (*in potentia*), because Christ died for them also, and though they have not the true faith, they receive actual graces through His merits. Even the unborn infants are potential members of the Redeemer's mystic body, for the reason that, at least mediately, through the prayers of their parents and those of the Church, they are brought under His influence. Christ cannot, however, be called the Head of the reprobate sinners in hell. He is their rigorous Lord and avenging Judge, but not their Head, because, being irrevocably cut off from His mystic body, they are no longer capable of being His members.

It is a matter of debate among divines whether or not Christ was also the Head of the human race in Paradise. The Thomists deny,[143] whereas the Scotists and Suarez [144] affirm it, either absolutely or hypothetically, each according to his individual attitude with respect to the predestination of the Incarnation.[145]

2. The question whether or not Christ by virtue of the *gratia capitis* is also the Head of the Angels, is answered in the negative by some of the Fathers and Scholastics, who maintain that between Christ as man and the angelic spirits there is lacking that homogeneity of nature and that influence of grace which constitute the essential characteristics of a head in the supernatural

---

142 Cfr. Palmieri, *De Romano Pontifice cum Prolegom. de Ecclesia*, pp. 47 sqq., 2nd ed., Prati 1891.

143 Cfr. Billuart, *De Incarn.*, diss. 9, art. 2, § 3.

144 *Comment. in S. Theol.*, III, disp. 23, sect. 1, n. 5.

145 For a discussion of this point we must refer the student to Soteriology.

sphere. As Christ became incarnate solely for man's
sake, they say, the graces He merited are applicable to
men only, the supernatural state of grace and glory enjoyed by the Angels being a gratuitous gift of the
Blessed Trinity.[146] In the opinion of Billuart, however, with which we are inclined to agree, it is little
less than temerarious to deny that, in a certain sense
at least, the Godman is also the Head of the angelic
hosts. "*Christum esse caput angelorum aliquo modo,
puta quoad externam gubernationem, sicut Papa dicitur
caput Ecclesiae,*" he says,[147] "*non videtur posse negari
sine errore, tum propter apertissima s. Scripturae testi-
monia et s. Patrum, tum quia esset negare Christum esse
principem ac Dominum angelorum atque totius Ecclesiae
triumphantis, quae ex hominibus et angelis constat.*"   In
matter of fact Christ's headship over the Angels can be
rigorously demonstrated by a threefold argument.   First,
He is by dignity the Head not only of men, but of all
creatures, which as such owe Him homage, obedience,
and adoration, as the Apostle testifies in Heb. I, 6:
"*Et quum iterum introducit primogenitum in orbem ter-
rae, dicit: Et adorent eum omnes angeli* — And again,
when he bringeth in the first begotten into the world,
he saith: And let all the angels of God adore him."
Again, since that which is more perfect rules over that
which is less perfect, there is every reason to assume that
the Angels are subject to Christ even *qua* man.   While
the infernal spirits tremble with fear and rage because
they are compelled to serve Christ, the blessed Angels

---

146 Thus Gabriel Biel, Driedo,
Soto, and others. Suarez comments
on this opinion as follows: "*Cui
sententiae videntur favere multi Patres, qui ubicumque Paulus dicit
Christum esse caput hominum et*
*angelorum, explicant hominum esse
caput secundum humanitatem, angelorum vero secundum divinitatem*" (l. c.).

147 *De Incarn.*, diss. 9, art. 3.

gladly do His bidding and are proud to acknowledge Him as their Ruler and Lord. Cfr. Matth. IV, 11: "And behold angels came and ministered to him." [148]

It is somewhat more difficult to decide whether the Godman is the Head of the angelic hosts also from the third point of view, *i. e.,* as the source of grace. Theologians disagree on this question. One group holds with Scotus that all graces without exception, and consequently also the grace bestowed upon the Angels, are exclusively attributable to Christ and His merits. Another, under the leadership of St. Thomas, defines the grace of Christ purely as redemptive grace in which the Angels do not share. But even in the Thomistic hypothesis Christ retains such a far-reaching accidental influence of grace over the Angels that He can still be called their Head. For even if He had not merited for them the full state of grace and glory which they enjoy, He would yet undoubtedly be in a position to communicate to them an accidental increase of light and happiness from the infinite thesaurus of His grace. When the angelic intellect turns towards the luminous soul of the Godman, it is flooded with light and enriched with prolific concepts. This truth is entirely independent of the theory of the three " hierarchic acts " (*illuminare, purgare,* and *perficere*) which Pseudo-Dionysius attributes to the Angelic intellect.[149] Since, however, the Angels, unlike the members of the human race, are not of the same species with Christ, De Lugo finds the ultimate cause of our Lord's headship over them in the two prerogatives of His infinite dignity and exalted dominion.

---

148 διηκόνουν αὐτῷ. Cfr. De Lugo, *De Myst. Incarn.,* disp. 30, sect. 1, n. 7.

149 *De Cael. Hier.,* VII, 3; cfr.

St. Thomas, *Comment. in Quatuor Libros Sent.,* III, dist. 13, qu. 2, art. 2.

3. As regards the third and last category of creatures, *viz.:* those which constitute the material uni/erse, the infinite dignity and supreme dominion of the Godman undoubtedly give Him a natural claim to rule as *primogenitus omnis creaturae et primatum tenens* over the entire universe. Inasmuch, however, as the title of "headship" connotes a certain willingness, docility, and manageableness on the part of the subject members, it is more appropriate to call Christ the Lord than the Head of material creatures. And the same principle applies to His headship over the demons and reprobate sinners in hell. He is their Lord rather than their Head. The devils, who are intelligent creatures, *will* not obey Him; the irrational brutes and matter, being destitute of reason, *can* not obey Him. Both serve Him under compulsion.

Some theologians hold that Christ's humanity exercises a physical influence over all creatures without exception. But this theory rests on false assumptions and is philosophically untenable. For, as Suarez pertinently observes," *hoc non pertinet ad dignitatem assumptae humanitatis nec est necessarium ad manifestationem nominis Christi.*" [150] It will be sufficient to say, therefore, that Christ, as man, ranks infinitely above the created universe, and that all creatures are subject to Him and compelled to do His bidding. Cfr. Matth. VIII, 27: "The winds and the sea obey him." [151]

READINGS : — Bougaud-Currie, *The Divinity of Christ,* pp. 66 sqq., New York 1906.—* L. Atzberger, *Die Unsündlichkeit Christi,* München 1883.— K. Hennemann, *Die Heiligkeit Jesu als Beweis*

150 *Comment. in Quatuor Libros Sent.,* III, disp. 23, sect. 1, n. 9.
151 On the *gratia capitis* cfr. St. Thomas, *S. Theol.,* 3a, qu. 8; also

L. Janssens, *De Deo-Homine,* Vol. I, pp. 374 sqq.; Franzelin, *De Verbo Incarn.,* thes. 41; Stentrup, *Soteriologia,* thes. 169 sqq.

seiner Gottheit, Würzburg 1898.— Wilhelm-Scannell, *A Manual of Catholic Theology,* Vol. II, pp. 149 sqq., 2nd ed., London 1901. — W. Humphrey, S. J., *The One Mediator,* pp. 238 sqq., London *s. a.*

ARTICLE 2

THE HUMAN KNOWLEDGE OF CHRIST

Having dealt in a previous treatise with the divine knowledge of Christ, *qua* Logos (*i. e.* God),[1] we may here confine ourselves to a consideration of His human knowledge.

The nature and extent of Christ's human knowledge is one of the most difficult problems in Christology. While the Church in her controversies with various heretics was repeatedly compelled to concern herself in a special manner with the will of our Divine Lord, she never had any particular occasion to decide the questions that have arisen in regard to His intellect.

The Hypostatic Union is the source and fountainhead of all the prerogatives and graces with which the soul of Jesus is endowed. It goes without saying that these prerogatives and graces are the highest and noblest of which a creature is capable. Since, however, no creature can ever become God, (this would involve a contradiction), the humanity of Christ is not God. The Hypostatic Union did not result in an apotheosis of the assumed manhood, but only in what is technically termed θεοποίησις. The mystery enveloping the Hypostatic

---

1 Pohle-Preuss, *God: His Knowability, Essence, and Attributes,* pp. 327 sqq.

Union makes it difficult for us to find the correct mean between these two extremes. It is probably due to this circumstance that certain theologians [2] have left the beaten track of traditional teaching in this important question. There can be no doubt that the universal and constant teaching of Catholic theologians in matters of faith constitutes the best source of certainty.

Generally speaking, man is capable of a threefold knowledge: (1) that derived from the beatific vision of God, (2) infused knowledge, and (3) acquired or experimental knowledge, derived from sense perception and experience. The first kind of knowledge (*scientia beata*) is a prerogative of the elect in Heaven, who participate in the divine knowledge of the Blessed Trinity through the medium of the so-called *lumen gloriae*. Acquired or experimental knowledge is conditioned by the present constitution of human nature and therefore peculiar to man as a wayfarer. The supernatural gifts of faith and grace do not dispense him from dependence on the material world. Midway between these two species stands the knowledge infused by God (*scientia infusa*). This kind of knowledge is connatural to the angelic intellect, and theologians commonly hold that it was conferred as a supernatural gift on Adam and Solomon.

---

2 This group comprises the school of Günther, the Modernists, H. Schell, and also a few divines of unquestioned loyalty to the Church, *e. g.*, Klee and Laurent.

The soul of Christ simultaneously possessed all three kinds of knowledge, as we shall now proceed to demonstrate.

Thesis I: From the first moment of its existence in a human body the soul of our Lord Jesus Christ enjoyed the beatific vision of God.

If the soul of Christ on earth was constituted in the possession of the beatific vision, and of such knowledge of God and the created universe as that vision implies, then His state, in this respect, was not so much that of a wayfarer, but rather the *status termini* proper to the elect in Heaven.

Hence the theological axiom: "*Christus erat viator simul et comprehensor.*" Modernistic theologians contend that this axiom involves a contradiction, or at least that the simultaneous possession of these two kinds of knowledge is incompatible with the life and passion of our Lord in His capacity as Mediator between God and man. To escape this alleged contradiction they deny Him the *visio beata*. As Sacred Scripture and Tradition teach nothing definite on the matter and the Church has never put forth a formal definition, this denial does not involve heresy; but it runs counter to a theological conclusion which, supported as it is by the unanimous consent of older theologians and the belief of the faithful, may be regarded as certain. Suarez says: "I regard the contrary opinion as erroneous, nay even as bordering on heresy (*proximam haeresi*), because the testimony of Sacred Scripture in connection with the teaching of the Fathers and the consensus of all

Catholic doctors is sufficient to produce certainty." [3] One may think this censure too rigorous, but it is hard to escape the force of the argument formulated by such a cautious and unprejudiced theologian as Petavius: "*Nemo hactenus bonâ fide christianus, i. e. catholicus scriptor exstitit,*" he says, "*qui de Christo aliter existimaret quam eum numquam, ex quo vivere coepit, divino aspectu caruisse; nec hodie quisquam est, rudis licet literarum et idiota, qui si utcumque quid Christus sit noverit, non idem de eo rogatus respondeat.*" [4] A further motive for adhering to the traditional teaching is that the Scholastics and later theologians, though fully cognizant of the difficulties which prompt modern writers to reject the older view, never swerved from the path mapped out by the Fathers.

Proof.—a) To construct a solid Scriptural argument we must find texts which treat expressly of the human knowledge of Jesus; such as merely prove His divine knowledge,[5] or can be interpreted by the Communication of Idioms,[6] are manifestly inconclusive.

Some divines [7] appeal to John III, 13: "*Nemo ascendit in coelum, nisi qui descendit de coelo, Filius hominis qui est in coelo* — No man hath ascended into heaven, but he that descended from heaven, the Son of man who is in heaven." To "be in heaven," they say, means to "be constituted in the possession of the beatific vision." But this interpretation is by no means cogent.

3 *De Incarn.*, disp. 25, sect. 1.
4 *De Incarn.*, IX, c. 4, n. 8.
5 For example, Matth. XI, 27; Luke X, 22.

6 *E. g.*, John XII, 26, XIV, 3, XVII, 24.
7 Prominent among them Cardinal Billot.

By virtue of the Communication of Idioms the " Son of man " is as much " in heaven " as the " Son of God," because both are identical with the Divine Person of the Logos.[8]

A more apposite text is John I, 17–18: *" Quia lex per Moysen data est, gratia et veritas per Iesum Christum facta est. Deum nemo vidit unquam, unigenitus Filius, qui est in sinu Patris, ipse enarravit —* For the law was given by Moses; grace and truth came by Jesus Christ. No man hath seen God at any time: the only begotten Son who is in the bosom of the Father, he hath declared him." Though this passage refers primarily to the divine vision of the only begotten Son in the bosom of the Father, the Evangelist seems to include also the human vision of His soul. Had he meant only the divine vision of the Logos as such, " He who declares the Father " would be either a mere automaton or at best a prophet enlightened by Revelation. In the former hypothesis Christ would rank beneath Moses, in the latter assumption He would certainly not surpass that inspired Jewish law-giver, because without divine inspiration it is impossible for any prophet to declare the mysteries of God. But what the Evangelist wishes to accentuate in the above quoted passage is precisely that Christ's superiority over Moses is not merely one of degree, but essentially different, as different as the Old Testament is from the New. Wherein does this essential difference consist? " He who declares," *i. e., the Son of man as such,* really saw God. Consequently the soul of Christ was constituted in the possession of the beatific vision.

8 Cfr. Chr. Pesch, *Praelect. Dogmat.,* Vol. IV, 3d ed., p. 139, Friburgi 1909; L. Janssens, *De Deo-Homine,* Vol. I, pp. 410 sq.

St. Thomas Aquinas [9] successfully appeals to John VIII, 55: "*Et non cognovistis eum* [*scil. Patrem*], *ego autem novi eum.*[10] *Et si dixero quia non scio eum, ero similis vobis mendax. Sed scio eum* [11] *et sermonem eius servo* — You have not known him [*i. e.*, the Father], but I know him. And if I shall say that I know him not, I shall be like to you, a liar. But I do know him, and do keep his word." In this passage the phrase " I know him " describes a clear, intuitive knowledge of the Father, and consequently of the entire Trinity; but such knowledge is impossible except through the beatific vision. Now our Divine Saviour claims this knowledge not only as God, but also as man, for it is only as man that He can "keep the word" of His Heavenly Father and say of Himself, as He does in the verse immediately preceding: "If I glorify myself, my glory is nothing. It is my Father that glorifieth me." [12]

b) The Patristic texts that can be adduced in confirmation of our thesis are too meagre to allow us to speak of a strict argument from the writings of the Fathers.

St. Augustine in his allegorical explanation of the resuscitation of Lazarus observes that Lazarus lying in the tomb and wrapped in a shroud is a figure of our earthly knowledge of God, whereas Lazarus released from his grave and restored to life symbolizes the knowledge of God which we are to enjoy in Heaven.[13] He adds that this simile applies to all men with the sole exception of Christ, who enjoyed the beatific vision as a wayfarer here on earth.[14]

9 S. Theol., 3a, qu. 9, art. 2.
10 οἶδα αὐτόν.
11 οἶδα αὐτόν.
12 John VIII, 54.
13 Cfr. 1 Cor. XIII, 12.
14 Lib. 83 Quaest., qu. 65: "Ipse

Pope St. Leo the Great teaches: " *Quum simplex et incommutabilis natura deitatis tota sit semper in sua essentia nec damnum sui recipiens nec augmentum et sic naturam assumptam beatificans, ut glorificata in glorificante permaneat."* [15]

The only ecclesiastical writer who has treated this question *ex professo* is St. Fulgentius of Ruspe. He holds that the soul of Christ, because of its divine dignity derived from the Hypostatic Union, must necessarily have been constituted in the possession of the beatific vision: " *Caveamus ne, quum anima Christi totum Patrem nosse non creditur, ipsi uni Christo ex aliqua parte non solum Patris, sed etiam sui et Spiritus S. cognitio denegetur; perquam vero durum est et a sanitate fidei alienum, ut dicamus animam Christi non plenam suae deitatis habere notitiam, cum qua naturaliter creditur habere personam."* [16]   Had St. Fulgentius contented himself with explaining, as St. Thomas did several centuries later, that the soul of Christ on earth saw, but did not adequately comprehend the Blessed Trinity,— because no creature can have an adequate comprehension of the Godhead,— he would deserve to be called, in respect of Christology, " a Scholastic before the days of Scholasticism."   But he grossly exaggerates when in the process of his argument he identifies simple vision with adequate comprehension,— a proceeding which has scandalized more than one later theologian.[17]   Fulgentius himself appears to have realized that he had overshot the mark, since he says further on: " *Possumus plane dicere, ani-*

---

solus in carne non tantum in monumento non est oppressus, ut aliquod peccatum in eo inveniretur, sed nec linteis implicatus, ut eum aliquid lateret aut ab itinere retardaret."
15 *Ep. 25 ad Iulian.*

16 *Ep. 14 ad Ferrand.,* n. 26.
17 *E. g.,* Petavius (*De Incarn.,* VI, 3, 1 sqq.), Thomassin (*De Incarn.,* l. VII), Ruiz (*De Scientia Dei,* disp. 6, sect. 2), and Stentrup (*Christologia,* thes. 72).

mam Christi habere plenam notitiam deitatis suae; nescio tamen, utrum debeamus dicere quod anima Christi sic suam deitatem noverit, quemadmodum se ipsa deitas novit, an hoc potius dicendum est, quia novit quantum illa, sed non sicut illa? . . . Anima vero illa ab ipsa deitate, quam plene novit, accepit ut noverit." [18] Needless to add, this distinction does not sufficiently safeguard the dogma of God's absolute incomprehensibility.[19]

For the rest, we may claim the authority of the Fathers in favor of our thesis at least in so far as they teach: (1) That Christ made no intrinsic advance in either His divine or His human knowledge [20] any more than in holiness or grace, and (2) that His human intellect did not admit of ignorance in the strict sense of the term, as claimed by the Agnoëtae. Of these two propositions the first postulates, while the second favors the doctrine that the human soul of our Lord enjoyed the beatific vision.[21] Since the Fathers base these two propositions on the Hypostatic Union, they must have held that Christ was constituted in the possession of the beatific vision at the instant of His conception, *i. e.,* the creation of His soul.

c) As the reader will have inferred, the argument for our thesis rests mainly on theological grounds, and these grounds are very weighty indeed.

α) The Hypostatic Union is the principle and

18 *Ep. 14 ad Ferrand.,* n. 31.
19 Cfr. Pohle-Preuss, *God: His Knowability, Essence, and Attributes,* pp. 107 sqq.
20 On the one exception to this rule see Third Thesis, *infra,* pp. 273 sqq.
21 For the necessary Patristic texts consult Chr. Pesch, *Praelect. Dogmat.,* Vol. IV, pp. 141 sqq., 153 sqq.

measure of our Lord's human knowledge in the same way in which it is the principle and measure of His created holiness.

Though the beatific vision is not a metaphysically necessary effect of the *gratia unionis,* the moral claim which the soul of Christ has to that vision is so strong that the burden of proof rests entirely with those who deny it. It is unthinkable that the soul of Christ should not from the very beginning of its existence have known the Logos with whom it was united in the most intimate manner conceivable, *i. e.,* by Hypostatic Union. And if Christ's sacred humanity was endowed with the sublimest of all gifts in the order of grace, *viz.:* personal communion with the Godhead, it could not possibly have been deprived of the lesser gift of beatific vision in the light of glory. The soul of our Lord was constituted in the full possession of created sanctity and the perfection of grace,[22] and consequently was elevated to the highest summit of accidental grace, which is the beatific vision of the Divine Essence. It is a theological axiom that " Glory is grace consummated." [23] " The man Jesus," says Kleutgen, " is true God by virtue of the Hypostatic Union, because by this union His humanity is elevated, not to a higher degree of divine resemblance, but to the personal being of the Son of God. The Hypostatic Union, therefore, is not, like the beatific vision of God, a consummation of sanctifying grace. It is something far superior to both. Consequently grace cannot be the cause but must be an effect of the Hypostatic Union. . . . This is the only correct conception of the relation between grace and the Hypostatic Union, and it naturally leads us to conceive

22 *V. supra,* pp. 207 sqq.
23 " *Gloria est consummata gratia.*"

of grace in Christ as in the state of consummation.   For
grace was not given to Christ, *qua* man, to enable Him
to attain to a certain predestined dignity, but because He
had already attained to the highest dignity which it is
possible for us to conceive.   Grace in its consummation is
precisely the light of glory which elevates the soul to the
vision of God.   If, on the contrary, the Hypostatic Union
be wrongly defined as a vital commerce effected by intellectual activity, we fail to distinguish its nature from that
union with God into which grace permits the soul to enter.
We should then be easily tempted to assume a gradual advance in both, and, to be consistent, should have to place
the consummation of the Hypostatic Union in the beatific
vision.   From all of which it is easy to see why the school
of Günther, though it does not expressly draw this inference, yet hotly attacks the thesis which we defend." [24]

β) St. Thomas argues that Christ "would not
be the Head of all creatures if some creature at
any time surpassed Him in mental perfection." [25]

Jesus was the Mediator between God and man, and
as such was to introduce men to the beatific vision of
the Divine Essence.   Hence it was necessary that His
human nature (as the *instrumentum coniunctum divinitatis*) should enjoy the highest and fullest measure
of that eternal life which He was to communicate to
others.   "Let it not be said," writes Kleutgen,[26] " that
He does not dispense eternal life until after His glorification; for it was not in His glorification that He was

24 *Theologie der Vorzeit*, Vol.
III, 2nd ed., p. 276, Münster 1870.
25 Wilhelm-Scannell, *Manual*, II,
p. 147.

26 *Theologie der Vorzeit*, Vol. III,
2nd ed., p. 280.

the author of our salvation, but in the hardships and pains He endured from the manger to the Cross."

It has been objected that if a passible Saviour was able to merit for us the glory of the Resurrection, there is no reason why the beatific vision should not come to us through the merits of a Redeemer who Himself lacked this prerogative. There is no parity between the two cases. Christ's mediatorial office, which was incompatible with a glorified life in the body, made it necessary for Him to postpone His bodily transfiguration until after the Resurrection. The beatific vision, however, did not interfere with the possibility of our Lord's agonizing passion and death, and, on account of His dignity and mission as the *caput gratiae,* had to be His from the very moment of His conception. Hence Aquinas justly argues: *"Homo est in potentia ad scientiam beatorum, quae in Dei visione consistit et ad eam ordinatur sicut ad finem. . . . Ad hunc autem finem beatitudinis homines reducuntur per Christi humanitatem, secundum illud (Heb. 2, 10): 'Decebat eum, propter quem omnia et per quem omnia, qui multos filios in gloriam adduxerat, auctorem salutis eorum per passionem consummari.' Et ideo oportuit quod cognitio beata in Dei visione consistens excellentissime Christo homini conveniret, quia semper causam oportet esse potiorem causato."* [27]

But how are we to reconcile Christ's life and suffering on earth, especially the agony of His sacred Passion, with the beatitude essentially involved in the immediate vision of God? Some theologians attempt to solve this difficulty by saying that the human soul of our Lord was filled with beatific joy in its upper, while sadness and pain and sorrow afflicted its lower region.[28] But

[27] *S. Theol.,* 3a, qu. 9, art. 2.
[28] Cfr. *Prop. 13 Fenelonii damn.*
a. 1699 ab Innocentio XII (Denzinger-Bannwart, *Enchiridion,* n.

this theory hardly deserves serious consideration. Joy
and sadness, happiness and sorrow, may co-exist in the
spiritual soul of man, if they are due to different motives and directed towards different formal objects. The
blessed martyrs exulted in the midst of cruel tortures.
However, we must draw a sharp distinction between spiritual joy and bodily pain on the one hand, and spiritual
joy and spiritual pain on the other. Spiritual joy is compatible with bodily pain,[29] but the simultaneous co-existence of spiritual joy and spiritual affliction has always
been regarded as a most difficult problem in Christology.
The fact that theologians generally have ranged it among
the inscrutable mysteries rather than recede from their position, is a strong proof of the vital importance which they
attach to the doctrine we are expounding. Among the
manifold solutions that have been offered probably the
most widely known is that of Melchior Canus. Canus
draws a real distinction between the action of the intellect
(*actus intellectus = visio*) and the action of the will
(*actus voluntatis = gaudium*) in the *visio beatifica*, and
holds that Jesus on the cross continued to enjoy the vision
of God, though without the beatitude ordinarily attending
it.[30] This not altogether unlikely explanation had been
adumbrated by St. Ambrose [31] and was adopted by Greg-

1339): *"Inferior Christi pars in cruce non communicavit superiori suas involuntarias perturbationes."*

29 Cfr. St. Thomas, *S. Theol.*, 3a, qu. 15, art. 5, ad 3: *"Virtute divinitatis Christi dispensative sic beatitudo in anima continebatur, quod non derivabatur ad corpus, ne eius passibilitas et mortalitas tolleretur; et eadem ratione delectatio contemplationis sic retinebatur in mente, quod non derivabatur ad vires sensibiles, ne per hoc dolor sensibilis tolleretur."*

30 Cfr. *De Locis Theol.*, XII, 13: *"Sicut per totam vitam Dominus gloriam animae quasi premebat, ne in corpus efflueret, sic saltem in cruce retinuit [= repressit] gaudium, quod suapte naturâ ex clara Dei notitia prodiret."*

31 *In Luc.*, l. 10, n. 56: *"Pro me doluit, qui pro se nihil habuit quod doleret et sequestratâ delectatione divinitatis aeternae, taedio meae infirmitatis afficitur."*

ory of Valentia, Salmeron, and Maldonatus. But it hardly satisfies the enquiring mind. The intuitive vision of God is so inseparably connected with beatitude that, so far as we know, neither can exist apart from the other.

A way out of the difficulty is offered by the theory that the will of the Elect reacts differently, (1) towards the uncreated Good and (2) towards created good. Besides the essential happiness which flows from the beatific vision, the Elect in Heaven also enjoy a species of accidental happiness derived from the spiritual contemplation of created goodness. Like their respective objects, these two operations are numerically and formally distinct, though in the blessed state both rigorously exclude sorrow and sadness. Yet, the incompatibility of joy and sadness is due to a natural rather than an essential contrariety. There is at least no ontological reason why the soul of Christ, though in the full enjoyment of the beatific vision, should not have been plunged into sadness and sorrow at contemplating the innumerable sins of mankind and the painful way of the Cross. A miracle of divine omnipotence may have temporarily suspended the natural, though not essential, nexus between essential and accidental beatitude.[32]

γ) A third argument is related to the problem concerning the origin of the Messianic and divine consciousness of Christ. Our Saviour must have been fully conscious of His Divinity and Messiahship from the very beginning, else there would be reason to doubt the infallibility of His testimony to the truths of salvation, especially to His own

[32] Cfr. Chr. Pesch, *Praelect. Dogmat.*, Vol. IV, 3rd ed., pp. 146 sqq.

divine Sonship and Divinity, and the meritoriousness of the atonement.

If we deny that Christ was constituted in the possession of the beatific vision from the first moment of
His existence, we shall find it difficult to determine
in what manner and at what time His soul attained
to an infallible consciousness of its Messiahship and
personal union with the Godhead. We shall have to
face this dilemma: Either Christ's human consciousness was originally and inseparably bound up with His
Messianic and divine consciousness, or there was a time
when His self-conscious soul was not yet aware of its
being constituted in the possession of the Messianic dignity and the Hypostatic Union with the Divine Logos.
In the first assumption there existed no other, surely no
safer or more direct way of attaining to divine consciousness than the beatific vision of God, which would
include the contemplation of the Logos and the Hypostatic Union. Any other means of communication inferior to this one would have compelled the soul of
Christ to walk in the obscurity of faith with regard
to its own Divinity, and for thirty-three long years
firmly to hold it as a mere truth of faith, not as a matter of intuitive knowledge. Such an assumption is
hardly compatible with Christ's repeated assertion
(which sharply differentiates Him from all the prophets)
that he testified only to that which He had Himself
seen.[33] Let it not be objected that He testified as man
to what He had seen as God; for it is not the Divine
Logos that speaks and testifies in such passages as John
III, 11 sqq., III, 27 sqq., VIII, 38, etc., but the man

33 Cfr. John I, 17, III, 11 sqq., III, 27 sqq., VIII, 38 sqq., and nu-merous other passages of similar tenor.

Jesus, and He speaks and testifies as one who understands perfectly what He has seen. Even Schell, probably the ablest defender of the new theory, admits that " faith had no room in Christ, but its place was taken by a most penetrating knowledge." [34] This " penetrating knowledge," freed from the limitations of faith, must be conceived as intuitive vision, for intuitive vision alone annuls faith.

To hold that Christ's human consciousness awoke before His divine consciousness, or to assert with the Modernists that " Christ did not always possess the consciousness of His Messianic dignity," [35] is equivalent to saying that the soul of the Redeemer had to learn the fact of His Messiahship from elsewhere, since, according to this theory, it never enjoyed the beatific vision on earth. From what source could such knowledge have come? Not from a study of the prophets who had clearly predicted our Lord's Messiahship and Divinity, for Holy Scripture tells us that Jesus without any schooling knew " His Father " at the age of twelve, and had a thorough command of Sacred Scripture. He did not receive this knowledge by divine illumination from within. Apart from the beatific vision, in what could such illumination have consisted except enlightened faith? But faith, no matter how enlightened, does not see or know; it gropes in the dark amid doubts and temptations.

Consequently, the divine consciousness in the human soul of our Saviour can have been derived from no other source than the beatific vision. As this divine con-

[34] *Dogmatik,* Vol. III, 1, 183, Paderborn 1892.
[35] Cfr. Denzinger-Bannwart, *Enchiridion,* n. 2035. The best refutation of this Modernist error is by Hilarin Felder, O. M. Cap., *Jesus Christus. Apologie seiner Messianität und Gottheit gegenüber der neuesten ungläubigen Jesus-Forschung,* Vol. I: " *Das Bewusstsein Jesu,*" Paderborn 1911.

sciousness is intimately bound up with Christ's human consciousness, which reaches back to His childhood, nay to the very instant of His conception, the divine consciousness of our Lord and the beatific vision with which He was endowed, must have had their inception at precisely the same moment.[36]

d) Of considerably less importance than the questions just discussed are the Scholastic speculations regarding the extent of Christ's knowledge of God and the created universe, as included in the *visio beatifica*.

It is of faith that God is absolutely incomprehensible to the created intellect even in the state of glory.[37] The soul of Christ was a finite creature, and therefore the beatific knowledge which it enjoyed, no matter how highly it may be rated, cannot have been equivalent to an adequate comprehension of the Divine Essence. The true doctrine of the Church on this point was trenchantly defended by St. Thomas against Fulgentius,[38] Alcuin,[39] and Hugh of St. Victor.[40] "*Est impossible,*" says the Angelic Doctor, " *quod aliqua creatura comprehendat divinam essentiam, eo quod infinitum non comprehenditur a*

[36] *Cfr. Concil. Colon. a. 1860*, tit. 5, cap. 19 (*Collectio Lacensis*, t. V, p. 308): "*Fuisse in anima Christi praeter scientiam acquisitam etiam scientiam infusam, imo et visionem beatorum, et quidem inde ab ortu, magno consensu docent theologi.*"—The embarrassment of modern Protestant theology through its false conception of the Messianic consciousness of Christ, is well described by A. Seitz, *Das Evangelium vom Gottessohn*, pp. 194 sqq., Freiburg 1908. Cfr. also Felder-Stoddard, *Christ and the Critics*, Vol. I, London 1924, pp. 121 sqq., and F. G. Hall, *The Kenotic Theory*, New York 1898.

[37] Cfr. Pohle-Preuss, *God: His Knowability, Essence, and Attributes*, pp. 107 sqq.

[38] *V. supra*, pp. 253 sq.

[39] *De Trinit.*, II, 12.

[40] *Opusculum de Scientia Animæ Christi.*

finito. Et ideo dicendum est quod anima Christi nullo modo comprehendit divinam essentiam." [41] Justly, therefore, did the Council of Bâsle reject the proposition of Augustine of Nazareth, that "the soul of Christ sees God as clearly and intensely as God sees Himself." [42]

This decision also affords us a key for the solution of the question whether or not the soul of our Lord was endowed with the *scientia simplicis intelligentiae, i. e.,* a knowledge of those things which are possible to God's omnipotence, but never realized. To affirm this proposition would be to attribute to the human soul of Christ an adequate comprehension of the Divine Essence itself.[43] The affirmative opinion is therefore quite generally rejected. Theologians are agreed, however, that Christ had a knowledge of all those things which fall under the *scientia visionis, i. e.,* all really existing things, past, present, and future, including the most hidden cogitations of the human heart.[44] This eminent though finite mode of knowledge safeguards the creatural character of the soul of Christ and corresponds to His twofold capacity of Head of the present economy and Judge of the living and the dead.[45]

Thesis II: Besides the scientia beata, the soul of Christ from the moment of its conception also possessed a knowledge immediately infused by God (scientia infusa).

Proof. Beatific knowledge is the immediate or intuitive vision, through the *lumen gloriae,* of

41 *S. Theol.,* 3a, qu. 10, art. 1.
42 "*Anima Christi videt Deum tam clare et intense, sicut Deus videt seipsum.*" (Sess. XXII.)
43 Cfr. St. Thomas, *S. Theol.,* 3a, qu. 10, art. 2: "*Hoc enim esset*

comprehendere divinam virtutem et per consequens divinam essentiam."
44 Luke IX, 47. Cfr. W. Humphrey, "*His Divine Majesty,*" pp. 268 sqq.
45 Cfr. St. Thomas, *S. Theol.,* 3a,

God and His creatures as mirrored in His Essence. Infused knowledge is a knowledge of those creatures in themselves. Infused like beatific knowledge is independent of the senses, though it cannot dispense with intellectual concepts (*species intelligibiles*).

As distinct from acquired or experimental knowledge, infused knowledge is connatural to the Angels, whereas man can enjoy it only as a preternatural prerogative of grace.[46] St. Augustine calls it " evening knowledge " (*cognitio vespertina*) in contradistinction to the " morning knowledge " (*cognitio matutina*) by which the Angels intue all things natural and supernatural immediately in the Divine Essence. Infused knowledge, therefore, differs widely from our ordinary knowledge, which depends on sense perception and intellectual concepts abstracted from phantasms. When granted to a human soul (as it was granted, for instance, to Adam and Solomon), infused knowledge adapts itself to the specific nature of the recipient. St. Thomas says of the infused knowledge of Christ: " *Et ideo sicut in angelis secundum eundem Augustinum ponitur duplex cognitio, una scil. matutina, per quam cognoscunt res in Verbo, et alia ves-*

qu. 10, art. 2: " *Unusquisque intellectus creatus in Verbo cognoscit non quidem omnia simpliciter, sed tanto plura, quanto perfectius videt Verbum. Nulli tamen intellectui beato deest, quin cognoscat in Verbo omnia quae ad ipsum spectant. Ad Christum autem et ad eius dignitatem spectant quodammodo omnia, inquantum ei subiecta sunt omnia. Ipse etiam est omnium iudex constitutus a Deo, quia Filius hominis* est, ut dicitur Io. 5, 27; et ideo anima Christi in Verbo cognoscit omnia existentia secundum quodcumque tempus, et etiam hominum cogitatus, quorum est iudex.*" On the views of St. Bonaventure with regard to this question see L. Janssens, *De Deo-Homine*, Vol. I, pp. 444 sqq.

46 Cfr. Pohle-Preuss, *God the Author of Nature and the Supernatural*, pp. 207 sqq.

pertina, per quam cognoscunt res in propria natura per species sibi inditas [*=infusas*], *ita praeter scientiam divinam et increatam est in Christo secundum eius animam scientia beata, qua cognoscit Verbum et res in Verbo, et scientia infusa sive indita, per quam cognoscit res in propria natura per species intelligibiles humanae menti proportionatas."* [47] This passage effectively refutes Schell's objection that " the body is merely an external additament designed to create the semblance of a human nature. A spirit who incidentally happens to have a body, even though he animates this body as his substantial form, is at most a compound of angel and man." [48] The unity and harmony of the inner life of the soul is no more disturbed by the possession of two higher modes of cognition than by the coexistence of sense and intellect. For the soul even after its separation from the body attains to heavenly beatitude in two ways: primarily through the vision of God, and secondarily through a twofold knowledge of the objects which are distinct from God, first as mirrored in the Divine Logos, and secondly as they are in themselves. After the resurrection of the flesh man will possess a third kind of knowledge, *i. e.,* an experimental knowledge which depends on sense impressions (see Eschatology). Why should these three modes of knowledge be incompatible in Christ?

We do not propose this thesis as theologically certain. But whoever admits that the soul of Christ was constituted in the possession of the beatific vision from the moment of its creation, cannot consistently deny that it was also endowed with infused knowledge. A denial of the latter proposition would not, however, incur

---

47 *S. Theol.,* 3a, qu. 9, art. 3.   48 *Dogmatik,* III, 1, 111.

theological censure, because we are dealing with a speculative deduction and not a revealed truth. The case
would be otherwise were one to assert that the human soul
of Christ possessed neither beatific nor infused, but only
acquired or experimental knowledge. This would be repugnant to the Catholic faith. The Church has always
held against Nestorius, Leporius, and the Agnoëtae, that
the human nature of Christ was endowed with the
highest wisdom and absolutely exempt from ignorance
and error. It is the common teaching of theologians that
our Lord's human knowledge was both beatific and infused.

a) While our thesis cannot be rigorously
demonstrated from Sacred Scripture, it derives a
high degree of probability from such texts as Is.
XI, 2: *"Requiescet super eum Spiritus Domini,
spiritus sapientiae et intellectus . . . consilii
. . . scientiae* — And the spirit of the Lord shall
rest upon him: the spirit of wisdom and of understanding, the spirit of counsel, and . . . of
knowledge." St. Thomas comments upon this
manifestly Messianic passage as follows: *". . .
sub quibus comprehenduntur omnia cognoscibilia;
nam ad sapientiam pertinet cognitio omnium di-
vinorum; ad intellectum autem pertinet cognitio
omnium immaterialium; ad scientiam autem pertinet cognitio omnium conclusionum, ad consilium
autem cognitio omnium agibilium."* [49] "The spirit
of the Lord shall rest upon him" means that

49 *S. Theol.,* 3a, qu. 11, art. 1.

Christ shall be constituted in the possession of all knowledge and that His knowledge shall be infused.[50]

The human knowledge of Christ is relatively infinite in extent, *i. e.,* it is the highest and most complete knowledge which it is possible for any creature to have in the present economy, and consequently, both with regard to natural and supernatural things, it is the ideal of all knowledge.

This conclusion is confirmed by the words of St. John the Baptist as recorded in John III, 34: "*Quem enim misit Deus, verba Dei loquitur; non enim ad mensuram* [51] *dat Deus spiritum* — For he whom God hath sent, speaketh the words of God: for God doth not give the spirit by measure." St. Fulgentius commentates this text as follows: "*Ipse enim est qui dat, ipse est qui accipit; et quia potens est ab mensuram dare, ideo non potuit ad mensuram accipere. In forma enim Dei manens Spiritum dat, formam servi accipiens Spiritum accepit; sed quia ipse ad mensuram dat, ideo non ipse ad mensuram accepit; ipsum enim, quem ad mensuram dat, totum accepit.*" [52]

Whether Col. II, 3 can be quoted in support of our thesis is more than doubtful.[53]

b) Ecclesiastical Tradition favors the proposition that the soul of Christ had an inerrant knowledge of all things past, present, and future, and that this knowledge positively excluded igno-

---

50 Cfr. John I, 14, II, 25, VII, 15.   53 Cfr. St. Thomas, *S. Theol.,* 3a,
51 ἐκ μέτρου.   qu. 9, art. 3.
52 *Ep. 14 ad Ferrand.*

rance. But it is not so decisive on the question whether this knowledge is derived from the *scientia beata,* or the *scientia infusa,* or both. Though the main point of contention between the Agnoëtae and the Church has not yet been fully cleared up,[54] the history of this heretical sect justifies certain important conclusions.

a) A sort of Agnoëtism was propagated by the Arians,[55] and also by the Nestorians,[56] but the name of Agnoëtae [57] is commonly applied to a sixth-century sect, whose chief tenet is supposed to have been that Christ was ignorant [58] of certain things, especially the day of judgment.[59] It is, however, uncertain whether the subject to which they attributed this ignorance was the human nature of our Lord or a fictitious Monophysitic compound of Divinity and humanity. Whereas the Monophysite opponents of Themistius, *e. g.,* Timothy and Theodosius, represent Agnoëtism as consistently Monophysitic, the Severians and Nicephorus Callistus [60] understood them as attributing ignorance to the sacred humanity of Jesus. In any case it is certain that the champions of Catholic orthodoxy against the Agnoëtae rigorously excluded all error and ignorance from

54 Cfr. Fr. Schmid in the Innsbruck *Zeitschrift für katholische Theologie,* 1895, pp. 651 sqq. For a well documented sketch of the Agnoëtae and their condemnation the student is referred to J. Lebreton, *Les Origines du Dogme de la Trinité,* pp. 458 sqq., Paris 1910.

55 *E. g.,* Eudoxius of Constantinople.

56 *E. g.,* Theodore of Mopsuestia and Nestorius himself.

57 They are also called Themistians, from their founder, Themistius, a Monophysite deacon of Alexandria.

58 ἄγνοια, *ignorantia.*

59 Cfr. Mark XIII, 32.

60 Cfr. Nicephor. Callist., *Hist. Eccles.,* XVIII, 50: οἱ καὶ λέγουσι τὸν Θεὸν Λόγον πάντα μὲν γινώσκειν, πάμπολλα δὲ ἀγνοεῖν τὴν ἡνωμένην αὐτῷ καθ' ὑπόστασιν ἀνθρωπότητα.

the human soul of Christ by ascribing to it a relative omniscience in regard to all actually existing things, due to its Hypostatic Union with the Logos. Agnoëtism they regarded as a positive heresy. The most prominent and the ablest among these champions of Catholic orthodoxy was Eulogius, Patriarch of Alexandria,[61] who, according to Photius,[62] taught that "*Neque humanitas Christi* [63] *in unam inaccessibilis et substantialis sapientiae hypostasim admissa quidquam ut rerum praesentium ita futurarum poterit ignorare.*[64] . . . *Quicumque enim vel divinitati ipsius vel humanitati ignorantiam adscribit, numquam certissimae temeritatis crimen effugiet.*" [65] St. Sophronius calls Themistius "*ignorantiae pater et genitor atque seminator nefandissimus.*" [66] Pope St. Gregory the Great in two letters extolled Eulogius as a brave and clever champion of the Catholic faith. "*De doctrina vestra contra haereticos, qui dicuntur Agnoitae,*" he says, "*fuit valde quod admiraremur, quod autem displiceret, non fuit. . . . Ita autem doctrina vestra per omnia latinis Patribus concordavit, ut mirum mihi non esset, quod in diversis linguis Spiritus non fuerit diversus. . . . Res autem est valde manifesta, quia quisquis Nestorianus non est, Agnoita esse nullatenus potest.*" [67] The last sentence is very important. In point of fact, though of Monophysitic origin, Agnoëtism is ultimately reducible either to Arianism, which denies the Divinity of Christ, or to Nestorianism, which rejects the Hypostatic Union. If Christ were a mere creature, as the Arians hold, He would necessarily be subject to

---

61 Died 608. Cfr. Bardenhewer-Shahan, *Patrology*, pp. 575 sq.

62 *Bibl. Cod.*, 230, n. 10 (Migne, P. G., CIII, 1069 sqq.).

63 τὸ ἀνθρώπινον.

64 ἀγνοήσει οὔτι, ὥσπερ τῶν παρόντων οὔτω δὴ οὐδὲν τῶν μελλόντων.

65 Cfr. Lebreton, *Les Origines du Dogme de la Trinité*, pp. 460 sq.

66 *Ep. Syn. ad Sergium.*

67 *Epist.*, l. X, 39.

ignorance and error; the same would follow from the Nestorian assumption that He was a person distinct from the omniscient Logos. It was for this reason, no doubt, that long before the time of Themistius the African bishops compelled the Gallic monk Leporius, who had incurred suspicion, to abjure Agnoëtism as heretical. Among other things in which Leporius had gone astray is the question of the human knowledge of Christ. He states that when he had heard Christ charged with ignorance, he had always considered it a sufficient answer to say that the Lord was ignorant " *secundum hominem*," but now he anathematized this opinion.[68]

Since, according to ecclesiastical Tradition, the relative omniscience of Christ, as man, has its source, principle, and measure in the Hypostatic Union, it follows that it must have begun simultaneously with the Hypostatic Union, *i. e.,* at the moment of His conception.[69]

β) The Fathers differed in their interpretation of Mark XIII, 32: "But of that day or hour no man knoweth, neither the angels in heaven, nor the Son, but the Father."

As long as it was necessary to combat the Arian heresy that the Logos was subject to " ignorance " because He was a creature, the Fathers confined themselves to de-

68 Cfr. Leporius, *Libell. Emend.,* n. 10 (Migne, *P. L.,* XXXI, 1229): " *Nunc non solum dicere non praesumo, verum etiam priorem anathematizo in hac parte sententiam, quia dici non licet, etiam secundum hominem ignorasse Dominum prophetarum.*"

69 On the Agnoëtism of the Protestant Reformers cfr. Bellarmine, *De Christo,* IV, 1–5; on the false teaching of Günther, J. Kleutgen, *Theologie der Vorzeit,* Vol. III, pp. 244 sqq., Münster 1870; on the view defended by H. Schell, L. Janssens, *De Deo-Homine,* Vol. I, pp. 418 sqq., Freiburg 1901; on the errors of the Modernists see the Syllabus of Pius X (Denzinger-Bannwart, *Enchiridion,* n. 2032 sqq.) and Felder, *Jesus Christus,* Vol. I.

fending Christ's *divine* nature against the charge of ignorance, and some passages in their writings create
the impression that they did it at the expense of His
sacred humanity. Leontius Byzantinus in his controversies with the Agnoëtae went so far as to admit that the
testimony of the earlier Fathers [70] was practically worth-
less in consequence of their having made this mistake.
Eulogius excused them on the plea that " If sundry
Fathers have admitted ignorance in the humanity of
our Saviour, they have not set it down as an article of
faith, but [made this admission] merely to reject the
folly of the Arians, who shifted all human attributes to
the Divinity in order to prove that the Divine Logos is
a creature." [71]   Petavius [72] takes a similar view, while
Suarez,[73] Kleutgen,[74] and Stentrup,[75] vigorously defend
the orthodoxy of the early Fathers.

Some of the Fathers explain Mark XIII, 32 in a mystic
sense, referring Christ's " ignorance " to His mystic body,
i. e., the Church.[76]   Others hold that when Christ said he
did not know the day of judgment, He meant that He had
no knowledge which He was free to communicate
(*scientia communicabilis*),[77] nor any knowledge derived
from His human intellect, abstracting from the Hypostatic Union.[78]   Of these three interpretations the
second and third are simple and natural, whereas the
first strikes one as factitious.   It is perfectly consonant
with the economy of salvation as proclaimed by our

---

70 Notably   Athanasius,   Basil,
Gregory   Nazianzen,   and   Cyril of
Alexandria.

71 In Photius' *Cod.*, 240.

72 *De Incarn.*, XI, 1.

73 *In Summam Theol.*, III, qu.
10, art. 2.

74 *Theologie der Vorzeit*, Vol.
III, pp. 258 sqq.

75 *Christologia*, thes. 73.

76 Thus   Origen,   Gregory   the
Great, etc.

77 This   theory   is   held   by   St.
Hilary, St. Augustine, and others.

78 Thus Gregory Nazianzen, John
Damascene, and others.

Lord on other occasions,[79] that the determination of the time of the last judgment should be reserved to the official sphere of the Father, and that the Son had consequently no right to reveal it.[80]   On the other hand it is obvious that the humanity of Christ, being a creature, could not of itself know the hidden counsels of Providence, though our Lord no doubt possessed this knowledge by and through the Hypostatic Union, because He was the " Son of man " and destined to be the Judge of the living and the dead.[81]

c) The theological argument for our thesis is based on the fact that, though a true man, Christ was not a mere man, but the Godman.   As Godman He had a formal claim to the most perfect knowledge of which His soul was capable.[82] As a wayfarer He cannot have been less perfect than Adam, who was endowed with infused knowledge,[83] nor less wise than Solomon, whose mind was directly enlightened by God.

79 Cfr. Matth. XX, 23; Acts I, 7.
80 Cfr. St. Augustine, *Enarr. in Ps.*, 36, Serm. I, 1: " *Quia vero Dominus noster Iesus Christus magister nobis missus est, etiam Filius hominis dixit se nescire illum diem, quia in magisterio eius non erat, ut per eum sciretur a nobis.*"
81 Cfr. Gregory the Great, *Ep.*, X, 39: " *In natura quidem humanitatis novit diem et horam iudicii, sed tamen hunc non ex natura humanitatis novit.*"— Additional arguments in Kleutgen's *Theologie der Vorzeit*, Vol. III, pp. 256 sqq.; Chr. Pesch, *Praelect. Dogmat.*, Vol. IV,

pp. 157 sqq.— On the exegetical interpretation of Mark XIII, 32, see A. Seitz, *Das Evangelium vom Gottessohn*, pp. 251 sqq., Freiburg 1908; W. T. C. Sheppard, O. S. B., " The ' Kenosis ' according to St. Mark," in the *Irish Theological Quarterly*, Vol. V (1910), No. 19; J. Lebreton, *Les Origines du Dogme de la Trinité*, pp. 447-458.
82 St. Thomas, *S. Theol.*, 3a, qu. 9, art. 3.
83 Cfr. Pohle-Preuss, *God the Author of Nature and the Supernatural*, pp. 207 sqq.

St. Paul teaches that Christ was from the very instant of His conception elevated to the headship of the angelic creation,[84] and that it was therefore congruous that His soul should know the purely spiritual beings subject to His rule not *per species alienas,* but *per species proprias infusas,* though of course only in so far as this angelic mode of knowledge is supernaturally communicable to a human soul.[85]

Thesis III: The soul of Christ likewise possessed a progressive experimental or empiric knowledge (scientia acquisita).

This thesis may be said to voice the common teaching of theologians.

Proof. Besides the divine knowledge which Jesus, *qua* man, enjoyed by virtue of the beatific vision, and besides the angelic knowledge infused immediately into His human soul, He also possessed acquired knowledge, *i. e.,* that specifically human knowledge which is gained through sense perception and the natural use of reason.

This kind of knowledge was not, it is true, indispensable to the perfection of His intellect. But along with the state which was His by virtue of the beatific vision, Christ had also assumed what theologians call the wayfaring state, namely that in which men are constituted during their mortal lives here upon earth, while on

---

84 *V. supra,* pp. 243 sq.

85 Cfr. St. Thomas, *S. Theol.,* 3a, qu. 11, art. 4. On the extent of this infused knowledge cfr. Suarez, *De Incarn.,* disp. 27 sq.; on the distinction between *scientia infusa per se* and *per accidens,* and the controversies incident thereto, see De Lugo, *De Myst. Incarn.,* disp. 21, sect. 1.

the way to their heavenly home.[86] As a wayfarer He was entitled to the mode of knowledge appropriate to the state of earthly pilgrimage. Although by virtue of the *scientia beata* and the *scientia infusa* Christ knew everything that experience could teach Him, still He was after a fashion able to "learn," that is, to become acquainted with what He already knew, as it were from a different point of view, *i. e.,* that of human experience. Such a knowledge, though limited in value, is not without its usefulness. As the "morning knowledge" of the Angels by no means renders their inferior "evening knowledge" valueless, though the two differ only in mode and origin but not in content, so the acquired knowledge of Jesus may have added new and valuable momenta to what He already knew from other sources. Was not His personal experience of actual suffering something totally different from the concept of His Passion previously existing in His human intellect? Cfr. Heb. V, 8: *"Et quidem quum esset Filius Dei, didicit ex iis, quae passus est, obedientiam —* And whereas indeed He was the Son of God, he learned obedience by the things which he suffered." [87]

a) That our Lord really possessed acquired knowledge can be proved from the fact that He was a perfectly organized man, equipped with all the natural faculties of a human being, both sensitive and intellectual. His nature demanded experimental knowledge. To deny this would savor of Docetism.[88]

---

86 Cfr. W. Humphrey, S. J., *The One Mediator*, p. 262.

87 G. Pierse, "Our Lord's Experiential Knowledge," *Irish Theol. Quarterly*, Vol. XV, No. 58, pp. 113 sqq.

88 The Docetae held that the sacred humanity was fictitious and apparitional. *V. supra*, pp. 41 sqq.

Basing his argument on the Aristotelian and Scholastic distinction between the *intellectus agens* and the *intellectus possibilis*,[89] St. Thomas argues out this point as follows: "*Nihil eorum, quae Deus in nostra natura plantavit, defuit naturae assumptae a Dei Verbo. Manifestum est autem, quod in humana natura Deus plantavit non solum intellectum possibilem, sed etiam intellectum agentem. Unde necesse est dicere, quod in anima Christi fuit non solum intellectus possibilis, sed etiam intellectus agens. Si autem in aliis Deus et natura nihil frustra faciunt, . . . multo minus in anima Christi aliquid fuit frustra. Frustra autem est, quod non habet propriam operationem. . . . Propria autem operatio intellectus agentis est facere species intelligibiles actu, abstrahendo eas a phantasmatibus* [= process of abstraction]. *Sic igitur necesse est dicere, quod in Christo fuerint aliquae species intelligibiles per actionem intellectus agentis in intellectu possibili eius receptae: quod est esse in ipso scientiam acquisitam, quam quidem experimentalem vocant.*"[90] Expressed in modern terms this means: The human soul of Christ, like any other human soul, acquired universal ideas by abstracting intellectual concepts from sensible phantasms. St. Luke tells us[91] that Jesus "advanced in wisdom," which, when applied to natural experience, must be understood not merely of a gradual outward manifestation, but of real inward increase.[92] "*Quomodo proficiebat sapientia Dei?*" asks St. Ambrose, and answers: "*Doceat te ordo verborum. Profectus est aetatis et profectus sapientiae, sed humanae est. Ideo aetatem ante praemisit, ut secundum hominem*

---

89 On the Aristotelian theory of abstraction as developed by the Scholastics, cfr. M. Maher, S. J., *Psychology*, pp. 303 sqq., 8th ed., London 1906.

90 *S. Theol.*, 3a, qu. 9, art. 4.

91 Luke II, 52: προέκοπτε σοφία καὶ ἡλικίᾳ.

92 *V. supra*, p. 237.

credenes dictum; aetas enim non divinitatis, sed corporis est. Ergo si proficiebat aetate hominis, proficiebat sapientiâ hominis, sapientia autem sensu proficit." [93] St. Thomas says: *" Tam scientia infusa animae Christi quam scientia beata fuit effectus agentis infinitae virtutis, qui potest simul totum operari; et ita in neutra scientia Christus profecit, sed a principio eam perfectam habuit. Sed scientia acquisita causatur ab intellectu agente, qui non simul totum operatur, sed successive; et ideo secundum hanc scientiam Christus non a principio scivit omnia, sed paulatim et post aliquod tempus, scil. in perfecta aetate: quod patet ex hoc quod Evangelista simul dicit eum profecisse scientiâ et aetate."* [94]

b) As appears from the last sentence of the preceding quotation, the Angelic Doctor holds that there was a true advance in the experimental knowledge of Christ, and that this knowledge gradually increased until it had exhausted all those objects which can be known by means of the *intellectus agens*. In order to show the possibility of such a " natural omniscience " (which is not omniscience in the strict sense of the term) sundry theologians have had recourse to more or less fantastic theories. Suarez, De Lugo, and among modern writers Tepe, adopted the theory of a *scientia per accidens infusa,* which St. Thomas had taught in his youth but retracted in the *Summa Theologica.*[96] Others, like Cardinal Cajetan, held that the natural experimental knowledge of Christ was brought to the highest state of perfection by the successive presentation to His senses (through the ministry of angels) of all the various objects that go to make up the physical universe (fish, birds, brute beasts, the stars, etc.). Duran-

[93] *De Incarn.,* VII, 71.
[94] *S. Theol.,* 3a, qu. 12, art. 2, ad 1.
[95] Cfr. also *S. Theol.,* 3a, qu. 12, art. 1.
[96] *S. Theol.,* 3a, qu. 9, art. 4.

dus, Marsilius, Gabriel Biel, and Cardinal Toletus took middle ground between these two extremes. They maintained that the knowledge which our Lord gained by the exercise of His natural faculties, though ineffably perfect, was not and never became absolutely infinite. It seems indeed sufficient to hold that Christ represents the unattainable ideal of all empirical knowledge and natural science. What Adam and Solomon were unable to learn by natural means and knew only by virtue of the *scientia per accidens infusa,* was part of the connatural perfection of Christ and acquired by Him gradually in proportion to His advance in age. This theory safeguards the dignity of the Divine Logos and at the same time does full justice to the dogma of the genuinity of the human nature of Jesus. Experimental knowledge is comparatively less perfect than either beatific or infused knowledge, but even though finite, it perfects and ennobles its possessor.

READINGS: — W. Humphrey, S. J., *The One Mediator,* pp. 252 sqq., London *s. a.*—J. M. Harty, "The Modern Kenotic Theory," in the *Irish Theological Quarterly,* Vol. I (1906), Nos. 1 and 2.—For the history of the "Kenotic problem" consult E. J. Hanna, "The Human Knowledge of Christ" in the *New York Review,* Vol. I (1905-6), Nos. 3 and 4; Vol. III (1908), Nos. 4 and 5; also E. Schulte, O. F. M., *Die Entwicklung der Lehre vom menschlichen Wissen Christi bis zum Beginn der Scholastik,* Paderborn 1914.—Lépicier, *De Incarn. Verbi,* Vol. I, pp. 395 sqq. —M. Lepin, *Christ and the Gospel,* Philadelphia 1910.—J. Kleutgen, S. J., *Theologie der Vorzeit,* Vol. III, pp. 244 sqq., Münster 1870.—Bellarmine, *Controversiae de Christo,* l. IV, c. 1-5.— J. Lebreton, *Les Origines du Dogme de la Trinité,* Note C, pp. 447 sqq., Paris 1910.—F. J. Hall (Anglican), *The Kenotic Theory,* pp. 176 sqq., New York 1898.—M. Waldhäuser, *Die Kenose und die moderne prot. Christologie,* Mainz 1912.—J. Marić, *De Agnoëtarum Doctrina,* Zagreb (Croatia) 1914.—V. Kwiatkowski, *De Scientia Beata in Anima Christi,* Warsaw 1922.— S. Szabó, O. P., *De Scientia Beata Christi* (*Xenia Thomistica,* VII), Rome 1925.

ARTICLE 3

THE ADORABLENESS OF CHRIST'S HUMANITY

1. PRELIMINARY NOTIONS.—Worship is rever-
ential respect paid to another. It requires two
numerically distinct beings: a person who exhibits
respect and another person, or a thing, to whom
or to which it is exhibited. There are as many
ways of paying respect and homage as there are
perfections which call for worship. The worship
due to God is called adoration (*cultus latriae*).
That worship to which creatures are entitled by
reason of such supernatural excellences as they
may possess in the order of sanctification and
union with God, is called *cultus duliae*. Corresponding to the unique excellence of the Blessed
Virgin Mary as Mother of God, there is a special
worship, which, to distinguish it from the inferior
cult due to lesser saints, is called *hyperdulia*.

Adoratio (Gr. προσκύνησις), in the usage of the Church
and of Scholastic theology, is a generic term, denoting
sometimes *latria,* sometimes *dulia.* The true sense must
in each instance be determined from the context. To
render divine worship to a creature is idolatry and a most
grievous sin.

These different forms of worship admit of
other distinctions, according as they are directed
to a prototype or a mere ectype.

By a prototype we understand the original and proper possessor of adorable prerogatives or excellencies. A prototype in this technical sense is always a person, never an object. Worship rendered to a prototype is called absolute (*cultus absolutus*). Absolute worship may again be subdivided into absolute *latria* and *dulia*. When exhibited to an ectype,— which is always an object, never a person,— worship is called relative (*cultus relativus*). Relative worship may also be subdivided into *latria* and *dulia*. Relative *latria* is the worship rendered, *e. g.*, to an image of Christ or of the Blessed Trinity; relative *dulia* is the worship rendered to a relic, the picture of a saint, a flag, etc.

A distinction of special importance lies between the material and the formal object of worship. By the material object of worship we understand the person or thing honored; its formal object is the immanent reason or motive for which honor is rendered. Since there can be no worship without some reason, material and formal object are always bound up together. The connexion between the two may be either (1) *per modum identitatis,* as in the case of Almighty God, in whom nature and adorability coincide; or (2) *per modum unionis physicae,* as in the case of the humanity of our Lord, which becomes adorable by its Hypostatic Union with the Logos; or (3) *per modum unionis moralis,* as in the case of images and relics of saints, which owe their character as objects of worship to the relation they bear to their respective prototypes. Worship *per modum unionis moralis* is always strictly relative.

A kind of subdivision of the formal object of worship is the so-called *obiectum manifestativum,* which plays such an important part in the beautiful devotion to the Sacred Heart of Jesus. By *obiectum manifestativum* we understand a formal object of worship which, though in itself rather remote, is particularly effective in its appeal to the worshipper.

A beggar who kisses the hand of his benefactor does so for the reason that the goodness and liberality of the almsgiver manifest themselves in a special manner through that particular organ of the body. Such veneration is at bottom nothing else than veneration of the benefactor himself. So we may prefer to adore God as our benefactor rather than as the Supreme Being, because His mercy touches our hearts and gives concrete expression, as it were, to the adorability of His Divine Majesty. Similarly, we adore the Five Wounds of our Divine Saviour, because they manifest His infinite love for us in a special manner; but the real and ultimate object of our worship is the Godman as such.[1]

2. THE DOGMA.—The divine worship which we render to the Logos as such (Λόγος ἄσαρκος) is identical with adoration of the *one* true God. The only two questions which can concern us here

---

1 Cfr. Franzelin, *De Verbo Incarn.*, thes. 45; Billuart, *De Incarn.*, diss. 23, art. 1.

are these: Are we justified in adoring Christ as the Word Incarnate (Λόγος ἔνσαρκος) ? and are we in duty bound so to adore Him?   These questions resolve themselves into three others, namely: (1) Is the Godman (*i. e.,* Christ in both His natures) entitled to divine adoration (*latria*) ?   (2) Must we also adore the man Jesus, *i. e.,* the concrete sacred humanity of Christ?   (3) Is it permissible to render divine worship (*latria*) to the several members of Christ's sacred humanity, in particular to His Sacred Heart?   We shall answer these questions in three distinct theses.

Thesis I: Christ as the Godman is entitled to divine worship.

This thesis embodies a truth which is of faith.

Proof.   To adore Christ in a different way as man than as Son of God would be to countenance the heresy of Nestorius that there are two persons in the Godman.   The Council of Ephesus (A. D. 431) formally defined the true relation of the two natures by adopting the eighth anathematism of St. Cyril, to wit: *"Si quis audet dicere assumptum hominem coadorandum Deo Verbo . . . tamquam alterum cum altero,*[2] *. . . ac non potius unâ supplicatione*[3] *veneratur Emmanuel, . . . iuxta quod Verbum caro factum est, anathema sit* — If anyone dare to assert that the man assumed

[2] ὡς ἕτερον ἐν ἑτέρῳ.   [3] μιᾷ προσκυνήσει.

into the Divine Logos must be adored as a Person distinct from the Logos . . . and that Emmanuel is not worshipped by one and the same act, . . . according as the Word was made flesh, let him be anathema." This same truth was still more clearly defined by the Fifth Council of Constantinople (A. D. 553): *"Si quis in duabus naturis adorari dicit Christum, ex quo duas adorationes introducunt separatim Deo Verbo et separatim homini,*[4] *vel si quis . . . non unâ adoratione Deum Verbum incarnatum cum propria ipsius carne*[5] *adorat, . . . talis anathema sit —* If any one say that Christ is adored in two natures, separately as the Divine Word and separately as a man, or if any one do not adore God the Word Incarnate together with His own flesh by one act of worship, . . . let him be anathema."[6] Hence it is an article of faith that the Godman as such is entitled to the same worship as the Divine Logos.

a) The Biblical argument for this thesis rests partly on the divine adoration rendered to our Lord by the magi,[7] the man born blind,[8] etc., and partly on Christ's positive claim to divine worship, which is echoed by His Apostles. He Himself commands "all men [to] honor the Son as

---

[4] ἰδίᾳ τῷ Θεῷ Λόγῳ καὶ ἰδίᾳ τῷ ἀνθρώπῳ.

[5] μετὰ ἰδίας αὐτοῦ σαρκός.

[6] Cfr. Denzinger-Bannwart, *Enchiridion,* n. 120 and n. 221.

[7] Matth. II, 11.

[8] John IX, 35 sqq.

they honor the Father." [9]   St. Paul says: "Let all the angels of God adore Him," [10] and lays it down as a divine precept "that in the name of Jesus every knee should bow, of those that are in heaven, on earth, and under the earth." [11]

b) The Fathers base the doctrine of the *unica adoratio* due to the Godman on the fact that He was the Son of God and true God after His Incarnation as well as before. The Divine Logos became man in virtue of the Hypostatic Union, consequently the man Jesus is true God and worthy of divine adoration. As St. Cyril told Nestorius: "We do not adore a man who is the bearer of a God,[12] but God made man." [13]   Even Theodoret of Cyrus,[14] who was suspected of Nestorian leanings, confesses: "After (as before) the Incarnation [15] we adore the one Son of God,[16] our Lord Jesus Christ, and call those infidels [17] who think otherwise."

Thesis II: Because of its Hypostatic Union with the Logos, the humanity of our Lord is entitled to divine worship in itself, though not for its own sake.

This proposition, though not an article of faith, is generally held to be a revealed truth (*fidei proximum saltem*).

9 John V, 23.

10 Heb. I, 6; cfr. Ps. XCVI, 7.

11 Phil. II, 10. Cfr. Apoc. V, 11 sqq. For other instances of divine worship rendered to Jesus in the Gospels see A. Seitz, *Das Evangelium vom Gottessohn*, pp. 263 sqq., Freiburg 1908. For further information consult Pohle-Preuss, *The Divine Trinity*, pp. 73 sqq.

12 θεοφόρον ἄνθρωπον.

13 ἐνανθρωπήσαντα Θεόν.

14 *Ep. ad Flav.*, 104. Other Patristic texts in Petavius, *De Incarn.*, XV, 3. Cfr. St. Thomas, *S. Theol.*, 3a, qu. 25, art. 1.

15 καὶ μετὰ τὴν ἐνανθρώπησιν.

16 ἕνα προσκυνοῦμεν υἱὸν τοῦ Θεοῦ.

17 δυσσεβεῖς.

Proof.   Let us first determine the state of the
question.   There is a large distinction between
the two propositions: "The humanity of Christ
is adored in itself," and "The humanity of Christ
is adored for its own sake."

The former proposition means that the human nature
of Christ is the immediate terminus or object of divine
worship (*obiectum materiale, sed partiale*); the latter,
that it is its motive or formal object.   To assert the
latter would be false and blasphemous, because the
sacred humanity of Christ is essentially a creature.   The
adorability of Christ's human nature does not rest upon
a Monophysitic deification, but simply and solely on the
Hypostatic Union.   Christ's humanity did not exist
apart from the Logos, but was assumed into the latter as
a quasi-part.   Whatever belongs to a person substantially (as in this case the humanity of Christ), is
worthy of the same specific veneration as the person
himself.   The veneration exhibited to a monarch, *e. g.*,
is not limited to his soul, but extends to his body, and
is in both respects a *cultus absolutus*, directed primarily
to the royal personage and only in a secondary manner to
whatever essentially belongs to that personage.   Hence
John Wiclif was wrong in asserting that the sacred humanity of our Lord is entitled to relative worship only.
The union of Divinity and humanity in the Godman
creates more than a mere moral bond.

The malicious insinuation of the Jansenist Council of
Pistoia (1794), that "direct adoration of the manhood
of Christ is equivalent to rendering divine honors to a
creature," was formally condemned by Pope Pius VI.[18]

---

[18] "*Falsa, captiosa, pio ac debito   praestito et praestando detrahens et
cultui humanitati Christi a fidelibus   iniuriosa.*" (Bull "*Auctorem Fi-*

a) That the sacred humanity of our Lord is a fit material object of divine adoration (*obiectum materiale partiale*) can be proved from Sacred Scripture and the unanimous teaching of the Fathers.

Cfr. Apoc. V, 12: "The lamb that was slain is worthy to receive power, and divinity, and wisdom, and strength, and honor, and glory, and benediction."

The Fathers adduce the following reasons:

a) If we were not permitted to adore the sacred humanity of our Redeemer directly, *i. e.,* in itself, the Second Person of the Most Blessed Trinity, *i. e.,* the Divine Logos, since the Incarnation would be deprived of the worship of *latria;* for the Incarnate Word exists only as Godman. This argument is made much of by St. Athanasius, who says among other things: "We by no means adore a creature; this is an error of the heathen and the Arians. But we do adore the Lord of the creature, the God-Logos made flesh. For although the flesh is of itself something created, it has become the body of God. But in adoring this body we do not separate it from the Logos, nor do we detach the Logos, when we wish to adore Him, from His flesh. . . . Who, then, is so foolish as to say to the Lord: 'Depart from Thy body, that I may adore Thee'?"[19] St. Epiphanius expresses himself in similar language. "Let no one say to the Only-begotten: Put away Thy body, that I may adore Thee,[20] but adore the Only-begotten One with the

dei," quoted by Denzinger-Bannwart, *Enchiridion,* n. 1561.)

19 *Ep. ad Adelphium,* n. 3.

20 ἀφὲς τὸ σῶμα, ἵνα σε προσκυνήσω.

body,[21] the Uncreated One with the temple which He assumed at His descent." [22]

β) The assertion of the Apollinarists that those who worship the sacred humanity of our Lord adore a man and mere flesh,[23] is a shameless calumny which St. Athanasius thus indignantly repels in the first of his Two Books Against Apollinaris: "Again you say: 'We do not adore the creature.' Ye fools! Why do you not consider that the created body of the Lord must receive more than the veneration which is due to the creature? For it has become the body of the increate Logos, and you adore Him whose body it is. [This body], therefore, is adored with due divine worship, because God is the Logos whose body it is. Thus the women . . . embraced his feet and adored. They held the feet, but adored God." [24]

γ) Since the sacred humanity of Christ is in itself adorable, we must also render divine worship to His body and blood as really and truly present in the Holy Eucharist. In an explanation of Psalm XCVIII, 5 St. Ambrose remarks: "*Per scabellum terra intelligitur, per terram autem caro Christi, quam hodie quoque in mysteriis [sc. Eucharistiae] adoramus et quam Apostoli in Domino Iesu adorarunt. Neque enim divisus est Christus, sed unus.*" [25] St. Augustine expounds the same text as follows: "*Adorate scabellum pedum eius. Fluctuans converto me ad Christum, quia ipsum quaero hic, et invenio quomodo sine impietate adoretur terra . . . et scabellum pedum eius. Suscepit enim de terra terram, quia caro de terra est et de carne Mariae carnem*

---

21 σὺν τῷ σώματι τὸν μονογενῆ.
22 *Ancor.*, 4.
23 ἀνθρωπολάτραι, σαρκολάτραι.
24 *Contr. Apollin.*, I, 6. There are, however, reasons for doubting the genuineness of this work. Cfr. Bardenhewer-Shahan, *Patrology*, p. 256.

25 *De Spiritu Sancto*, III, 11, 79.

suscepit. Et quia in hac ipsa carne hic ambulavit et ipsam carnem nobis manducandam ad salutem dedit — nemo autem illam carnem manducat, nisi prius adoraverit — inventum est, quemadmodum adoretur tale scabellum pedum Domini et non solum non peccemus adorando, sed peccemus non adorando." [26]

δ) The worship we render to the sacred humanity of our Lord is not idolatry, because we do not adore mere flesh, but flesh hypostatically united with the Divine Logos. St. John Damascene develops this thought with an acuteness which might almost be termed Scholastic. "The flesh is not to be adored in its own nature," he says, "but it is adored with the Incarnate Logos, not indeed for its own sake, but for the sake of its Logos, with whom it is hypostatically united. For we do not profess that it is the naked, simple flesh which is adored, but the flesh of God, or God made flesh." [27]

b) It is, however, a matter of debate among divines whether the sacred humanity of Christ considered in itself, *i. e.,* without regard to the Hypostatic Union, besides *latria* is also entitled to the worship of *dulia,* or, more specifically, *hyperdulia,* directed solely to His created perfections, *e. g.,* sanctifying grace and the seven gifts of the Holy Spirit. [28]

The Thomists [29] take the affirmative side.

Suarez, who agrees with them, says that Christ's title

---

26 *In Ps.,* 98, 5.

27 *De Fide Orth.,* IV, 3. For additional Patristic evidence consult Vasquez, *In S. Theol.,* III, disp. 95 sq.; Petavius, *De Incarn.,* XV, 3 sq.;

Schwetz, *Theol. Dogmat.,* t. II, 2nd ed., pp. 62 sqq., Vindobonae 1880.

28 *V. supra,* Article 1.

29 Cfr. Billuart, *De Incarn.,* diss. 23, art. 3.

to the worship of *hyperdulia* is based upon the innumerable and exalted creatural prerogatives, both natural and supernatural, of His sacred humanity.[30] But this theory is open to the grave objection [31] that such an inferior species of worship might easily lead to a disparagement of Our Lord's divine dignity. The theoretical truth that our Lord is entitled to various kinds of worship does not justify us in actually exhibiting to Him a cultus which, at its lowest, sinks below the level of *latria,* to which His sacred humanity has a strict claim. No good Catholic would dream of honoring the Sovereign Pontiff merely in his capacity of Bishop or Cardinal, though these titles and the dignity corresponding to each are no doubt included in the papal prerogatives. Similarly, though Christ's sacred humanity is endowed with certain prerogatives which in themselves are entitled to no more than hyperdulic worship, we do not worship Him merely with the veneration which we exhibit, *e. g.,* to His Blessed Mother, because to render Him this lower kind of worship would be equivalent to denying Him the strictly divine adoration to which He also has a right, just as the recognition of an adoptive sonship in the man Jesus consistently leads to a denial of His natural Sonship.[32] Billuart is therefore guilty of a sophism when he says: "*Humanitas sic praecisa potest amari et laudari, ergo et adorari (scil. hyperduliâ).*" [33] To consider Christ's created pre-

---

[30] "*Si Christus ut homo praecise adoretur propter dignitatem et excellentiam, quam eius humanitas habet ex vi unionis, illa adoratio non erit perfecta latria, sed inferior . . . et proprie hyperdulia dicitur.*" (*De Incarn.,* disp. 53, sect. 2, n. 7.)

[31] Emphasized especially by Vasquez (*In S. Theol.,* III, disp. 96, c, 4), De Lugo (*De Myst. Incarn.,* disp. 35, art. 3), Chr. Pesch (*Praelect Dogmat.,* Vol. IV, 3rd ed., pp. 114 sqq.).

[32] *V. supra,* pp. 196 sqq.

[33] *De Incarn.,* disp. 23, art. 3.

rogatives abstractly for themselves, to admire, to love and to praise them, is not the same as to render them the worship of *hyperdulia*. Since it is impossible to separate these prerogatives from the Person of the Logos and to argue that, if Christ's sacred humanity, which is endowed with so many graces, existed in a separate human person apart from the Logos, it would be entitled to a higher degree of hyperdulic worship than the Blessed Virgin Mary, is dogmatically inadmissible for the reason that the sacred humanity with all its prerogatives is inseparably (ἀχωριστῶς) united to the Person of the Logos.

St. Thomas seems to admit that we may render to our Lord and Saviour Jesus Christ the worship of *dulia* side by side with that of *latria*. "*Adoratio humanitatis Christi*," he says, "*dupliciter potest intelligi: uno modo, ut sit eius sicut rei adoratae, et sic adorare carnem Christi nihil est aliud quam adorare Verbum Dei incarnatum. . . . Alio modo potest intelligi adoratio humanitatis Christi, quae fit ratione humanitatis Christi perfectae omni munere gratiarum, et sic adoratio humanitatis Christi non est adoratio latriae, sed adoratio duliae, ita scil. quod una et eadem persona Christi adoretur adoratione latriae propter suam divinitatem et adoratione duliae propter perfectionem humanitatis.*"[34] This passage has been variously interpreted. Franzelin understands St. Thomas as teaching that the sacred humanity of Christ is simply the *obiectum manifestationis* of the only kind of worship which we are permitted to render Him, *viz.: latria*.[35] Chr. Pesch holds that in the opinion of the Angelic Doctor the worship of *latria* virtually includes that of *dulia* and *hyperdulia* respectively, but that

34 *S. Theol.*, 3a, qu. 25, art. 2.
35 Franzelin, *De Verbo Incarn.*, thes. 45, coroll. 2.

the permissibility of the former does not argue the permissibility of the latter.[36] But such interpretations seem unwarranted. Medina, Billuart, L. Janssens, and others explain the passage literally, so that for once we find ourselves compelled, with all due reverence, to deviate from what on the face of it appears to be the teaching of the Angelic Doctor. At the present time there is a special reason for taking a different view of the question than did Aquinas. Despite the innumerable hyperdulic excellencies proper to the Sacred Heart of Jesus, the Church regards the worship paid to this particular organ of our Lord's human body as exclusively latreutic.

Thesis III: The sacred humanity of Christ as a whole, and its several members, especially His Sacred Heart, are entitled to divine adoration (latria).

This thesis embodies a well-established theological conclusion.

Proof. The adorability of Christ's human nature in its totality is entirely due to its Hypostatic Union with the Logos. This applies *a fortiori* to its constituent parts, such as, *e. g.,* His soul, His Precious Blood, the Five Wounds of His Sacred Body, all of which are inseparably united with the Logos.

a) Devotion to any one of these parts, therefore, properly takes the form of adoration (*cultus latriae*). Though immediately directed to these separate parts or organs, the formal object or motive of such adoration is the Godhead itself, or, concretely, the Divine Logos, who is hypostatically united with Christ's sacred hu-

[36] *Praelect. Dogmat.,* Vol. IV, p. 115.

manity, both in its totality and in its several parts. The
Acts of the Nicene Council, which were cited by the
Council of Ephesus, though their authenticity is not
entirely beyond doubt, contain this passage: " *Confite-*
mur D. N. Iesum Christum . . . totum adorabilem
etiam cum corpore, sed non secundum corpus adorabilem,
. . . totus quippe ergo Deus etiam cum corpore, non
secundum corpus; totus adorandus etiam cum corpore,
non propter corpus." [37]

Upon this principle is based the devotion to the Sacred
Heart, inaugurated by Sister Margaret Mary Alacoque,
of Paray-le-Monial in Burgundy (d. 1690). Blessed
and nurtured by the Roman Pontiffs, this devotion has
spread over the Christian world and proved a rich source
of blessings. Though opposed by the Jansenists, it was
officially approved in 1765, and soon became immensely
popular. On August 26th, 1850, Pope Pius IX raised
the Feast of the Sacred Heart to the rank of a festival of
the Universal Church, and at the dawn of the twentieth
century, the immortal Leo XIII, by a solemn act of consecration performed in all the churches of the universe,
dedicated the entire human race to the Sacred Heart of
Jesus.

The Jansenistic Council of Pistoia referred to the
adoration of the Sacred Heart as " novel, erroneous, or at
least dangerous," but Pope Pius VI, in his dogmatic
Bull "*Auctorem Fidei*" (1794), denounced this opinion
as " false, venturesome, pernicious, offensive to pious
ears, and injurious to the Apostolic See." [38] In the same
Bull the insinuation that the faithful adore the Heart of

37 Cfr. Hardouin, *Concil.*, Vol. I, p. 1639.

38 "*Falsa, temeraria, perniciosa, piarum aurium offensiva, in Apo-stolicam Sedem iniuriosa.*" (Den-zinger-Bannwart, *Enchiridion*, n. 1562.)

Jesus apart from the Godhead was condemned as "captious and injurious to the faithful worshippers of the Sacred Heart," who, in the words of the Pontiff, adore this organ of our Lord's human body "as the Heart of the Person of the Logos, with which it is inseparably united." [39]

The dogmatic reasons alleged in these pontifical decisions fully coincide with those we have adduced in confirmation of our Second Thesis. The Sacred Heart is the material and partial, though not the formal object, of divine adoration (*latria*). In other words, we worship it "in itself, but not for its own sake." The sole formal object and motive of adoration is its Divinity, due to the Hypostatic Union.

It may be asked: What particular motives prompt the Church to urge the faithful to worship the Sacred Heart of Jesus in preference to other organs of His body? She must have special reasons for doing this, since not every devotion that is dogmatically unobjectionable is recommended for general adoption. We can conceive of devotions which, though dogmatically correct, might even cause disedification and scandal.

The worship of any special organ of our

[39] ". . . quasi fideles cor Iesu adorarent cum separatione vel praecisione a divinitate, dum illud adorant ut est cor Iesu, cor nempe personae Verbi, cui inseparabiliter unitum est: . . . captiosa, in fideles cordis Iesu cultores iniuriosa." (Const. "Auctorem Fidei," in Denzinger-Bannwart's Enchiridion, n. 1563.)

Lord's sacred Body does not hinge entirely on the question whether that particular organ is adorable in itself, but primarily on the question whether the worship rendered to it is apt to manifest our Lord's condescension and love for humankind, and to bring Him nearer to us. From this point of view it may safely be asserted that no organ of our Saviour's body is so apt to serve as *obiectum manifestativum* as the Sacred Heart, regarded as the material seat of Christ's theandric love for mankind. In the languages of all nations, and particularly in that of the Sacred Scriptures of both the Old and the New Testament, the heart is the symbol of love.[40]

The teaching of the Church was misinterpreted by Camillus Blasius, an auditor of the Rota, who published a shallow dissertation at Rome in 1771 under the title *Dissertatio de Festo Cordis Iesu*. He claimed that the symbolic, not the material Heart is the object of our adoration, which is tantamount to saying that the Church proposes to the worship of the faithful an intangible metonymy, a substanceless metaphor, an abstract symbol. Can this be possible? It is true that the Sacred Congregation of Rites, in the decree by which it instituted the Feast of the Sacred Heart (February 6th, 1765), employed the phrase: " [*Hoc cultu*] *symbolice renovari memoriam illius divini amoris, quo unigenitus Dei Filius humanam suscepit naturam.*" But this phrase

---

40 The circumstance that modern physiology assigns the ganglia as the seat of love as a sensitive affection, does not impair this argument. Cfr. Leroy, *De SS. Corde Iesu eiusque Cultu*, pp. 22 sqq., Leodii 1882.

must be interpreted in accordance with the petition of the Bishops of Poland, to which the decree was a reply. In that petition we read: *"En res, quam Iesus colendam proponit, nimirum cor suum sacrosanctum, non tantum ut est symbolum omnium interiorum affectionum, sed ut est in se."* [41] The matter was cleared up beyond a peradventure by Pope Pius VI in his Bull *"Auctorem Fidei"*: *". . . illud adorant [fideles],"* he says, *" ut est cor Iesu, cor nempe personae Verbi, cui inseparabiliter unitum est ad eum modum, quo exsangue corpus Christi in triduo mortis sine separatione a divinitate adorabile fuit in sepulcro."* [42] Surely it was not the " symbolic " Heart that was " inseparably united with the Person of the Logos," any more than it was the " symbolic " body of the Saviour that reposed for three days in the tomb.[43]

The Church has solemnly approved the worship of the Sacred Heart of Jesus and sanctioned it liturgically by the incorporation of special prayers in her Breviary and Missal. Hence Catholics are no longer free to reject this admirable devotion as incorrect or inadmissible. All good Christians will hail with joy and join in the adoration of that Divine Heart which beats for us in undiminished love both in Heaven and on our altars. Amid the spiritual afflictions of our cold and unbelieving age nothing is so well

41 Cfr. N. Nilles, *De Rationibus Festorum SS. Cordis Iesu et Purissimi Cordis Mariae,* 4th ed., pp. 120 sqq., Ratisbon 1885.

42 Cfr. Denzinger-Bannwart, *Enchiridion,* n. 1563.

43 On the divergent opinions held by different theologians in regard to the *proximate* object of the worship of the Sacred Heart, cfr. Chr. Pesch, *Praelect. Dogmat.,* Vol. IV, pp. 124 sq.

justified as the ardent petition: "Sacred Heart of Jesus, have mercy on us!"

READINGS: — Wilhelm-Scannell, *A Manual of Catholic Theology,* Vol. II, pp. 117, 2nd ed., London 1901.— S. J. Hunter, S. J., *Outlines of Dogmatic Theology,* Vol. II, pp. 497 sqq., 2nd ed., *s. a.*—*L. Leroy, *De SS. Corde Iesu eiusque Cultu,* Leodii 1882. — J. Jungmann, S. J., *Die Andacht zum hl. Herzen Jesu und die Bedenken gegen dieselbe,* 2nd ed., Freiburg 1885.—N. Nilles, S. J., *De Rationibus Festorum SS. Cordis Iesu et Purissimi Cordis Mariae,* 2 vols., 5th ed., Ratisbon 1885.— IDEM, *The Devotion to the Sacred Heart* (tr. by W. H. Kent, O. S. C.), London 1905.— H. J. Nix, S. J., *De Cultu SS. Cordis Iesu Notiones quaedam Theologicae,* 2nd ed., Aug. Vindel. 1886.— W. Humphrey, S. J., *The One Mediator,* pp. 272 sqq., London *s. a.*—J. V. Bainvel, S. J., *La Dévotion au Sacre-Coeur de Jésus, Doctrine, Histoire,* 7th ed., Paris 1923 *(English tr. by E. Leahy, *Devotion to the Sacred Heart; The Doctrine and its History,* ed. by G. O'Neill, S. J., London 1924).—J. de Gallifet, S. J., *The Adorable Heart of Jesus,* 3rd ed., London 1908.—J. J. C. Petrovits, *Devotion to the Sacred Heart, its Theology, History, and Philosophy,* St. Louis 1918 (a good bibliography, pp. 277–281).—E. R. Hull, S. J., *Devotion to the Sacred Heart,* London 1904.—K. Richstätter, S. J., *Die Herz-Jesu-Verehrung des deutschen Mittelalters,* 2nd ed., Ratisbon 1924.—Ch. G. Kanters, *Le Coeur de Jésus, Étudié dans la Tradition Catholique,* 2 vols., Bruxelles 1926.—P. Galtier, S. J., *De Incarnatione et Redemptione,* Paris 1926, pp. 246–253.

APPENDIX I

THE TEACHING OF NESTORIUS

In the text (pp. 90 sq.) we have given the traditional view of the teaching of Nestorius. This view is based on the writings of his opponents, especially St. Cyril. More recently the publication by Loofs, of over three hundred fragments of Nestorius' own writings, and by Bedjan and Nau, of a hitherto unknown work written by him during his exile under the pseudonym of "Heraclides of Damascus," [1] has given rise to a controversy, in which the orthodoxy of Nestorius was vehemently defended against Pope Celestine I by Bethune-Baker, Harnack, and Duchesne. The majority of Catholic savants, however, hold that the traditional account of Nestorianism requires no correction in the light of the newly discovered writings of the unfortunate patriarch, especially since it is not at all likely that his Christological teaching differed in any essential respect from that of his master Theodore of Mopsuestia.

The meaning which Nestorius attached to πρόσωπον remains obscure, and the term, as used by him, may be interpreted in different ways. This is not surprising, as Nestorius was an exegete and a historian, not a philosopher. M. Jugie probably comes nearest the truth when he says [2] that the ἓν πρόσωπον resulting from the ἕνωσις προσώπων is simply a very intimate union of the divine with a human person. According to this view there are

---

1 Nestorius, *Le Livre de d'Héra-clide de Damas,* Paris 1910.

2 *Nestorius et la Controverse Nestorienne,* pp. 94 sqq., Paris 1912.

actually two distinct persons in Christ. Junglas [3] holds
that the essence of Nestorianism consists not so much in
the assumption of a twofold personality, as in the proba-
tionary theory peculiar to the Antiochene school, *viz.:*
that Christ was compelled to merit the so-called hypostatic
union, which began only with His glorious Resurrection,
by patient suffering and obedience to the will of God; in
other words, that, though he may by a sort of prolepsis
be called " Son of God " from the moment of His conception, He did not become true God until after His
death. It is in accord with this theory, according to
Junglas, that the term θεοτόκος must be interpreted in the
writings of Nestorius: Mary was not really the mother
of God, though she may be called thus *per anticipationem,*
just as the mother of a man who is raised to the episco-
pate may be called the mother of a bishop. Whether
this explanation can be made to square with Nestorius'
teaching on the Holy Eucharist (where he neglects to
emphasize the hypostatic union of the two natures), is
not for us to decide. But no matter how the Christology
of the unfortunate patriarch be interpreted in the light
of his own writings, he certainly did deny that Christ
was true God from the moment of His conception, and,
furthermore, drew so sharp a line between the divine and
the human attributes of our Lord that they can no longer
be ascribed to one person. In other words, it is an
inevitable corollary of Nestorianism that there are two
persons in Christ, and consequently the system was justly
condemned as heretical in the anathematisms of St. Cyril.[4]

[3] *Die Irrlehre des Nestorius,* Treves 1912.

[4] Cfr. C. Pesch, S. J., *Nestorius als Irrlehrer,* Paderborn 1921.

APPENDIX II

THE CONTROVERSY BETWEEN JULIAN OF HALI-CARNASSUS AND SEVERUS OF ANTIOCH

Dr. R. Draguet, in his recent work, the full title of which is cited on page 73, note 5, *supra,* attacks the traditional interpretation of the Julian position, which rests upon some letters and certain anathemas among the scanty writings of Julian hitherto known. Dr. Draguet avails himself of some hitherto unpublished writings in Syriac from Antiochian sources, in which the Severian polemists incidentally quote Julian, and in the light of the documents offers a new interpretation of Julian's teaching. This teaching, according to Draguet, was that, in becoming Man, Christ, the Son of God, was preserved from the stain of hereditary sin, thus escaping the tyranny of corruption and death, while retaining in his bodily nature all the human infirmities which served as satisfaction in redeeming mankind. If this interpretation is correct, it follows that the differences between Julianists and Severians are to be sought in a misunderstanding of the technical dogmatic terminology, rather than in any actual difference of doctrine. (See the review of Draguet's book in the *Ecclesiastical Review,* May, 1925, Vol. LXXII, No. 5, pp. 546 sq.)

Against Draguet, M. A. A. Jugy (*Julien d'Halicarnasse et Sévère d'Antioche,* Paris 1925) upholds the traditional view of Julian's teaching.

INDEX

"Ἕνωσις καθ᾽ ὑπόστασιν, 115.
Ἐντολή, 217 sqq.
Ephesus, Third General Council of, 73, 87, 89, 91, 96, 101, 103, 105, 108, 115, 147, 183, 185, 191, 211, 281, 291.
Ephraem, St., 151.
Epiphanius, St., 62, 100, 102, 285.
Epistula Dogmatica ad Flavianum, 149, 155, 158.
Epistula Dogmatica ad Imperatores, Pope Agatho's, 156, 157.
Erasmus, 77.
Esse essentiae, 138.
Esse subsistentiae, 138.
Estius, 199.
Etchmiadzin, 149.
Ethiopian liturgy, 169.
Eucharist, The Holy, 85, 109, 194, 242, 286.
Eudoxius of Constantinople, 268.
Eugene IV, 43, 50, 74, 208.
Eulogius, Patriarch of Alexandria, 269, 271.
Eusebius, 23.
Eusebius of Vercelli, 6.
Eutyches, 112, 147 sqq., 183.
"Evening knowledge," 264, 274.
Existence, 137 sqq., 141.

F

"*Factus ex muliere*," 66, 167.
"*Factus ex semine David*," 167.
Father, God the, Could He have become man instead of the Son? 135 sqq.
Faustus of Reji, 131.
Feast of the Sacred Heart, 291, 293.
Feder, A. L. (S. J.), 24.
Felder, H. (O. M. Cap.), 37, 97, 261, 262, 270, 277.
Felix III, Pope, 193.
Felix of Urgel, 196, 197, 202.
Fend, L., 115.
Fenélon, 257.

Filiation, No twofold in Christ, 196 sqq., 201 sqq.
Florence, Council of, 43, 50, 74.
Fomes peccati, 208, 210.
Fonck, L. (S. J.), 37.
Forma Dei, 95, 150, 192.
Forma existentiae, 137.
Forma servi, 45, 95, 150, 192.
Fraidl, 30.
Frankfort, Council of (A. D. 794), 60, 192, 197, 202, 203.
Franzelin, Card., 5, 8, 54, 68, 88, 103, 104, 111, 127, 129, 131, 135, 139, 143, 144, 145, 146, 172, 178, 194, 217, 220, 246, 280, 289.
Fraser, R., 37.
Freddi-Sullivan (S. J.), 37, 39, 177, 178.
Friedrich, Ph., 229.
Fulgentius, St., 7, 57, 66, 168, 195, 205, 214, 253, 262, 267.
Funk, 21, 22, 42, 46, 49, 62, 115, 149, 155, 157, 176.

G

GABRIEL, Archangel, 212.
Gajanus, 73.
Galatia, 176.
Garnerius, 115.
Γεννηθέντα, 64.
Γέγγησις, 203, 204.
Giannoni, K., 206.
Gibbon, 41.
Gilmartin, T., 115, 155, 206.
Glory, 255.
Gnostics, 41, 61.
Godman, 94.
Gonet, 138, 140, 141, 223.
Grace, 202, 214, 232.
Graffito Blasfemo, 105.
Granbery, J. C., 47.
Gratia capitis, 236, 239 sqq., 243, 246.
Gratia unionis, 226, 230 sqq.
Graun, 39.
Greeks, 69.

Monas prodigiosa Ehrenberg, 173.
Μόνη φύσις, 148.
Monergetae, 154.
Monogamy, 224.
Monophysitism, 72, 73, 102, 105, 106, 107, 109, 111, 113, 121, 125, 128, 147 sqq., 153, 158, 162, 183, 185, 189, 193, 268.
Monothelitism, 108, 154 sqq., 183, 210.
"Morning knowledge," 264, 274.
Morris, J., 40.
Moses, 90, 251.
Mozarabic liturgy, 196, 201.
Mulier, 68 sqq.
Müller, G. A., 70, 84.
Münscher, 54.
Muratorian Fragment, The, 22.
Mysteries, Theological, 116.
"Mystery of Christ," The, 116.

N

NATURE and Person, The mutual relationship of, 124 sqq.
Nau, F., 115.
Neander, 54.
Neo-Adoptionism, 197.
Nerva, Emperor, 21.
Nestorianism, 89 sqq., 102, 110, 112, 113, 120, 125, 147, 149, 183, 185, 191, 193, 196, 197, 200, 268, 269, 283.
Nestorius 90 sqq., 96, 97, 101, 103, 111, 112, 114, 120, 128, 168, 183, 186, 189, 197, 266, 268, 283, 296 sq.
Neury Saint-Sepulchre, 173.
Newman, Card., 10, 23, 37, 101, 108, 109, 111, 113, 115, 122, 161, 163, 164, 167, 174, 176.
Nicæa, First Council of, 27, 96, 114, 291; Second Council of, 195.
Nicene Creed, 175.
Nicephorus Callistus, 167, 268.
Nilles, N. (S. J.), 294, 295.

Nix, H. J. (S. J.), 295.
Noëtus, 102.
Nominalists, 213.
Νοῦς, 49.

O

Obiectum manifestativum, 280, 289, 293.
Ointment, 227.
Olivet, Mount, 174.
Omniscience, Natural, 276.
Operatio deivirilis, 161.
Ophites, 41.
Origen, 26, 27, 105, 167, 227, 271.
Original Sin, Christ's exemption from, 208 sqq.
Ὁρίζειν, 199.
Oswald, J. H., 8, 88, 178, 180.
Οὐσία, 113 sq.
Oussani, G., 30.

P

PALESTINE, 148.
Pallavicini, 218, 223.
Palmieri, 243.
Paradise, 243.
Passibility of Christ, 72 sqq., 217.
Passiones, universales and *particulares,* 81.
Passion, The, 30, 165, 170, 173, 218, 257, 274.
Πάθη, 81.
Patiss, G. (S. J.), 84.
Patripassianism, 73, 133.
Paul, St., 8, 65, 67, 75, 83, 95, 96, 114, 118, 150, 175, 192, 198, 199, 209, 212, 227, 241, 273, 283.
Paul V, Pope, 214.
Paulicians, 62.
Paulinus of Aquileja, 196.
Pelagianism, 91, 103.
Perichoresis, Trinitarian, 134, 135, 179 sq.; Christological, 179 sqq.
Person, 114, 120, 124 sqq.

S